P R A I S E   F O R
HEART OF A GREAT PASTOR

Our heart beats in the same rhythm as *The Heart of a Great Pastor*. This great book should be on the shelf of every pastor. Ministry is all about pastors as servant leaders valuing people and focusing on a mission with an emphasis on the future while taking the risk to trust disciples. This edition challenges and encourages pastors to reach for their dreams while energizing those around them. A must-read!

Tommy Barnett
PHOENIX FIRST ASSEMBLY OF GOD
PHOENIX, ARIZONA

Matthew Barnett
LOS ANGELES DREAM CENTER
LOS ANGELES, CALIFORNIA

I have known H. B. London for many years and have always been encouraged by his dedication to helping pastors. *The Heart of a Great Pastor* is just the latest installment from a life dedicated to helping us pastors carry out the Great Commission. Dr. London and Neil Wiseman have captured the essence of the pastor's heart. If you as a pastor have become discouraged and frustrated in ministry, you must read this book. It will strengthen your passion for ministry and rejuvenate your passion for souls.

Jerry Falwell
PASTOR, THOMAS ROAD BAPTIST CHURCH
LYNCHBURG, VIRGINIA

In a world in which people are becoming distracted from their true purpose in life by the dizzying schedules they keep, even pastors are starting to lose sight of what true ministry is all about. H. B. London and Neil Wiseman have once again joined forces to give us special insight into what it means to be a servant of Christ. I encourage every pastor and church leader to spend some time soaking in the truths found within the pages of *The Heart of a Great Pastor*. It will help us all to get back to our first love!

Jonathan Falwell
EXECUTIVE PASTOR, THOMAS ROAD BAPTIST CHURCH
LYNCHBURG, VIRGINIA

As a multigenerational pastoral family, we have discovered *The Heart of a Great Pastor* to be a timely and important book for every pastor-leader. H. B. London and Neil Wiseman combine their lifelong experiences in the local church along with years of investing in the lives of pastors to present the timeless principles of sustaining effective leadership in the local church in a fresh, contemporary and practical way. H. B.'s musings to a new generation of pastors at the end of each chapter is worth the investment alone. The Church in America today is searching for a new generation of leaders whose hearts beat with the heart of our great God. If that divine call resonates in your heart, you owe it to yourself and to the church you serve to read *The Heart of a Great Pastor*.

Dr. Gene Fuller
RETIRED PASTOR AND
DISTRICT SUPERINTENDENT
CHURCH OF THE NAZARENE

Mark Fuller
SENIOR PASTOR
GROVE CITY CHURCH OF THE NAZARENE
GROVE CITY, OHIO

H. B. London and Neil Wiseman have hit on a focus that is often missed by many authors writing about pastoral leadership in the Church. H. B. can get to the heart of a pastor because he knows what is in our hearts. He is one of us. The challenge to "be pastors who are holy, whole, blameless, loving and filled with all the goodness of God as we do our work like He did" challenges us to the core as shepherds of the flock of the One we are to imitate. With so much restlessness in the ministry today, I share the view that "the secret is to make your assignment ideal by blooming where God plants you." We have shared 41 years together in this ministry and still must go back to the fountain and drink again and again to keep growing. Thanks for some cool, fresh water! We will drink together.

Rev. Dr. Daniel Mercaldo
SENIOR PASTOR AND FOUNDER
GATEWAY CATHEDRAL
STATEN ISLAND, NEW YORK

Rev. Timothy J. Mercaldo
ASSOCIATE PASTOR, WORSHIP LEADER
GATEWAY CATHEDRAL
STATEN ISLAND, NEW YORK

The Heart of a Great Pastor is a classic in my opinion. It encourages, inspires and challenges pastors to make a difference for the Kingdom. I look forward to the impact this updated edition will have on a new generation of pastors as they embrace these principles and creative methods to reach the lost with the timeless and relevant Word of God.

Ed Young
PASTOR, SECOND BAPTIST CHURCH
HOUSTON, TEXAS

THE HEART OF A
GREAT
PASTOR

H. B. LONDON, JR.
NEIL B. WISEMAN

Regal

From Gospel Light
Ventura, California, U.S.A.

PUBLISHED BY REGAL BOOKS
FROM GOSPEL LIGHT
VENTURA, CALIFORNIA, U.S.A.
PRINTED IN THE U.S.A.

Regal Books is a ministry of Gospel Light, a Christian publisher dedicated to serving the local church. We believe God's vision for Gospel Light is to provide church leaders with biblical, user-friendly materials that will help them evangelize, disciple and minister to children, youth and families.

It is our prayer that this Regal book will help you discover biblical truth for your own life and help you meet the needs of others. May God richly bless you.

For a free catalog of resources from Regal Books/Gospel Light, please call your Christian supplier or contact us at 1-800-4-GOSPEL *or* www.regalbooks.com.

Library of Congress Cataloging-in-Publication Data
The Library of Congress has cataloged the first edition as follows:
London, H. B.
    The heart of a great pastor : making the most of the unique opportunities that can only be found where God has planted you/H. B. London, Jr., Neil B. Wiseman.
        p. c.m.
    Includes bibliographical references.
    ISBN 978-0-8307-4281-3 (trade paper)
    1. Clergy—Office. 2. Pastoral theology. 3. Evangelicalism.
    I. Wiseman, Neil B. II. Title.
    BV660.2.L66 1994
    253—dc20   94-12657
                                                                                    CIP

Rights for publishing this book in other languages are contracted by Gospel Light Worldwide, the international nonprofit ministry of Gospel Light. Gospel Light Worldwide also provides publishing and technical assistance to international publishers dedicated to producing Sunday School and Vacation Bible School curricula and books in the languages of the world. For additional information, visit www.gospellightworldwide.org; write to Gospel Light Worldwide, P.O. Box 3875, Ventura, CA 93006; or send an e-mail to info@gospellightworldwide.org.

Especially for young pastors everywhere,
including the perpetually young.

The world and the Church await the achievement
of your dreams and the miracles your Christ-empowered
ministry will bring to reality.

CONTENTS

WHAT MATTERS TO YOU MATTERS TO US

Tough times call for heroic action by great souls. That is why this book was written: to help pastors renew their sense of self-worth and to revive their passion for ministry. This book praises pastors and encourages them to dream new dreams, impossible dreams.

As the authors, we believe pastors are indispensable to society and the Church. We appreciate what every pastor does for the Kingdom. We also want to challenge pastors to realize they are part of society's best spiritual hope and their church is an important part of the everlasting Body of Christ. We believe every pastor can bloom where God has planted him.

About the Title

The Heart of a Great Pastor salutes pastors everywhere. The title also seeks to encourage pastors who are well on their way to greatness—the way that God counts it. The potential of marshaling an army of active-duty pastors throughout the world astounds us. Think of what we can accomplish together.

This magnificent, righteous army could revolutionize the nation and the world. In a time of moral hand-wringing and cultural confusion, we must not allow ourselves to forget that the combined impact of individual actions is what most affects any society and any church. Let's make the most of the unique opportunities in the place where God has planted us.

Pastors with Great Hearts

Pastors, we believe that you are great for many reasons. Start with your abiding desire to make a difference in the world. Think of the size of this pastoral army—more than 350,000 strong in the United States alone. Think of the incredible amount of good that pastors accomplish every day.

Your faithfulness, sacrifice, tenacity, courage, hard work and compassion have an impact on the world in immeasurable ways. You are great because of your loyalty to your Commanding General. His empowerment enables you to achieve spiritual accomplishments that really matter to Him and to our world.

Today's crises cry out for this shared greatness to be poured out in sacrificial service that leads people to Christ, builds healthy churches and redeems society. As pastors, our challenges and problems reach in two directions—to the Church and to the culture.

Society Needs Great Pastors

In our society, a coarse, moral civil war causes people to shed values, depreciate goodness and forsake righteousness. As a result, dysfunction, violence and alienation have denigrated our families, schools, communities and governments. We cannot minimize the depth of this moral decay or the difficulty of transforming it. But reformation and renewal have to come, and God promises to empower and enable us to make it happen.

Ministry in the best and in the worst of times offers unprecedented opportunities even as it causes tyrannizing trauma. Although the problems appear tougher than ever before, the possibilities have never been greater. The needs are monumental. Anyone who cannot be stirred by the conditions facing us today has forgotten the amazing power of the gospel or is too battle weary to realize what winning the war could mean to the cause of Christ.

Why This Book Was Written

Our purpose in writing this book is to encourage pastors to see unparalleled opportunities in every situation. We hope to provide a useful road map for people who want to reenergize their ministry.

There are several things that you will notice in this book. When we, the authors, speak from personal experience, we will use the pronoun "I" and then identify ourselves as H. B. or Neil. We have used the masculine pronoun throughout the book, even though we know that approximately three percent of churches are led by women. Please be merciful.

There are many illustrations and names used in the various chapters. To be sensitive to people and places, we have changed actual names and locations to ensure privacy.

Move to the Front Lines

We challenge you to respond fully to the incredible needs for the gospel that shout from every cranny of society. Take courage: Divine strength for every battle is just a prayer away. Make the promise personally your own: "God can do anything, you know—far more than you could ever imagine or guess or request in your wildest dreams!" (Eph. 3:20, *THE MESSAGE*).

Sound the battle call loud enough so that all can hear. Enlist the troops. Move to the front. Get ready for the toughest battle of your life. Personalize Paul's charge to Timothy as your own: "Teach believers with your life: by word, by demeanor, by love, by faith, by integrity. Stay at your post reading Scripture, giving counsel, teaching. And that special gift of ministry you were given when the leaders of the church laid hands on you and prayed—keep that dusted off and in use" (1 Tim. 4:12-14, *THE MESSAGE*).

Miraculous achievements are ignited by new dreams for the place where God has providentially placed you. Straight ahead for the Kingdom. What matters to you, matters to us.

H. B. London, Jr.
Neil B. Wiseman

TO THE NEW GENERATION
ARE YOU READY FOR THE CHANGING OF THE GUARD?

I (H. B.) watched a television tribute to my friend Adrian Rogers. It was a program to honor his ministry in Memphis as one of the leaders in the Southern Baptist Church. Though he had been gravely ill, those who knew him—either personally, through his radio/television program, or as their pastor—were shocked at his passing. I knew Dr. Rogers through his involvement as a Focus on the Family board member and because of our mutual love for the clergy.

As I watched the tribute, I thought to myself, *Who will replace a man like that?* Remember, when Moses died, the Lord said to Joshua, "As I was with Moses, so I will be with you" (Josh. 1:5). So I am sure someone will come along, but who? Then I thought about all of the other leaders of the church who are in their "fourth quarter." When the time comes, who will replace them?

When I say "replace," I am not talking about filling their place with just another body. I have in mind a person of quality and character whose resolve is not to better himself and his image—one whose focus is on Jesus more than his own ministry. The Lord gave us a hint of the qualifications in Micah 6:8—men who act justly, love mercy and walk humbly with God.

The Body of Christ faces impending transition of leadership in the next decade, or sooner. Who will accept the baton? And who is worthy to take it?

It will likely come from a new generation of pastors coming on the scene. They are young, well educated and highly motivated, but very vulnerable. So many of them (and perhaps you fit in this category) have failed to count the cost of serving Christ and His Church, and they are now in the process of dropping out.

Although the average age of pastors is 47 years, there are great numbers who are in their mid-twenties and thirties. To the new generation, I ask you sincerely: Do you have a mentor? Have you examined your unique call and place in society? Do you have buy-in from your spouse and children? Do you spend as much time in the Word and study as you do in the entrepreneurial pursuits of your ministry? Have you determined what kind of shepherd you will be? Do you genuinely love people? Do you understand the concept of servant-leadership? Are you willing to walk through the valley, weep with those who weep, and rejoice with those who rejoice? Do you really understand how invested God is in you and how important it is for you to make it? I pray so.

Some say the new generation doesn't read much. I'm not sure about that report, but we urge you . . . no, beg you . . . to take a few hours out of your schedule and give *The Heart of a Great Pastor* a thorough going over—a kind of heart-to-heart talk about what really matters. We want you to take your ministry to the cutting edge of imaginative newness for Christ while keeping it anchored to the abiding adventures of the eternal gospel.

The changing of the guard is almost here. Are you ready?

JESUS, THE PASTOR
OUR MODEL FOR MINISTRY

Jesus, the Pastor. That title sounds strange when we hear it or say it for the first time, like an overstated stretch of the imagination. After more careful scrutiny, however, it seems clear that many expressions of pastoral ministry started with Jesus—something He said, something He did, or something He challenged His disciples to do or be.

That being true, it can easily be said that Jesus was the first pastor of the Christian era. And what a pastor He was!

Jesus taught His original team of disciples how to do ministry by pastoring them—trusting them, teaching them, inspiring them, boosting them, stimulating them, challenging them, praying with them, and showing them their future.

He spent time—lots of time—with His disciples. He ate with them. He sometimes even taught them pastoral ministry lessons that they could never forget as they walked together to the next ministry site. He loved them. He modeled ministry for them. And they learned as much about the "whys" as well as the "hows" of ministry as they watched Jesus minister to people in different settings—a kind of "this is what I mean" hands-on, traveling, informal seminar that continued day after day. Jesus taught them ministry by doing ministry before them and by ministering to them.

STRONG REASONS FOR CALLING JESUS "PASTOR"

Calling our Lord "Pastor" seems right, maybe even overdue, when these four reasons are considered:

1. **Shepherd = pastor.** The two words, "shepherd" and "pastor," are virtually synonymous. Pastor John Frye explains, "Our common English word 'pastor' made its way to us through Latin and is simply the semantic equivalent of the biblical word for 'shepherd.'"[1] And New Testament scholar William Barclay wholeheartedly agrees with this conclusion.[2]

2. **"I am the good shepherd" testimony.** In John 10:11, Jesus says of Himself, "I am the good shepherd. The good shepherd lays down his life for the sheep." A few verses later He says it again: "I am the good shepherd; I know my sheep and my sheep know me—just as the Father knows me and I know the Father—and I lay down my life for the sheep" (vv. 14-15).

3. **Scriptural support.** Other verses in the Bible also refer to Christ as the Shepherd. For example, Peter calls Jesus the shepherd of men's souls (see 1 Pet. 2:25) and Chief Shepherd (see 1 Pet. 5:4). The writer of Hebrews calls Jesus the Great Shepherd of the Sheep (see Heb. 13:20).

4. **Love exam.** Jesus uses the shepherding theme again in His post-resurrection meeting with His disciples on the seashore (see John 21). He met them for breakfast on the beach to celebrate the extravagant catch of fish that came when they dropped their nets on the other side of the boat in response to His directive.

Some biblical specialists believe that Jesus planned this last incident with its emphasis on loving service in order to restore Peter, who before the crucifixion had so disappointed himself and others by His denial of Christ. Planned or not, Peter was reconciled to Christ that day.

At the meeting by the sea, Jesus asked the big fisherman one soul-searching question three times. Facing the questions and forming answers shaped Peter's pastoral ministry for the rest of his days. From your own study of Scripture, you likely remember the dialogue:

Jesus said to Simon Peter, "Do you truly love me more than these?"
"Yes Lord," he said, "you know that I love you."
Jesus said, *"Feed my lambs."*
Again Jesus said, "Simon son of John, do you truly love me?"
He answered, "Yes, Lord, you know that I love you."
Jesus said, *"Take care of my sheep."*
The third time he said to him, "Simon son of John, do you love me?"
"Lord, you know all things; you know that I love you."
Jesus said, *"Feed my sheep"* (John 21:15-17, emphasis added).

Several significant pastoral issues surfaced in the dialogue. One has to wonder if Jesus was not also thinking of other biblical settings that describe the Shepherd (see Gen. 32; Ps. 23; 80:1; Isa. 40; Jer. 31; Ezek. 34).

The dialogue between the Lord and Peter underscores how much Jesus valued what is inside a pastor—motive, affection and intention. He wanted Peter, the others in the disciple group and us to know how inner heart issues affect or even determine a pastor's usefulness and satisfaction.

The conversation also shows that mere words are not enough to express our love for Christ: He wants us to demonstrate our love for Him by caring for His lambs and His sheep. And in the process, He believes that our service to others will help us grow spiritually stronger, while at the same time increasing our spiritual stamina.

Interestingly enough, there is another fact in the biblical account that is sometimes overlooked when studying this love examination that Jesus gave to Peter. Although the conversation was obviously intended to be a life-changing moment for Peter, it was also a teaching moment for six other disciples who witnessed the event at the seaside breakfast. It has a powerful message for contemporary pastors as well.

HOW JESUS DID PASTORAL MINISTRY

In addition to the hands-on influence that Jesus had on His disciples, He continually ministered to those who came to Him with their needs. He demonstrated what He taught. Memories of those experiences sustained and directed the disciples through thick and thin all the days of their ministry. Here is a partial list of what made Jesus' ministry authentic and replicable then and now:

- **Jesus valued people.** Jesus went to where people were, and they knew that He cared for them. He went to a tax collector's booth to recruit Matthew and stayed for supper. Before the event was over, He had given His critics fodder for their gossip that He ate with tax collectors and sinners (see Matt. 9:9-12). With Jesus, people came first, and loving them unconditionally was at the top of His list.

- **Jesus focused on mission.** Those who followed Jesus knew much about His purpose and mission. Perhaps the most succinct of His statements about mission comes from His words to Zacchaeus: "Today salvation has come to this house. . . . For the Son of Man came to seek and to save what was lost" (Luke 19:9-10). There are many other statements about Jesus' purpose sprinkled throughout Scripture.

- **Jesus thought of Himself as a servant.** Jesus' strategy was to present Himself as a servant who asked for nothing—no money, no privilege, no home, no leisure and no privacy. He knew that it was possible for spiritual leaders to hinder the gospel by wanting to be king or queen rather than a servant.

- **Jesus emphasized the future.** Although Jesus used history and traditions appropriately, He focused His message and movement on the future. Then as now, His message to His disciples is to get ready for the new things that God wants to do in them and through them.

- **Jesus took risks by trusting His disciples.** Jesus risked the whole Christian movement on the abilities and commitments of ordinary people. After three short years with the disciples,

He turned the movement over to them. With the help of the life-giving Spirit, they carried on—and so can we.

FOLLOWING THE JESUS PATTERN TODAY

Look for a moment over the shoulders of the disciples as Jesus shows them how to be a pastor. What do you see? Of course, a contemporary pastor may never be able to give sight to the blind, raise someone like Lazarus from the dead, or heal someone like the crippled man who had been at the side of the pool at Bethesda for 38 years. And of course, a contemporary pastor will never have to endure the wilting criticism of the Pharisees for doing good on Sunday. But every contemporary pastor can emulate the Lord in loving people. He can focus on mission and view himself as a servant of God and the people. He can emphasize the future and risk placing the church into the hands of its youth and new converts.

At a time when thousands feel disenchanted by the church, authentic Christlike leaders are needed who emulate these characteristics. Why not follow the Lord's pattern to connect human beings to the abundant grace of Christ? Let's be pastors who are holy, whole, blameless, loving and filled with all the goodness of God as we do our work like He did.

I love this description of our Lord's earthly ministry: "Then Jesus made a circuit of all the towns and villages. He taught in their meeting places, reported kingdom news, and healed their diseased bodies, healed their bruised and hurt lives. When he looked out over the crowds, his heart broke. So confused and aimless they were, like sheep with no shepherd. 'What a huge harvest!' he said to his disciples. 'How few workers! On your knees and pray for harvest hands!'" (Matt. 9:35-38, *THE MESSAGE*).

"His heart broke"—what a powerful sentence.

He saw them as "sheep with no shepherd"—He had compassion for their confusion.

And His command to them and to us—"On your knees and pray for harvest hands!"

CHAPTER 1

EVERY ASSIGNMENT IS HOLY GROUND

God of the burning bush
I take off my shoes of distractions and foggy focus,
I take off my shoes of pride and phony professionalism,
I take off my shoes of ignorance and blindness,
I take off my shoes of hurry and worry.
Let the burning bush remind me of your
grace and power.

> TAKE OFF YOUR
> SANDALS, FOR THE
> PLACE WHERE
> YOU ARE STANDING
> IS HOLY GROUND.
>
> EXODUS 3:5

YOU'RE STANDING ON HOLY GROUND

Eight young pastors and their wives sat in front of a roaring fireplace. Any thought of venturing outdoors for some afternoon exercise was erased by a howling blizzard that swirled around their Rocky Mountain retreat.

When the conversation began to lag, Ted, a bit like a brash, modern-day Peter, blurted out a suggestion: "Let's make up a game in which each person describes the phase of ministry that irritates him the most."

Why-spoil-the-fun looks greeted Ted's suggestion. The others reminded him that a retreat should offer temporary sanctuary from thoughts of assignments awaiting back home. But Ted's persistence prevailed, and he volunteered to start the game.

"My biggest problem," Ted said, "is a lay leader who is related to nearly everyone in the church. Dignified. Selfish. Hard to reach. Domineering. World War III starts if anyone crosses him, so he gets his way through negative intimidation." Several heads nodded, acknowledging that Ted's experience was not unique.

Sarah, at first a bit hesitant, confessed that her husband never lets down his preacher image. "He walks, talks and thinks like a preacher. Even at home, he uses his stained-glass voice for table prayers. Romance with a reverend often isn't very exciting." Several participants muffled nervous laughs.

"My work is never done," said Max. "Like Los Angeles freeway traffic, it never quits. Another sermon to write. A phone call to return. Another brush fire to stomp out. And I don't know about you, but money is tight every day. I have thousands of dollars of college and seminary loans to pay, and the salaries of most beginning pastors aren't big to begin with. The pressure to make ends meet never lets up."

"You're not alone," Dan responded. "My wife and I deal with discouraging financial pressure every day. We are about $2,000 a year away from living a fairly normal life, but no one in the church seems to understand our money problem. Key players say absurd things like, 'God will provide.' That makes me want to scream, 'God only raises pastors' salaries through lay leaders.' I never saw dollars drop from the sky."

Grievances began to pile up as participation in the game intensified: crowded parsonages, demands on family, apathetic leaders, broken promises. As the share-the-misery therapy session progressed, a collective mood of self-pity began to brew.

Then David, tears streaming down his face, shared, "My situation is tougher than I can describe. People are brittle, demanding, unresponsive, touchy. I often want out, and I complain to God. But I know God sent me there. And He keeps me there. He expects me to be a Christ-exalting leader, but I wish I were somewhere else. Humanly, I want to quit.

"But a few good parishioners stand by me," David continued. "They care about my wife and me. They care about God and His work. Even though I might want to bail out at times, I just can't leave. It's like . . . well . . . it's like I stand on holy ground."

The room grew hushed as the group of couples in ministry looked into the dancing fire.

"I never thought of our setting for service from that perspective," Sara said. "This discussion puts our situation in a new light and makes it sound like holy ground, too."

"Ours, too!" Tom chimed in.

"Yeah," Andy said. "I guess you could say it's that way with us. But it's the strangest holy ground I've ever seen. Sometimes, it seems as if God has deserted the place."

During the two hours of conversation that followed, seven of the eight couples agreed that God had led them to their places of ministry, to holy ground.

The boisterous Ted, now more subdued, observed, "This conversation has caused me to think of my childhood. My mother—a pastor's wife—used to sing, 'Where Jesus is, 'tis heaven there' when times were tough. As I grew up, I always thought the words were overstated—exaggerated, really. But there's enough truth in that song to make me realize that every assignment may become holy ground."

The song and the insights gained during that afternoon around the fireplace accompanied the couples as they left the Colorado conference center. They knew that God was not finished with them. People still needed their ministry. And they had God's promise that He would empower them where they served.

QUESTIONS A PASTOR MUST ANSWER

Like the group members at the retreat, every pastor in the thick of the struggle must answer significant questions, the answers to which will shape his ministry and determine his effectiveness:

- What difference will I make?
- Why am I here?
- Who sent me?
- Is this assignment sacred because God placed me here?
- What does God want to accomplish through me?

Every assignment is holy ground because Jesus gave Himself for the people who live there. Every place is important because God wants something incredibly important to be accomplished there through us. Every situation is special because ministry is needed in that place. Like Queen Esther, we have come to the Kingdom for a time like this.

Think of the awesome possibilities. Our assignment may be holy ground because of a specific need in the local congregation. God may want a fresh vision started there or a reconciliation to occur. Perhaps some front-line opportunity awaits us—a neighbor to be led to Christ, a ministry to be started, a church to be refocused on biblical priorities.

Moses discovered during his lifetime that even in tough places God's presence turns ministry into an adventure. As the evangelist Luis Palau suggests, "Any old bush will do because it is not us doing something for God, but God doing something through us."[1] The Bible reminds us, "When you're joined with me and I with you, the relation intimate and organic, the harvest is sure to be abundant" (John 15:5, *THE MESSAGE*). What an extravagant promise. What amazing potential. What an unconquerable force for changing the world for Christ.

You are needed. You are important. You are empowered by God. You serve in the middle of the action. God wants to enable you to transform your present assignment into holy ground—a place where He accomplishes supernatural achievements through ordinary people like you.

EVERY ASSIGNMENT HAS SEVEN RESOURCES WAITING TO BE USED

Seven resources are available for use in every assignment, congregation and community. Although sometimes unrecognized, these resources are never limited by geography, finances, facilities or creed. They are available in every church in every place and at any time.

Resource 1: Every Congregation Is Unique
Like resemblances in every family, every congregation will bear a likeness to all other churches. But just as little Tommy looks more like himself

than anyone else in his family, each church has more differences than similarities.

Consequently, using a church's uniqueness is an important factor in developing a flourishing ministry. God gives uniqueness to a church to achieve His purposes. He has created your church, like every snowflake and raindrop, to be unlike any other.

Resource 2: Every Congregation Responds to a Pastor's Love

Just as marriage partners must intentionally love each other to build a strong marriage, so a church must be loved by its pastor and must love its minister in return. Pastoring a church is more like a courtship in a marriage than the process of developing a business. Although productive pastors may employ work habits similar to those used by professional persons or business owners, they must also be loving—warm, friendly and accepting. Bishop Joseph McKinney calls us to a mature realism about loving people: "Anyone can love the ideal church. The challenge is to love the real church."[2]

Congregations seldom thrive without a pastor's love. The sheep grow restless without an attentive shepherd. This love is the radical New Testament *agape* love, which David Hansen believes is a requirement: "Pastors cannot do pastoral work for people they hate or even dislike. Love is our life's work. We must love our church in order to do our job. . . . *agape* is the decision to love to the point of giving our life away. *Agape* love transcends our human circumstances and instincts; it transcends our nature and our nurture."[3]

Agape love transcends human circumstances and instincts.

Resource 3: God Provides Supernatural Empowerment

Contemporary evil and human brokenness are not too much for the power of God. He can redeem a society as easily as He created the earth. Although murder, rape, violence, white-collar crimes, abortions, divorce and unwed births sadden the heart of God, they do not paralyze Him. If He can find a few faithful servants, He will work miracles.

Neither are complex problems in our church too much for Him. Divine empowerment and guidance are available in every setting and for every need. God's power is as effective in ordinary circumstances of ministry as in spectacular crunches. Most churches need much more reliance on supernatural empowerments for everyday ministry. It is, after all, His church.

Resource 4: Every Church Needs Bible Preaching

God has preserved the Bible as a supernatural guide for life and faith. Regrettably, many people consider the Bible and preaching to be lifeless and out of date. But better biblical preaching will make every church healthier.

The Bible, our source for preaching, needs no defense. When proclaimed in ways people understand, it always exonerates itself. Strange as it may seem, preaching—one anointed person speaking a fresh word from God amid the people of God—is one of the Father's favorite ways of communicating His will to believers.

Sound scriptural preaching can help every hearer and every preacher grow. Biblical preaching keeps molding the preacher into the image of Christ. For the hearers, as William Willimon says, "People are ripe for a voice that gives them something significant worth living and dying for."[4]

Resource 5: Every Pastor Is Distinctively Gifted

God whispers His call to ministry to committed people who often possess many diverse gifts. No two pastors are alike. In my (Neil) 20 years of teaching potential pastors, I always marveled at the kinds of person the Lord called into ministry. Many of these pastors would never have been called had that decision been left to me. However, I have lived long enough to see those whom I thought were the most limited come to full bloom as pastors and church leaders.

So the issue for the potential minister is to honor his call by giving himself the best possible education and personal development. The issue for the Church is to be sure that people are placed in assignments in which their giftedness will have its greatest effect. And the issue for the specific congregation is to cherish the pastor and seek to understand what God had in mind when He sent this pastor to this congregation at this time.

Resource 6: Every Setting Has Potential

Something special needs to be done in every setting. Within an amazingly short radius in every church, there is someone who needs the Savior and an opportunity to change. It's easy to visualize needy people in East Los Angeles or in parts of New York City, but unreached people can also be found on the next ranch in Montana, on the next farm in Missouri, on the next block in Minneapolis.

Although Kingdom opportunities are often measured by the masses, they can only be accomplished by winning individuals who live across the fence, up the street, down the freeway, or across town.

What appear to be insurmountable hindrances will seem insignificant when we consider how many unreached people are all around us. This might be a good time to revive the spirit of a pioneer pastor who described his work: "We went to people who didn't want us and stayed until they couldn't get along without us."

Try this test: Check the demographics in your town. Find out how many people live within easy reach but who have not come to know Christ. You will find there are more than enough for you to win scores of people to the Kingdom.

Resource 7: Every Church Has Something to Give People

In spite of apparent limitations, every church has something rich to offer constituents, visitors and neighbors. It may be friendship, fellowship or restoration. Every place turns into a holy center for productive ministry when a congregation believes it has something worthwhile for every person, even the first-time visitor.

We have been lulled into believing that the small church has little to offer. We have allowed the big-is-best mind-set to dilute the fact that when the church is the Church, regardless of its size, it is a mighty instrument in the hand of God.

NEEDED: A MODERN MOSES

Ideal conditions do not automatically create a satisfying ministry. Real meaning comes from developing an intimacy with the Lord Jesus. Accordingly, in every situation a pastor must ask himself the "ease versus need" questions: Do I wait for an ideal setting? Do I seek an easy place? Or do I ask God to empower me to make the assignment He has given me the opportunity I dreamed about?

The compelling issue is whether you want usefulness, ease, fruitfulness, opportunity or satisfaction. Sometimes opportunity and satisfaction fit together in an assignment. On the other hand, the most fruitful places may be demanding and difficult.

God may want you to be a modern Moses in Memphis, Los Angeles, Shreveport, Lansing or Ord Bend. He might want to empower you to find holy ground in a messy, noisy place where anarchy and brokenness and dysfunction reign. Or His plan for your holy ground might be a delightful church like Paul enjoyed at Philippi. In any event, it is not essential that you be happy, but that you matter—that you make a difference.

Lessons from Moses in the Badlands
Some modern ministry settings seem as barren as Moses' desert experience in Exodus 3, where he cared for smelly sheep in the scorching sun.

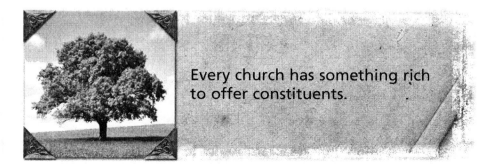

Every church has something rich to offer constituents.

His situation probably was boring and very much beneath his abilities and experiences.

But rethink the story for a moment. God impacted Moses at the burning bush in ways Moses never forgot—ways that instructed and inspired him all the rest of his days. How could he? God came to Moses while he was performing ordinary work in a simple place, miles from fame of any kind. Moses' setting was humdrum routine except for the burning bush. But that meeting with God in the arid lonely place made all the difference.

Miles from any action, God gave Moses a soul burden for his people. But Moses struggled to know what he could do about it. Like many present-day pastors, Moses was burdened for his people but didn't know how to help them.

Reading about Moses' encounter with the living God rekindles our motivation. Even a cursory reading of the story forces a reappraisal of our assignment and a reevaluation of our resources. What if Moses had been asked to figure out the logistics of moving all those people and their animals? From a human perspective, it would have been impossible. God intended to use Moses, and God had a plan.

How a pastor views himself, his competency, his spiritual maturity and God's direction also help determine outcomes in a specific setting. For example, in one church in Colorado, five pastors served during a 20-year span. Ministers stayed for 2 to 8 years. That congregation—housed in the same building and same town and attended mostly by the same people or their kin—fluctuated from surviving to sometimes almost thriving. Although the fluctuation might have been caused by a variety of factors, the difference seemed to revolve around whether the pastor believed that the church and its congregation could make a difference.

To put the idea in loftier New Testament terms, God has built resurrection life into the fabric of every church. This supernatural force offers hope for revolutionizing a morally twisted society and for again vitalizing a lethargic church.

Pastors hold the incredible energy of the gospel in their hands and in their hearts. Its power is amazing. It can penetrate the hardest soil. It's a supernatural power to cope with the minister's most demanding challenges. This makes spiritual triumphs possible in the toughest of places.

Affirmations to the Modern Moses

Moses' life provides a life-changing model for contemporary pastors. His awareness of being sent by God kept him faithful for a lifetime. His willingness to be consumed by a mighty cause far outweighed all other concerns. For Moses, usefulness to God was more important than standing or security.

Moses' awareness of holy ground came as he opened the routines of his life to God. His curiosity caused him to say, "I will go over and see this strange sight—why the bush does not burn up" (Exod. 3:3).

No one knows how Moses would have reacted to all the risks facing modern clergy, such as membership migration, loss of absolutes, dysfunctional people, and ever-changing paradigm shifts. We do know that complete dependence on God was the pattern of his life (see Exod. 3:11-12; 33:14-17). God's response was supernatural empowerment, as it always is (see Exod. 3:18-20).

Look Beyond Limitations

Looking beyond our limitations is a key point from Moses' life that can fire us up for ministry in our time. After hearing the I AM send him to blaze new trails of remarkable adventure and marvelous achievement, Moses could never view his situation in the same old way. The same is true for us after we hear God's summons and recognize the potential He sees in our setting.

Pastors hold the incredible energy of the gospel in their hands and hearts.

Even though Moses' problem of trying to lead stubborn people where they did not want to go may differ from ours, our need for God's empowerment is as intense as Moses' was. God's assurance to Moses— "I am the God of your father, the God of Abraham, the God of Isaac and the God of Jacob. . . . I will be with you" (Exod. 3:6,12)—is more than adequate for a minister to follow God's purposes for a lifetime. Being yoked with God in a holy cause makes every pastor a mighty vessel for righteousness in every setting.

Let's clarify the issues that all modern Moses-like pastors face. At this very moment, the future effectiveness of the gospel in thousands of settings is being determined by how pastors view their task and count their resources. Three pressing questions are before us:

1. Can we view our situation from God's perspective?
2. Can we believe every setting has more potential than anyone realizes?
3. Can we see ourselves as more than conquerors through the One who called and sent us?

God Seeks Cheerful Naturalized Citizens
When God sends out modern Moseses, they must willingly go to tough places. Two realities that we seldom discuss include:

1. There are not enough easy assignments to go around.
2. Most desirable places were difficult until a previous pastor loved the church into greatness. Face it—few Camelots exist in ministry.

This means that ministers must sink their roots where the Father providentially places them. The prophet Jeremiah, admonishing the surviving elders who were exiled in Babylon, wrote, "Build houses and settle down; plant gardens and eat what they produce. . . . Also, seek the peace and prosperity of the city to which I have carried you into exile. Pray to the LORD for it, because if it prospers, you too will prosper" (Jer. 29:5,7).

Pastors may find themselves in situations not to their liking and working among people they do not understand. Then it's easy to choose tears, self-pity and complaints. But why not choose joy, fulfillment and unconditional involvement? They can unpack their bags, stop longing for greener pastures, and assume spiritual responsibility for their place of ministry. They can claim the territory for God and for righteousness. God wants to transform endurance to adventure.

A pastor in Arizona once wrote to me (Neil), explaining how he considers his present assignment as a long-term commitment. He purchased cemetery plots for himself and for his wife in the town where they were serving. Pastors must commit to stay in an assignment until God gives them a genuine spiritual breakthrough or a clear-cut release. Many pastors need to become enthusiastic naturalized citizens of the place where they serve until they are used by God to establish a flourishing ministry.

God is pleased when a pastor welcomes a congregation into his heart and loves them as his extended family. He is pleased when a pastor learns to love an assignment as much as an ancestral home. He calls a pastor to be willing to live and to die for the congregation. Hundreds of churches have reason to think like a Methodist layman who once wondered, "Why does the bishop keep sending us pastors who do not want to come here?" This needs to be changed.

Just as every pastor is strengthened and affirmed when laypeople love him, so every congregation thrives when the members know their pastor loves them. This two-way pattern is the amazing love relationship of the shepherd and the sheep that Jesus explained in John 10.

God is pleased when a pastor welcomes a congregation into his heart and loves them as his extended family.

God Has Up-to-Date Plans

God's agenda is bigger than ours, and His plans are exceedingly in touch with contemporary needs. He is as fully acquainted with the future as with the past. He wants brokenness healed. He wants stony soils softened by selfless service. He wants secularists saved from themselves. He wants dysfunctional people and families made whole.

He also wants us to serve troublesome and immature church members, because we are the only pastors they have. Although God's blueprint may seem too big or too complicated, He plans to accomplish His purposes through ordinary people like us.

In God's plan, much needs to be accomplished outside the Church. One only needs to read the morning newspaper or listen to the evening news to be reminded of places where Christ must be taken. Think of Gen-Xers, immigrants, teens, single parents, homeless people, seniors, children, boomers and busters who have no life-transforming knowledge of Christ.

Consider violent city streets, dying rural towns, sophisticated centers of culture, and sprawling suburbs. Arid spiritual wildernesses wait to be transformed into lush gardens where the gospel seed will bear abundant fruit and where Jesus is the Master Gardener. Could we pray to be inspired to live out new commitments that override all questions about hardship, inconvenience and frustration?

God Uses Unconditional Commitment

Words about unconditional commitment are difficult for us to hear and even harder for us to live out in the details of ministry.

I (Neil) know a great pastor who during his pastoral prime moved to a troubled church in western Kansas. For 15 years, he had served a 500-member church in Yakima, Washington, with distinction. He had an impressive list of ministry achievements. He loved people and preached with a creative anointing. The church grew year after year in numbers and in spiritual vibrancy. He had no logical reason to move, but he did.

From the start, everything went wrong in the Sunflower State assignment. Some members of the church thought he was too progressive, while others thought he was too old-fashioned. After a couple of years of misery, the decision group requested his resignation, and he submitted it. He had no place to go, and he had little money.

The contrast between the loving congregation in Washington and his rejection in Kansas ate like a cancer at his sense of self-worth. He called his former district superintendent in the Northwest to discuss his dilemma. He was desperate and asked to be considered for any size church. The superintendent responded, "I would be glad to have you back in our area, but we have no openings. Sorry." The superintendent really meant that he had no openings that would fit the minister's capability and years of experience.

Throughout the night, the superintendent felt troubled as he pondered this great pastor's predicament. So he phoned early the next morning and said, "We have an opening in an isolated town. The church is so tiny that I'm embarrassed to even suggest that you go there. But I have an idea that will help you and this smaller church. Why don't you serve there for a few months until a stronger church opens? The smaller church will be flattered to have you even for a short time. In fact, you will be the most experienced pastor they have ever had."

My pastor friend accepted the challenge. He moved to that isolated town and to a church attended by fewer than 75 people. He told his friends that the challenge was as exciting as his first pastorate years before. Opportunities to move to larger assignments soon beckoned. But to everyone's amazement, he stayed in the community for 10 years.

His commitment and competence made holy ground out of a tough place. Soon, the little church was the talk of the town, and it grew. New people began attending. The pastor started a daily 6:00 A.M. radio program that gave people a spiritual jumpstart as they went to their jobs or to work on their farms.

In a short time, everyone in the county knew the pastor. He became chaplain of two service clubs. He was invited to speak during civic functions. He read books on writing and attended writing seminars. He wrote five books during the decade he served in that church. He also served as an inspirational model to younger pastors.

When asked about his tenure in such an ordinary place, he laughingly replied, "I found a secret here. People in this fine church were waiting for someone to love them, so I did. And they have loved me back."

My friend committed himself to the greatest thing in the entire world—to be used of God. One entry in his journal from those years is as follows: "As my contact with need increases, each completed project exposes me to many more waiting areas of service. Each task seems to open new opportunities of service and increases the circumference of my influence."

That pastor discovered the old but ever-new adventure of self-crucifixion to security, place and prominence.

God Nullifies Every Excuse

All of our self-centered rationalizations are questioned as we listen to the conversation between God and Moses at the burning bush. Listen again to lessons from Exodus 3 and 4.

- **Lesson 1:** No need for self-pity or to complain, "Why me?"
  God answers, "I will be with you, and that is enough" (see Exod. 3:11-22).

- **Lesson 2:** No use to sniffle, "What if they do not believe me or listen to me and say, 'The Lord did not appear to you'?"
  With unbelievable assurance, God tells Moses, "I'll give you a miracle or two to inspire you and to capture their attention" (see Exod. 4:1-9).

- **Lesson 3:** No need to point out inadequacies or low self-esteem and whine, "O Lord, I have never been eloquent, neither in the past nor since you have spoken to your servant. I am slow of speech and tongue."
  Weary of Moses' rationalizations, God responds with a command and a promise: "Go. I will help you speak and will teach you what to say" (see Exod. 4:10-12).

- **Lesson 4:** No use to suggest that God send someone else: "O Lord, please send someone else to do it."
  God answers with a promise: "I will give you someone to help

you, and I will give both of you resources to speak and will teach you what to do" (see Exod. 4:13-16).

Because the assets are significantly larger than the obstacles, let's refocus our vision. This time in human history promises to be one of frightening resistance and of incredible achievement for the gospel. We will maximize the possibilities only if we approach our task with creative imagination, alert competence and unconditional dependence on God.

Most of all, the task before us demands an abiding assurance that God is with us. It calls for vigorous confidence that the gospel is the only answer to the moral mess that society faces. The time has come to make Christ-centered character, spiritual wholeness and Kingdom service attractive and adventuresome again.

Elizabeth Barrett Browning sounds as if she is reading this chapter over our shoulders when she puts the issues before us in four lines of verse:

Earth's crammed with heaven,
And every common bush afire with God:
But only he who sees, takes off his shoes,
The rest sit round it and pluck blackberries.[5]

CONTEMPORARY CHALLENGE

Your Pastorate Is Holy Ground

- Every congregation and community has untapped potential.
- Potential awareness starts with an encounter with God.
- Every church is an instrument for righteousness God wants to use.
- Every church can enjoy supernatural resurrection power.

In communicating the gospel our confidence is not in the effectiveness of our techniques but in the inherent power of the message. —Eddie Gibbs[6]

Learn from Moses: Be Yourself— Your Best Self

Musings from H. B. London, Jr.

A recent magazine article described how two pastors felt after attending a three-day high-energy, high-profile pastors' conference. At the end of the conference, they felt so useless that they questioned whether they had misunderstood God's call in the first place. Although the magazine report may have been an overstatement, it mirrors what I have heard others say: "Encourage me—don't make me feel guilty."

In the article, the main confusion seemed to be that the pastors didn't see how they could become like the presenters. I have a suggestion: Be yourself—you don't have to be like anyone else. But be your *best* self.

I see many of our colleagues in ministry who have pretty much given up on their uniqueness. They have become like clones, almost afraid to venture out and be unique. I talk to many who live in such fear of failure that they never reach their potential.

Here are some stretching suggestions: Dare to dream an impossible dream for your ministry. Go out beyond your comfort zone. Invest in an original thought every day. Ask God for a challenge that will test every gift and skill you possess. Spend time with people who stimulate you to continual creative newness. Be a hero. Live a life others view as anointed.

Remember the Scripture, "I am fearfully and wonderfully made" (Ps. 139:14). God had you in mind before you took your first breath, and His intention was that you would live and minister uniquely—different than any other pastor. You are a wonderful original. Celebrate your uniqueness. Sharpen your mind, body, spirit and will to maximum usefulness.

CHAPTER 2

PARTNERSHIP WITH THE MASTER GARDENER

Living Lord, I rejoice in our relationship in which You are senior partner in my ministry. Help me to see Your plans for this place. Help me to follow Your will to the last detail. Sharpen my awareness of the potential around me. Save me from ego-driven self-sufficiency. Help me produce lasting fruit.

Amen.

> I CHOSE YOU AND
> APPOINTED YOU TO GO
> AND BEAR FRUIT—
> FRUIT THAT WILL LAST.
>
> JOHN 15:16

THE MASTER GARDENER HAS PLANS FOR YOUR SETTING

Jesus sets the agenda for holy-ground ministry with His directive to go everywhere and win everyone. This adventure of ministry in partnership with the Lord is brought into crystal-clear focus when we examine the Parable of the Sower in light of Jesus' directive to win the world.

You Are a Farm and a Field

A few years ago, author and speaker Bob Benson remarked during a Kentucky retreat that "we should be glad Jesus thinks of us as a farm as well as a field." Although being called a field or a farm may not sound too flattering, Bob's point was that few people, including pastors, hear the

Word of God without the message being garbled in some way.

Accurate listening can be thwarted by rootless enthusiasms, frightening persecutions, discouraging troubles, worries of life, deceitfulness of wealth or, for pastors, the deceitfulness of not having wealth.

Ministers as well as believers can be like the farm in our Lord's Parable of the Sower. In Luke 8:5-8, Jesus makes the field idea clear: "A farmer went out to sow his seed. As he was scattering the seed, some fell along the path; it was trampled on, and the birds of the air ate it up. Some fell on rock, and when it came up, the plants withered because they had no moisture. Other seed fell among thorns, which grew up with it and choked the plants. Still other seed fell on good soil. It came up and yielded a crop, a hundred times more than was sown."

Catch the message of the parable: We are made up of fields. Some are productive, while others are barren, rocky, packed down or overrun with thorns. I hope it does not push the meaning of the parable too far to suggest that some ministry crises might appear in a field that has become overly focused on troubles, persecutions or cares of this life.

Every pastor knows the feeling of having one or two fields flourishing for the cause of Christ while the other fields are weedy, stony and unproductive.

You Hold Incredible Seed in Your Hand

The law of harvest promises that we will reap the kind of fruit we plant. All of us need new confidence in what the gospel seed can reproduce.

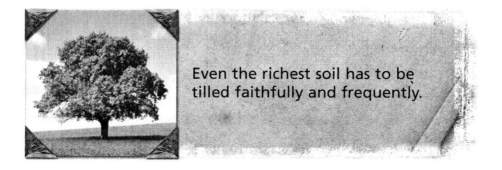

Even the richest soil has to be tilled faithfully and frequently.

Righteousness produces righteousness just as surely as onions produce onions. Too often, we mistakenly expect to reap righteousness by sowing something else.

Continue sowing the good news of the gospel. Although growing conditions may vary from year to year and from place to place, the gospel seed will eventually produce a harvest of redeemed people and renewed churches. Sometimes, it will even produce a bumper crop.

Cultivate Every Field

Even the richest soil has to be tilled faithfully and frequently. The same is true of the Church. In the agricultural world, even the best soil only produces a crop of grass and weeds until the ground is plowed, planted, watered, cultivated and harvested.

For ministers, this means that many apparently unattractive and overgrown church settings are rich in opportunity beyond their wildest imagination. In many places, a bumper crop awaits pastors who cultivate the land, plant the gospel seed, and stay long enough to experience a harvest.

Farming Is Hard Work

The Parable of the Sower also teaches another important fact about ministry: No harvest can be expected without effort. Ministry is hard work. This is not to say that it is without joy, adventure or effectiveness. But it is often tough and demanding.

A young pastor in his first assignment in a small growing southern Michigan church once said, "I never enjoyed hard work so much as I do in this ministry. I start early in the morning and work all day. But it is fun taking the transforming message of new life in Christ into people's lives in such a variety of ways."

Faithful farming is a continuous requirement throughout the entire growing season. All this compels a pastor to keep on planting, weeding, cultivating and fertilizing the soil to bring in the harvest before bad weather strikes.

Results May Sometimes Seem Slow

Once the seed has been planted, it may take a long time for it to grow so that it can be brought to harvest. Patient waiting can be one of the most frustrating experiences of ministry, but gospel planting and harvesting often require tenacious persistence.

Everyone knows at least one believer who for years delayed responding to the gospel. Yet in spite of no visible results in that individual's life, someone kept sowing and cultivating the seed until it finally germinated into a harvest of righteousness. That's the way it frequently happens. Keep working the fields. Keep planting the seed. A harvest is on the horizon.

It's Time to Break New Ground

One cynic's comment may be too close for comfort: "Futurists say knowledge changes every five years, but the Church takes 40 years to consider changing her Sunday morning schedule and then votes against it." Although this skeptic may have overstated the case, the Church has a well-earned reputation for resisting change or for seeing no need for it.

Throughout Church history, lay members, as well as pastors, have been notorious for believing modification of methods was a compromise of truth. In many people's minds, technique and truth are identical twins. It is easy to forget that today's traditional methods were often yesterday's controversial innovations.

Pastor Dale Burke offers a sure way to solve this dilemma: "If a church celebrates its methods, it becomes calcified and difficult to change. Celebrate mission over methods if you hope to build a culture of creativity that remains open to change."[1] Sadly, when a church resists change—even under the guise of lofty cautiousness—it can miss many golden opportunities. It can become so heavenly minded that it is no longer of any earthly good. As one pastor observed, "Holding the line often means missing the boat." New challenges, new populations and new centers of society are left untouched by the gospel.

In our confusion over rapid change in our culture, it is easy to overlook the fact that biblical accounts of the Early Church are packed with innovative strategies that took the Christian message to unevangelized places, nationalities, races and cultures. That is our task too!

WAYS TO CULTIVATE HOLY GROUND

Holy ground, in Moses' time and ours, is a way to describe an ordinary run-of-the-mill place or event God makes special by His presence. Sheep, desert, a few dried-up bushes—sometimes called tumbleweeds—and a lonely shepherd add up to ordinary in the extreme until the burning bush gets factored into the story. That presence in the burning bush made all the difference. Forever after that experience, Moses had a new alertness to what was happening around him and within him.

Our burning bushes may come in the form of new settings for the gospel, surprising Christian trends, and rapid societal changes that require us as pastors to be open and alert to see the opportunities.

Keep the Door Open to Innovation

Because change is ever present, why not start using it? Observe and use trends in society to shape new ways to minister. Watch for changes in the way people view life and how they respond to the work of the Church.

The changes occurring in today's society are more than cosmetic. Plainly, a new intensity of interest in religion is developing. We live in a time of massive social change, moral bankruptcy, religious curiosity and spiritual shallowness. How will we respond? Will we maximize the opportunities, resist the changes, or opt to be a modern-day Rip Van Winkle and sleep through the revolution?

Admit Everything Is Not Okay

To acknowledge frailties in the Church and failures in the ministry is a giant step toward renewal. Psychologists speak of a "professional denial reflex" in many occupations that occurs when rapid change and threats of job loss are present. This may be why some religious leaders are unwilling to admit that anything in the Church needs to be fixed.

I (Neil) heard a recognized clergy leader tell ministerial students in a college chapel that "the Church is doing a better job of fulfilling her mission now than at any time in Church history." A student asked a friend seated next to him, "I wonder if the speaker really believes that? If everything is right, why are so many giving up on the Church?"

Let's admit that the Church is not what it should be and not what it can be. Deep in our hearts, we all know that the Church needs to be renewed and refocused. There is a growing feeling among pastors that something has to be done about it.

Neither does it help to gloss over the Church's weakness by recounting the opportunities available to her. We often hear that these are days of golden opportunity for the Church, and so they are. Winston Churchill is quoted as saying that challenges are keys to self-renewal. If he was right, the Church is presented with the potential of an awesome awakening.

Restore the Supernatural

It is easy to forget ministry at its core has an omnipotent linkage with the resources of God. Although most of us can preach, counsel, visit, comfort, raise funds or lead without divine enablement, we all do these things much more effectively with God's help. All our efforts will be more lasting when divine anointing, presence, unction and guidance are restored to the daily activities of ministry.

God never intended a pastor's work to be mere human effort. A pastor once wrote to me (H. B.) at Focus on the Family that his frustrations with his decision-making group dropped to zero when he invited Christ to attend every meeting with him. "I should have known all along that God is as interested in those board meetings as I am," he rejoiced. "Now each meeting has become a ministry occasion where lay leaders openly seek to serve each other. It is a wonderful change!"

Commit to a Spiritual Awakening

Today, the moral chaos and ethical irrationality in our culture is mind-boggling. Society is drowning in immorality. As a remedy, we need more than syrupy spiritual sentimentality. We need a spiritual awakening.

An awakening of the magnitude we need depends on thousands of smaller revolutionary moral changes in every hamlet, crossroad, small town, suburb, city, county and state. The needed awakening won't come from imposing halls of government but from simple houses of worship. It won't come from centers of learning at the universities but from resurrection power proclaimed from hundreds of pulpits. It won't come from TV talk shows but from intercessory prayer meetings.

It will take pastors who challenge church members and communities to moral rightness and adventuresome faith. It will take pastors who believe and teach and live the reality that faith is not a luxury but the fulfillment of our reason for existence.

These could be the best of times for the cause of Christ if we know what to do with our opportunities. As a starting point for widespread revival and renewal, every gospel assignment must be viewed as holy ground. And every authentic minister of the gospel must commit to a moral awakening in his sphere of influence.

Abolish Meaninglessness

The Creator implanted a hunger in the human heart for us to make sense of life. Millions want to make a life as well as a living. They are bone weary of meaninglessness and cruelly disillusioned by the fact that

These could be the best of times for the cause of Christ if we know what to do with our opportunities.

they invested monumental energy and stress-producing allegiance to reach the top, only to find that it does not satisfy them or that someone else got there first. Albert E. Day, the devotional writer of an earlier generation, described the hunger and its satisfaction: "The real meaning of life is—not self-fulfillment or anything that the self can create—but God, finding God, and finding oneself in God, and adoring God, and loving Him, and being loved by Him."[2]

For individuals, the Christ way is the best possible life. This way of living provides ultimate payoffs on the *last* day when we stand before God. Between now and then, we enjoy an amazing quality of life as we become more like Christ. This kind of life is fulfilling and worthwhile. Such a focus in ministry on quality living and finishing well encourages people to seek a growing relationship with Christ.

"Repot" Your Ministry

To "repot" means to transplant a plant to a bigger pot so that it is not root-bound and the roots have room to grow. This term, when used in relationship to vocational issues, comes from author and statesman John R. O'Neil, who describes repotting as a purposeful choice to enjoy the excitement of doing something better, trying something new, or expanding one's interests to new fields.[3]

Repotting possibilities are nearly limitless for a pastor. We can improve our preaching or counseling skills. We can refresh our Greek. We can take a college course in human relationships or in creative writing. We can plan a day of spiritual retreat every month. We can give ourselves growing room in our present setting so that we can perform our work with more passion and people focus.

Try repotting your ministry. Allow the mental picture of a plant being given room to expand its root system affect your ministry and reshape your personal and professional growth.

Resist Cultural Intimidation

Secularism, sophistication and security are dead-end streets—even though much of society acts as if all three are worthy goals. As a result,

pastors sometimes feel browbeaten by society's values and even threatened when they are called on to offer ministry to people in higher social
strata than they are.

Paul pushed past any feelings of intimidation or inferiority when he
preached Christ to the Epicurean and Stoic philosophers at the
Areopagus. The biblical record shows that Paul started with familiar
ideas and then moved to the resurrection of Jesus:

> Paul then stood up in the meeting of the Areopagus and said:
> "Men of Athens! I see that in every way you are very religious.
> For as I walked around and looked carefully at your objects
> of worship, I even found an altar with this inscription: TO AN
> UNKNOWN GOD. Now what you worship as something unknown
> I am going to proclaim to you. The God who made the world
> and everything in it is the Lord of heaven and earth and does not
> live in temples built by hands. And he is not served by human
> hands, as if he needed anything, because he himself gives all men
> life and breath and everything else."

Note that Paul used verbal symbols his hearers easily understood;
he spoke the language of their social standing and class like a missionary using a native language dialect. In the process, he did not fear
cultural opposition, nor did he water down the gospel to please his
hearers.

Even as missionaries are needed to take the ministry into alien
nations and cultures, so the world needs spokespersons to take the
good news of Christ to every social and economic class. All people need
the gospel, and we must take it to them in words they understand
without any feelings of personal intimidation on our part.

More and more potential settings for the gospel message are being
misshaped by secularism, sophistication and security. Many people
will not understand the basic vocabulary of faith, nor do they have a
Christian memory. But they need us, and we must go to them, using
Paul's strategies:

- Speak so secularists understand.
- Take the gospel to every strata of society.
- Use transferable concepts.
- Start with familiar ideas.
- Emphasize resurrection power.
- Conquer fears of new cultural environments.
- Believe God wants to transform everyone.

Create a Future for Ministry

Demographics, social trends, expert research and investigative analysis are useful for helping us understand our world and our opportunities. But there is more.

To predict the future is passive, but to shape the future is active. Predicting the future means we attempt to explain what appears to be inevitable. But shaping and fashioning the future start by asking what God wants the gospel to accomplish in the new generation in our setting and then working to make it happen.

Every ministry site offers some opportunity to shape the future. I have in mind considering every decision in light of the future. I have in mind applying hope and expectation to every phase of ministry. Take heart—the same God who was present, active and victorious in all our yesterdays will be with us today and tomorrow.

George Gallup advises using the following prescription to shape the process:

- **Listen** to the remarkable spiritual experiences of people and help them understand and build upon those experiences.

- **Teach** people how to develop their faith, pray more effectively, bring the Bible into their daily lives and become better trained in leadership skills.

- **Encourage** small-group fellowships, which serve as a means for people to enter the faith community as well as a way to support current members.

- **Inspire** people to reach out to others in appropriate and loving ways.

- **Target** key groups for spiritual nourishment and religious instruction: people in business, the professions and other fields who constantly make ethical judgments; students, who receive an incomplete and distorted education if the vital role of religion is ignored; and people in the media, who often are ignorant about religion.[4]

Produce Magnificent Fruit

Many years ago, a clergy couple who were pastors to a mid-size church in Idaho took turns preaching on alternate Sundays. In addition to being a wife and mother, the woman was an interesting biblical expositor, and the people enjoyed listening to her. The man, though a highly appreciated pastor, was introspective, shy, sometimes melancholy, and not a gifted speaker.

When it was his Sunday to preach, the husband usually awoke with discouraging self-doubts. On those Sundays, it was his custom during breakfast to express his apprehension and ask his wife and children to pray for him. He freely admitted that he was unsure of his message, questioned his ability to speak, and wondered how close he really was to Christ. It was a bad scene for everyone in the family and a terribly discouraging way to begin Sunday.

"God, help Edward," his wife would pray as she helped the children prepare for church. "You know he can do it. And You will help him. He has served You faithfully all week, and You will help him now."

This pastor's wife has an important message for contemporary clergy persons. Even during confusing times, we can accomplish competent ministry because of God's enablement. Joshua 1:9 promises, "Be strong and courageous. Do not be terrified; do not be discouraged, for the Lord your God will be with you wherever you go."

Take strength for every part of your ministry as you consider God's remarkable record of helping ordinary people in difficult circumstances. Consider their victory as promises for your own victory:

- Daniel, who slept peaceably in a den of lions
- Joseph, who resisted a seductive woman
- David, who overpowered a giant
- Elijah, who defied a heathen cult
- John the Baptist, who redirected his prominence to Jesus
- Paul, who sang stress away at midnight in jail
- Jesus, who modeled God's love on the cross

This list contains enough encouragement to reenergize your ministry even in the most demanding of situations. Join hands and hearts with hundreds of self-renewing pastors who are committed to taking the gospel to the cutting edge of modern life. You will experience a magnificent soul-stretching sense of God's nearness in the middle of a ministry filled to the brim with incredible demands, challenging possibilities and remarkable achievements.

A MENTOR'S LETTER CONCERNING HOLY GROUND

Some time ago, I (Neil) wrote to a young pastor who was feeling shell-shocked at the first anniversary of his first pastorate. Nothing was the way he believed it should be. He wanted to quit and go back to school to learn how to train pastors. Here's part of my letter to him:

Finding holy ground for ministry is not to go, but to stay. It is not to look for something else, but to see what you already have. It is not to hunger for a new love, but to court an old one. It is not to long for ease, but to risk everything to cultivate your stony field until it produces an abundant crop.

Persevere until you would not consider leaving. Refuse to give your difficulties too much attention. Invest more energy in nourishing the center of your faith so God can use you for a radical renewal in the congregation you serve.

Your friend in the great adventure of ministry, Neil

There is sound counsel in that letter for every minister in every place.

A Prolific Partnership with God

- God's nearness makes ministry an adventure regardless of location.
- People in your setting have incredible spiritual needs.
- Your outlook limits or liberates ministry.
- The gospel seed penetrates the hardest soil.
- God has up-to-date plans for every setting.
- Everyone—pastor, parishioners and the world—needs a miracle.

No good work is done anywhere without aid from the Father of Lights.
—C. S. Lewis[5]

To a New Generation of Pastors
Great Expectations

Musings from H. B. London, Jr.

Hype takes expectations off the charts each year as Super Bowl season approaches or when a prominent team hires or fires a highly visible coach.

I think we all need moments when the expectations for our own ministry are given elevated status, too. I imagine that you were filled with great expectations when you entered ministry. I know I was.

Sadly, in time reality sets in and expectations are tempered by many variables. People, places and chemistry between you and those you serve seem to undermine your hopes and dreams. In some ways, your great expectations are at the mercy of others' expectations for you. I didn't like that part very much, but let me encourage you with a few timely passages from God's Word:

The LORD delights in a man's way, he makes his steps firm (Ps. 37:23).

Now to him who is able to do immeasurably more than all we ask or imagine (Eph. 3:20).

No eye has seen, no ear has heard, no mind has conceived what God has prepared for those who love him (1 Cor. 2:9).

Sometimes I think we forget how much faith God has in us. That's when we most often give in to our own self-doubt. Don't do that! His hopes and dreams for you are great—even greater than what you believe for yourself. You are a winner— live like it!

CHAPTER 3

BLOOM WHERE YOU'RE PLANTED

Master Gardener of my soul and ministry,
Open my eyes to opportunities in my assignment.
Open my love to all the people in this place.
And strengthen my skills to be Your junior gardener
to plant, water, cultivate, weed, prune and
harvest in this place.
Amen.

> # LET US NOT BECOME WEARY IN DOING GOOD, FOR AT THE PROPER TIME WE WILL REAP A HARVEST IF WE DO NOT GIVE UP.
>
> GALATIANS 6:9

MAXIMIZE OPPORTUNITIES

"Bloom Buster helped me grow these flowers, the greatest gardening success I've ever had," the shopkeeper in Red Stone, Colorado, said in response to my comments about her flowers. She had the most extraordinary red geraniums I (Neil) had ever seen. Garden catalog illustrations seem inferior by comparison.

At the first sign of spring, you can be sure I started shopping for Bloom Buster. And that year, my flowers were better than ever before.

The name "Bloom Buster" started me thinking about front-line pastors I know. They do everything they can to be effective shepherds for God in a hurting world. They work and pray and struggle. Yet in spite of their sacrificial commitments and demanding schedules, their churches often grow only slightly or even shrink a little every year. Like working in a wilting garden under a scorching August sun, their sizable efforts never break growth barriers. Nothing unusual happens in their congregations.

They feel like the tired old preacher who said, "My necessities ate up my possibilities." They starve for the reality they lost when ministry was allowed to become secularized, professionalized, miniaturized and marginalized. They hunger for a new grip on ministry and a new joy in serving.

They seek a new perspective and a fresh anointing. They want something to happen inside of them—something similar to what one 40-year-old pastor experienced after serving his church in rural Georgia for 10 years: "When I allowed myself to be fascinated by opportunities and by the grace of God, I started blooming in ways I never experienced before."

New ministry blooming in familiar places requires that we take a discriminating look at our existing ministry activities, even as we carefully examine our opportunities. Most settings have extraordinary possibilities that do not show on the surface. For example, outreach makes ministry grow faster than administrative activities, and marriage workshops usually are more effective than divorce-restoration counseling.

A beginning pastor from New England wrote to me (Neil), saying, "I don't have time for outreach because I am too busy studying for next Sunday's sermon, stomping out brush fires or trying to meet the unrealistic demands of people in the church." Could it be that more emphasis on outreach would change the focus of this pastor's ministry and would challenge the perceptions of the members of his small church? Making such a shift might be tough, but it is the only way new opportunities for his church will be set in motion.

LARGER BLOOMS AND LASTING FRUIT

One reality is obvious: God wants every ministry to bloom, to bear magnificent fruit and to have strong roots. He wants His people fed and loved in every place. He does not, however, expect each pastor to look alike, to grow at the same rate, or to have the same impact. That is why He planted us where we are.

Several key challenges must be faced if ministry in a specific place is to be renewed, reenergized or even revolutionized. Try scoring yourself on this checklist:

- Can a pastor change the world?
- What did God have in mind for me to accomplish in this place when He called me here?
- Can I take the life-changing power of the gospel to the cutting edges of life where the substitutes for faith have proven trivial and futile?
- Am I willing to refocus my ministry so it attracts contemporary people?
- Can I help secular people see the gospel as an appealing alternative to the security, sex, fame and power they chase?
- Can my ministry thrive in tough places where effective ministry has never occurred?

Everyone knows that flourishing gardens need quality seed, cultivating, watering, weeding and meticulous attention to soil conditions and temperature. But my gardener friend from Red Stone multiplied her success and satisfaction when she added generous amounts of tender loving care and nourishing plant food.

Ministry is like that—tender-loving care and bloom busters must be added to develop vibrant congregations. The following ideas might be useful to help you feed and lead your church. Try them for yourself.

MEASURE POTENTIAL GOD'S WAY

I loved the way one church described itself in an advertisement seeking a new pastor:

A DIAMOND IN THE ROUGH is searching for a master stone-cutter to unleash the potential that lies beneath its surface. This GEM TO BE can be found in a suburban neighborhood in South-Central Pennsylvania. . . . If you have a steady hand,

keen eye, and are willing to "strike the blow" to produce daz-
zling results, write to . . .[1]

Maybe every church is a diamond in the rough, waiting for a master
stonecutter to strike the blow that unleashes its potential.

View Your Church as a Living Cell

Take another careful look at your "diamond in the rough." In *Diary of a
Country Priest*, Georges Bernanos writes tenderly about his congregation:

> This morning I prayed hard for my parish, my poor parish, my
> first and perhaps my last, since I ask no better than to die here.
> My parish! The words can't even be spoken without a kind of
> soaring love. . . . I know that my parish is a reality; it is not a
> mere administrative segment, but a living cell of the everlasting
> Church.[2]

It is nearly impossible for a pastor to see his church as a living cell of
the everlasting Church when he is bogged down with the confusing
expectations of dear old Sister Smith or when he is dealing with the sad
sorrow of a dying teenager. This is probably the reason pastors often see
more problems than possibilities in the place where the Father has
planted them. The inability to see the forest because they are in the
midst of the trees certainly applies.

Can you see this clearly and believe it thoroughly? Your church is a
living cell of the everlasting Church.

Play Prospective Pastor

To clarify the possibilities in your present assignment, try viewing it
through the lens of a prospective pastor for a full day once or twice each
year. Drive or walk through your neighborhood as if you were seeing
it for the first time. Refocus on the potential you saw when you first visited this area.

Dare to dream your original dream. See your congregation as live,
flesh-and-blood people—some noble and some clueless, some saintly

and some sinful, some great and some not so great. The routines you experience day after day or year after year may become brand-new. Remember, God intends for ministry to thrive everywhere people reside.

Recently, a bored young pastor phoned to ask, "What comes next after pastoring? I've been thinking about trying teaching or law or social work." What comes next? This young pastor's question implies that he does not see the possibilities in his church the way that God does.

All things considered, who could be satisfied with the narrower spiritual opportunities that other occupations offer? The possibilities are enormous and eternal. To see these possibilities clearly, every minister needs to often pray, "God, show me what You want done in this living cell of your everlasting Church."

Opportunity blindness always worsens when a pastor considers each assignment as a steppingstone to something better. Such a stance forces him to consider every pastorate as semi-temporary. In some unexplainable, self-fulfilling way, his thinking causes the assignment to actually become restrictive or even suffocating. Yet the opportunities he hopes to find in another place often already exist where he resides.

Francis Bacon's advice helps us bloom: "A wise man makes more opportunities than he finds."[3] What a soul-expanding idea when applied to our ministries. *Every* faith community— regardless of its size, location or history—has opportunities and potential built into it that are just waiting to be discovered by its pastor.

Marking Time Costs Too Much

The human cost of marking time while waiting for something better can

When a pastor begins to see potential from Jesus' perspective, every congregation will possess possibilities.

be frighteningly high. Those whom we could have won for Christ continue in their sinful confusion. Broken marriages that we could have helped mend go to the divorce courts. Innocent children that we could have introduced to the Savior move on to adulthood without meeting the Lord. Church members atrophy. Our passion shrivels. Multiply these losses across a few thousand congregations and it adds up to alarming spiritual barrenness for a country and a culture.

But consider the strong underpinnings of ministry. Doesn't a call to ministry mean that God may send a pastor to tough situations that He wants to make new and to people whom He wants to save? Doesn't ministry mean that God sometimes sends people like us—inadequate though we may be—next door to hell? He has to have *someone* there as His agent of transformation and miraculous reconciliation.

Consider Two Perspectives from Jesus

Jesus viewed potential from two perspectives: service and sacrifice—using a towel for service and a cross for sacrifice. God often assigns us to places where we are especially needed. This might be a tough situation in which our salary will be small, the housing limited and the attendance of the church low. Perhaps He will assign us to places blighted by urban decay, social violence or moral desperation. Maybe He will send us to congregations splintered by broken relationships. Or He might want us to serve exploitative people because we are their only hope.

Perhaps God intends for us to love people and feed faith in places where even the best folks have given up. Let's face it, throughout the long, stirring march of Christian history, pastors have often bloomed the most in times of moral decay.

When a pastor begins to see potential from Jesus' perspective, every congregation will possess possibilities. Every community will seem ready for a spiritual awakening. Why be terrified or intimidated? We are linked in strength-giving partnership with Omnipotence.

Create an Ideal Assignment

Maybe every minister dreams of the perfect pastorate—whatever that is. Some expect to find such a congregation around the next bend. Others hope their sweetheart church will show up before Christmas.

Some pastors spend their entire ministry hoping for a model congregation made up of hundreds of good-natured people in a moderate climate, in an ideal town, with high pay.

For many, it seems to be about wanting what the other guy has without the problems that go with it. Apparently, the pastors who long for such greener pastures have never considered the reality that every good place was once a tough place that required someone to transform it into a special, desirable church by blooming there. The secret is to make our assignment ideal by blooming where God plants us.

To expand our views of the "ideal" assignment even more, consider the views of one young pastor, whose words suggest wisdom beyond his years: "I do not think a minister should move until he has experienced a spiritual breakthrough where he is." Careful—there is a surprising bear trap in his concept. No one would want to leave a place while an authentic spiritual breakthrough is happening.

This view helps us to see incredible new possibilities in every setting and undermines the human frustration and financial costs of moving to another church. An absolutely indispensable factor in sustaining a healthy ministry is the willingness to view one's setting from God's perspective.

A church leader in Canada suggests that "every church has a right to have a pastor who believes something spiritually significant will happen in that place under his leadership. If a pastor does not believe in the possibilities of his assignment, he should seek God until he sees the potential."

God counts on you to achieve a Christ-exalting ministry where He has planted you. He has no one else to lead the charge. Growing an effective ministry starts by discovering a need that breaks your heart and then motivates you to break your back to meet that need.

FIND FULFILLMENT WHERE YOU ARE

A yearning to be whole, to make his life count and to make a difference in the world are what make a potential pastor open to God's call into ministry in the beginning. And God provides the raw materials for us to discover fulfillment in every assignment.

A pastor on Florida's Gold Coast was called to a 100-member church made up of mostly elderly people. He followed a pastor who had served this congregation for more than 20 years. He had been there so long that few people in the congregation could remember the former pastor.

To complicate matters, many members of the congregation lived across the street from the church in a Social Security-supplement high-rise building. As a result, the new pastor faced unusually heavy demands for pastoral care. Some of his minister friends warned him that the situation was futile, but he saw beyond the limitations.

In eight years, the new pastor started Bible studies in the high-rise facility; recruited recent immigrants from Haiti, Cuba, Mexico and Finland to start six language churches; began a youth ministry; purchased five nearby houses for sanctuary expansion; and offered genuine friendship to the former pastor who lived nearby.

The new minister saw beyond age, color, language and limitation. After he had been there for several years, one of his friends who had advised him not to accept the pastorate offered this compliment: "You took lemons and made lemonade."

During an interview for a pastor's magazine in which he was asked about finding ministry fulfillment in tough assignments, this minister responded: "Complain about difficulties? Emphasize hardships? Bellyache about inconvenience? Many do and so could I. But what's the point? There's so much more to ministry. I choose to hope, explore, cherish, contribute and live. I enjoy seeing how much fun I can have in the ministry."

Growing an effective ministry starts by discovering a need that breaks your heart and then motivates you to break your back to meet that need.

This minister's ability to find meaning, fulfillment and satisfaction was a natural result of a long succession of doing the right things for the right reasons across years of cheerful, Christ-centered service. His formula for fulfillment: Expect every assignment to enrich our life and it will not disappoint us. The serendipity of selfless service is abiding satisfaction. Loving gives us love. Serving supplies satisfaction. Giving one's self away enriches us.

How to Increase Fulfillment

To increase satisfaction, rekindle your original motivations for ministry. Rejoice in your achievements. Celebrate your victories as God-given enablements that flow into the nooks and crannies of your ministry.

Tame your workaholic tendencies so that you can find time to grow a great soul. Read old and new books about ministry in order to establish a benchmark for your pastoral service. Find successful models to emulate. Doing these ecclesiastical calisthenics on a regular basis will prevent spiritual stagnation, professional passivity and superficial success.

Let's admit that every pastor stands at the center of what makes ministry meaningful for him. The springs of fulfillment are internal and personal. The whole thing starts with that first stirring in our soul about ministry—the dialogue and debate that no one else heard between God and us. Because God has called us, it means that we measure fulfillment differently from people in other occupations or other pastors. It means that we are most fulfilled when God is most pleased with our ministry.

Fulfillment Is an Inside Job

Unless ministers find a high level of meaning in their work, they almost never have a significant impact on a congregation or a community. Take the example of a subordinate on General George C. Marshall's staff during World War II, who reported that several officers were having low-morale problems. General Marshall retorted, "Officers don't have morale problems. Officers cure morale problems in themselves and others. No one looks after my morale."[4]

Marshall was probably right about military personnel, and this certainly says a lot to ministers. No pastor can depend on anyone else to feed his feelings of fulfillment. It is an inside job, but anyone can achieve it.

One pastor in a mid-Atlantic state—let's call him Tom—has served a series of congregations for 31 years. Tom is confused about when to expect his satisfactions. To a trusted friend, he sadly said, "All my life, I followed scripts suggested by my parents, wife, church members and even my bishop. When their scripts conflicted, I just tried harder. But I haven't experienced much fulfillment. I've done my duty, but it hasn't been too much fun. My life is melancholy and drab."

Now, at age 55, Tom keeps waiting for someone to give him his fulfillment, but he fears it will never come. And he's probably right. How tragic! Tom should have awakened years ago to the fact that no outside circumstance or person provides meaning for a pastor.

Genuine fulfillment is rooted in knowing what ministry is and then doing it energetically and creatively. You know better than anyone else when your ministry is vibrant and satisfying. You know what pleases God. This is what matters most in measuring meaning in ministry.

Fulfillment Is an Intentional Choice

Unfortunately, a pastor never gains an ounce of fulfillment by saying, "I know I should build a satisfying ministry, but I don't get the breaks or have the luck or possess natural abilities." It is far better to realize that every minister can have more meaning if and when he wants it.

One writer suggests that discovering fulfillment is like experiencing a hot stove. After touching a blistering flame, one can draw back forever

Giving one's self away enriches us.

and announce, "I will never touch a stove again." But a different reaction is more desirable. One can turn down the heat, follow the instruction book, have the stove repaired and become a gourmet cook. Then the cook has the satisfaction of serving a superb meal, and many are well fed. In a similar way, pastors can either settle into humdrum mediocrity or find ways to increase their effectiveness for God.

A warning must be considered: Most pastors easily discern God's fulfillment in their yesterdays, but they struggle about today. Why not watch carefully for God in our present moments? Why not turn today's troublesome circumstances into magnificent fulfillment? Spectacular blooming often depends on how we choose.

USE CHANGE INTENTIONALLY AND CREATIVELY

Like a raging river overflowing at flood stage, almost everything is changing. Old assumptions are being challenged and forsaken. Everything is heading downstream at breakneck speed to an unknown destination. And every local congregation stands in the center of this pandemonium.

Leadership shifts, member migrations, economic upheavals and doctrinal confusion multiply congregational changes. No congregation, regardless of how it resists change, is the same as it was a decade ago—or even the same as it was last year.

Some People Applaud Change

Ministers sometimes mistakenly begin a pastorate with the assumption that the entire congregation has its heels dug in against change. This is seldom the case. Sprinkled throughout many churches are allies waiting for progressive signs from the pastor as head of the organization.

Despite their stick-in-the-mud reputations, many congregations are no longer rigidly unchangeable. Thus, a pastor should learn to manage change, understanding that many people will resist change out of fear while others will welcome it as progress.

A wise old whittler who purposely tries to impress tourists as he kills time in a hotel lobby at Fairplay, Colorado, was overheard to say to a young man, "You better learn to like change, because life is just one miserable change after another." He is right. The question is not *if* the Church will change, but *how* it will change. The real issues are: Change for what? Change to what? And how will change impact Kingdom work?

Value Imagination and Innovation

Any pastor who wishes to constructively use change must possess pure motives and use creative imagination. Business authority and author Warren Bennis offers the following wise counsel that especially applies to pastors: "Positive change requires trust, clarity and participation. At this juncture in our world, all three seem as distant as Jupiter. But we have reached Jupiter, and so perhaps we can finally reach ourselves."[5]

Bennis's next sentence offers extraordinary challenge for pastors: "Only people with virtue and vision can lead us out of this bog and back to high ground."[6] Change is natural, normal and needed. Our problem in church and ministry is to know the difference between the changeless and the passing. The changeless message must be conserved, but it must always be communicated in ways that each new generation understands.

However, a possible gale warning must be posted in every pastor's thought processes. *Novel* change is not the same as *needed* change. Ministers must resist the temptation to become, as one bishop observed, "apostles of change for no reason." Change for its own sake can sometimes destroy a church.

For example, the pastor of a 125-member church in Northern California instituted change because he wanted to be known as a nonconformist. So he moved the pulpit to a closet, declaring, "Jesus never used a pulpit." He called hymnals "relics" and preached from a controversial Bible translation just because "it was not like the Bible my grandfather used." He strummed his guitar as the congregation sang from handmade overheads that were hard to read in broad daylight. He refused to take public offerings and asked people to place their gifts in a box at the rear of the sanctuary. He altered the starting time of the morning worship service, hardening his congregation's resistance to his changes even more.

When asked about these rapid changes, the pastor replied, "Tradition kills churches." Much to his surprise, he was later forced to move when his compulsions about change undermined his leadership.

If a church is to bloom, change must be used creatively to improve ministry for those who currently attend and to expand the church's impact on secular people who don't attend. Whether we love or loathe change, the writer of the song "Be Still, My Soul" offers this assurance: "In every change He faithful will remain."[7]

FOCUS ON MISSION AS FOUNDATION FOR VISION

Define ministry accurately and clearly. Sharpen your perspective through Scripture, church history, believers and fellow ministers. Know what the target is. Check the promises again. Then intentionally implement Christ's mandate in your ministry.

A clearly understood biblical mission keeps a church from being sidetracked. It helps a pastor create vision. It can produce such high motivation for genuine achievement that people can't be stopped from doing what they believe to be God's will for their church.

Many crises in troubled congregations whirl around misunderstandings concerning the Church's reason for being in our kind of world. A confused congregation led by a perplexed pastor never knows if it accomplishes anything worthwhile. The fundamental question is this: Does anyone have a clue about what God wants the Church to be and do in our setting now?

An Uncertain Purpose Always Hinders

Confusion about purpose has many jumbled roots. Bizarre and uninformed voices, outside and inside our congregations, offer unsolicited opinions about the Church's task in the world. The confusion deepens even more when alien groups such as gay activists and secular media experts tell the Church what her duty is while branding her members as crackpots and hatemongers for not following their agenda.

Another confusion arises when we use ministry as a label for too wide a range of church activities. These days, the designation "ministry" is applied to everything from rock music to abortion fights to basketball leagues to financial seminars to dinner parties to women's rights. This tendency to define ministry so broadly dilutes the Church's ability to focus on her bedrock basic objectives.

As a partial solution, a minister must know what business the church is in and must frequently communicate these priorities to the congregation. Without such understanding, the church may become bogged down in minutiae or overextended in nonproductive activities. Regrettably, when a church does not understand her reason for being, she is likely to vacillate between ingrown mediocrity or fad fascination or paralyzing apathy.

But do pastors know what the Church's mission is? It might be frightening to discover how few of us are able to accurately articulate the Church's mission. Without a clear focus, ministry activity is often done at the margins and too much concentration is invested in peripheral issues. As a result, many needs of contemporary life are left untouched by the impact of the gospel.

Vision and Mission Can Be Clear
To focus and clarify mission, the pastor must ask and answer several weighty questions: What is the essential core of modern ministry? What principles endure in every generation? Who sets the agenda? What criteria will we use to determine success?

Such a focus-clarifying process can be shared among lay leaders, church members and the pastor. In this effort, remember that congregations cannot rally to battle cries they do not hear or sacrifice for causes they do not understand.

Our Lord gave pastors and churches important raw materials for developing a mission statement. Taking three biblical references together gives us a clear picture of what He wants done.

First, in John 14:12-14, Jesus told His disciples, "Anyone who has faith in me will do what I have been doing. *He will do even greater things than these*, because I am going to the Father. And I will do whatever you ask in my name, so that the Son may bring glory to the Father. You may ask me for anything in my name, and I will do it" (emphasis added).

Second, after giving His disciples the Great Commission, Jesus helped them to see His mission and theirs in the world: "Go and make disciples of all nations, baptizing them in the name of the Father and of the son and of the Holy Spirit, and teaching them to obey everything I have commanded you. *And surely I am with you always, to the very end of the age*" (Matt. 28:19-20, emphasis added).

Third, in the Great Commandment, Jesus said, "'Love the Lord your God with all your heart and with all your soul and with all your strength and with all your mind'; and, *'Love your neighbor as yourself'*" (Luke 10:27, emphasis added).

Mission and the vision that grows out of the gospel help us get a clear focus and a good grip on what needs to be done next.

But still, the unknown future calls for a willingness to adjust to the new opportunities that no one could see earlier. Such an adjustment is easier to make when a mission/vision statement is in place, for then it's a matter of adjustment rather than starting from nothing.

UNDERSTAND YOUR IMPORTANCE

God needs you now more than ever. The human race cannot afford to lose one more committed pastor. Without the salt of your ministry, society could putrefy. Without your light, the darkness could grow darker still.

As we discussed in our book *Pastors at Greater Risk*, the number of pastors going AWOL has increased over the years, and everyone admits the parish ministry is harder now than it once was. The causes include membership migration, distracted church members, declining moral absolutes and unrealistic expectations from many sources. The resulting moral decline in society makes ministry difficult, but highlights how desperately you are needed.

Tony Snow, press secretary for President George W. Bush, sounded like a modern prophet when he wrote more than a decade ago: "While activists and judges have shoved religion from the public stage, usually under the guise of separating church and state, religious figures have made the task easy. They have committed the cardinal mistake of snuggling too close to power and submitting to compromises that have bought them respectability without earning them respect."[8]

Although these current days confuse us, we may be the only hope for faith, righteousness and truth to be chiseled into society's psyche. We must recognize how much our troubled world needs us. Here's a prayer to help us do it:

> *Give us enough lightning and storms*
> *to shake up our soil*
> *enough wind to keep us spirited*
> *enough death to bring us life*
> *and enough goodness*
> *to help us remember who we are.*[9]

Society Has Many Problems

Let's admit that no one knows how to deal with the moral decay and spiritual disintegration that is sweeping our nation and world. A serious sickness of the soul seems to be crippling individuals, families, churches and communities. Counterfeit ministries have nauseated the masses. Judeo-Christian values are being discarded without trial. Something must be done.

Civilization stands at a moral abyss. Newscasters, sounding like Old Testament holy men using the latest technology, predict that doomsday is just around the corner.

Without intending to be religious, the media remind us constantly that we are being destroyed, like the Roman Empire, from within. Chastity and character have fallen to a low point. Rooted in a permissive revolution, families, homes and society are reaping a toxic harvest. Although moderns call it a "social blight," earlier generations called it "sin." And that's what it is. This sounds like a society that needs the Church and our ministry more than ever before.

Churches Often Reflect Culture

To make matters worse, in many places the Church has allowed itself to become greatly influenced by the prevailing culture. In his well-researched book *The Transformation of American Religion*, Alan Wolfe says, "In every aspect of the religious life, American faith has met American culture—and American culture has triumphed."[10]

In light of these realities, it's too late for more opinion polls, focus groups and national conferences to speculate about morality, faith and righteousness. The time has come to speak to the deepest needs of the human heart and secular society with soul seriousness and supernatural biblical authority.

A miraculous spiritual revolution is needed to clean up this immoral cesspool. We must intercede for an awakening. We must speak of the gospel again with a divine anointing.

This cannot be accomplished by ministers who give up a day too soon, by those who suffer from professional inferiority, or by those who turn and run at the first sign of formidable opposition. Who will give our neighbors God's good news about forgiveness and grace and reconciliation if we don't?

The power to alleviate this darkness is in our hearts and in our hands. We can light the lamps, stay the course and stop cursing the darkness. The fact that the world needs us so urgently makes it possible for us to bloom in lots of dark places.

CONSIDER YOUR POTENTIAL IMPACT ON THE WORLD

Think of the impact that approximately 350,000 pastors could make on the United States and the world. Think of the potential. The responsibilities. The rekindling. The energizing. The reformation. The hope. It could mark the beginning of a moral revival, a new reign of righteousness, and even the preservation of our civilization.

With apology to John W. Gardner, former secretary of Health, Education and Welfare and author of the book *On Leadership*, the following paragraphs paraphrase a "become the change you want to see" for pastors:

YOU can have a significant role in re-creating the state of the Church.

YOU can become symbols of moral purity in our society.

YOU can express biblical values that make the Church great and allow her to redemptively impact the culture.

Most importantly, YOU can conceive and articulate goals that lift people out of petty preoccupations, carry them above the conflicts that tear a church and society apart and unite them in pursuit of objectives worthy of their best efforts.[11]

God has sounded a solemn wake-up call. The message is as clear as the morning sun: In this baffling epoch of human history, He needs you to be strong and courageous and effective. The Church—a vital, living, changing entity—is susceptible to rotting decay or open to revolutionary renewal. What she becomes depends on each of us.

This is the time to energize one church at a time—your church. This is the time to spiritually overhaul one pastor at a time—you. This is the time to pay any price to make ministry so ablaze with God's presence that perplexed, broken people will be drawn to your church and be transformed one at a time.

Bloom where God has planted you.

CONTEMPORARY CHALLENGE

How to Bloom in Your Ministry

- Take the gospel to the cutting edges of contemporary life.
- Measure potential God's way.
- View your church as a living cell of the everlasting Church.
- Refuse to merely mark time.
- Re-evaluate your opportunities.
- Find a cause that breaks your heart and then accept God's challenge to change it.
- Seek fulfillment as an intentional choice.
- Understand your significance in society.
- Define mission accurately and clearly.

Put yourself completely under the influence of Jesus, so that He may think His thoughts in your mind, do His work through your hands, for you will be all-powerful with Him to strengthen you. —Mother Teresa[12]

Divine Appointments

Musings from H. B. London, Jr.

Our lives are filled with divine opportunities—those times when we cross paths with a person or a situation that, as we reflect on it, could only happen by divine appointment.

A while ago, I was on a flight from Cincinnati to Chicago. It was scheduled to take 56 minutes, but it took nearly five hours! It was one of the most frustrating days I have had in a long time. But during those five hours, I was seated next to a lady from the East Coast who was going through marital problems. During the long delay, she shared some heartbreaking information about her family. I mostly listened. She needed someone to hear her out. I believe God placed me on that plane for that lady—a divinely directed moment.

With so much pain in our world and so many people needing to be helped to their feet, we as Christian leaders need to make the most of those divine moments when God places us in the right place at the right time to represent Him. We need to be like Christ for the moment to someone who needs "a cup of cold water in Jesus' name."

So be alert! Be available! Be sensitive! Be prepared! God has some divine appointments set for you. They may appear subtle at first, but in eternal terms, they will be life changing. "Be very careful, then, how you live—not as unwise but as wise, making the most of every opportunity" (Eph. 5:15-16).

CHAPTER 4

LIVE IN THE PRESENT FULLY

Lord of the present and God of the future,
Give me thanks for the past.
Give me hope for the future.
Awaken me to the glorious possibilities
of the present.
And give me fortitude to follow your
direction today.
Amen.

> ## AS LONG AS IT IS DAY, WE MUST DO THE WORK OF HIM WHO SENT ME.
>
> JOHN 9:4

TODAY IS THE DAY FOR ACTION

Somewhere in my notes and clippings for writing projects, I jotted this quote from some unknown writer: "Yesterday is a canceled check, tomorrow is a promissory note, and today is cash in hand. Spend it wisely." This is true and wonderful advice for a pastor.

History, heritage and tradition are important foundations of contemporary Christianity. But nostalgia about the good old days can be lethal if we allow it to keep us from a wholehearted commitment to effectively serve this present age.

Ministry never bursts into full bloom at some magic future moment when we have more experience, find the right town, or receive some favored advantage. It starts now. Our current post has a wealth of potential. Why not find it and use it?

REFUSE TO SQUANDER TODAY'S OPPORTUNITIES

Some of the most productive expressions of ministry in the Church's long pilgrimage of faith should be happening *today*. God wants pastors to make the gospel real in contemporary life. This is the precise reason why a pastor cannot pitch his tent in the past, misuse the present, or resist the future.

Too many of us waste years waiting for some nebulous something to occur. In our imagination, the future is wrapped in airy fantasy or flimsy ambition. As a consequence, we never fully live in the present.

Another squandering of present opportunities occurs when a pastor gives more time and thought to church politics than to proficient ministerial competence. Everyone, especially the pastor, loses when that happens. Although no one can honestly deny that political forces are at work in congregations, denominations and parachurch organizations, political maneuvering never saved one soul, fed a homeless child or gladdened the heart of God.

On the contrary, political jostling often actually hinders Kingdom work when it causes a pastor to misappropriate energies he could have invested in helping hurting people or in personal pastoral development. To maximize your effectiveness, live in the present and try to ignore the politics.

THE ENVIRONMENT FOR MINISTRY KEEPS CHANGING

Americans once thought they had it all: a healthy economy, good medical care, safe and secure schools. No one thought to ask whether the letter

God wants pastors to make the gospel real in contemporary life.

received in the mail today was safe to open or whether the tap water was safe to drink. And we could take a plane to grandmother's house without a second thought. Many people believed they had a good chance at the American dream.

Securities Crumble

Then our sense of security began to crumble as our nation experienced four catastrophes that symbolize the confusing changes that keep taking place in the environment in which we do ministry. Those catastrophes were Hurricane Katrina, the terrorist attacks of 9/11, the Columbine shootings and the Oklahoma City bombing.

- *Natural Disaster and Government Response.* Hurricane Katrina, which hit the Gulf Coast of the United States, caused catastrophic damage along the coastlines of Louisiana, Mississippi and Alabama and flooded approximately 80 percent of New Orleans. The hurricane became a symbol that natural disasters can be devastating, capable of destroying whole towns, and can leave millions homeless.

- *Money and Military.* The terrorist attacks against the World Trade Center in New York and the Pentagon on September 11, 2001, were ultimately an attack on our nation's military strength and financial might. These attacks became a symbol that security cannot be found in military or financial institutions.

- *School and Family.* The shootings that occurred at Columbine High School by two teenaged students forever changed the way Americans view the safety of their children in schools and focused awareness on cliques and bullying in schools. The Columbine school shootings became a symbol that security cannot be found in our schools and that we have a lot of room for improvement in relation to the children and youth of our country.

• *Home-grown terrorists.* The Oklahoma City bombing, which destroyed the federal building in downtown Oklahoma City, was the largest act of domestic terrorism in the history of the country. The bombing became a symbol that terrorism can be an inside job and made us aware that the person "next door" could be the cause of the next disaster.[1]

Check your own list of crumbling securities. The events listed here are only symbols of what is happening all around us—changes in the environment where ministry is done.

Surprises Keep Coming

Surprises keep invading our world that affect how ministry is to be done and how it will be received. Two big surprises are the thousands of seekers who are looking for something but don't know what and the increased involvement of evangelicals in the public square. Still other surprises include the sex scandals in Catholic churches, the millions of people involved in religious small groups, the continual hemorrhaging of members and influence in the mainline churches, the Christian publishing bonanza that has put religious titles on the best-seller lists, the rise of influence of the megachurches, the millions of serious Christians who have given up on the church, and the hundreds of thousands of people involved in a ministry of compassion that reaches across almost all theological systems.

Surprises keep invading our world that affect how ministry is to·be done and how it will be received.

Surprises in the Church Beyond the Local Congregation

A recurring question seems to startle each new generation. It starts with the old question that sounds so new: Does the church accept culture the way she finds it and work within that culture, or does the church become countercultural with a goal of redeeming the culture? Some in each generation decide to take another alternative—they withdraw from society.

From the time of Jesus until now, some pastors in every generation have found reasons that convince them that they live in the most sinful and despicable period the human family has ever experienced. As a response, some choose to cocoon themselves in a kind of stay-at-home self-imposed spiritual monasticism that makes them feel spiritually elite even as it isolates them from society. They decide to hunker down in social isolation to await the Lord's return or to await their own demise so they can go home to be with the Lord. Of course, those who choose this alternative shut themselves off from having any redemptive impact on society.

But in our time, something new is happening that may merit a more optimistic response from all of us in the ministry. It may be an authentic springtime for the work of Christ.

To understand the possibilities, it is necessary to consider two terms: "post modern" and "emerging church." Neither is easy to define or even describe because the realities behind the words change so rapidly.

Post moderns, a term that worries some Christian leaders, are thought to be more open to the gospel than the moderns before them. They are reported to want integrity, reality and authenticity in matters of faith. They are part of a society sociologist Wade Clark Roof calls the "quest culture characterized by a deep hunger for a self-transformation that is both genuine and personally satisfying."[2]

Then there is something some call "emergent" or the "emerging church." Whatever it is called, it represents a growing mood in the United States that calls for rethinking what the Church should be and do and look like in contemporary culture.

A composite description of the emerging church drawn from several journalists shows the new "something" as being a conversation or dialogue among interested pastors and churches. These conversations center on missional engagement with culture, theology based on the experience/narratives of the people, commitments to emulate Christlikeness in all relationships, and a call to believers to live an authentic faith.

The emerging-church movement claims to have no organization, no denomination, no set theology and no program or ritual to follow. They prefer an increased emphasis on the feeling-experience side of faith and are much less concerned about the rational, cognitive and logical. Many emphasize the ancient creeds of the Church. They take seriously their responsibility to live out their faith in the world. Technology, visual arts and performing arts are highly valued and used in worship that is likely to be participatory and multisensory.

Whatever else it means—and many of the meanings are unclear—the emerging church is a response to a growing disillusionment with the way evangelicals as well as old liners do church and how those groups apparently fail to practice their faith.

Who knows how long or deep or far the influence of this emerging-church mood will have on how and where we do church. At the least, it will cause thousands of churches to rethink how they do church, and at the most, its significant impact could revolutionize the work of the church in our time.[3]

Bring It Close to Home

While our examples of crumbling securities and surprises in the culture may not seem relevant in your situation today, there are some changes that are either present or about to happen near you that will shape the way you share the gospel and the way it is received.

Keep alert to ways you can use those changes for the sake of the gospel. Give careful attention to the emerging-church movement—it has so much help for making maximum impact on contemporary folks.

If you are one of the new young leaders in the church, remember changes have come so fast in the last two or three decades that some of the experienced pastors are somewhat fearful of proposed change that has not been proven anywhere else. Fear is different than antagonism or stubbornness; one gets over fear when one sees that it can happen.

If you are among the more experienced pastors who are afraid of the ideas of the younger pastors and staff people who want to reinvent the Church, rejoice in their commitment to the Savior and pray for deliverance from your fears. The newer generation probably won't change the Church as much as it needs to be changed. Encourage them. Mentor them and let them carry your influence into the next generation. Likely, they will modify the work of the Church with their unique perspectives and skills so that it speaks more to the coming generation—much like the young have been doing for two centuries of Christian history.

The following section on exegeting your environment could revolutionize your understanding of yourself and your situation. It will help you discover the facts about your situation rather than dealing with hunches or hearsay. Best of all, it will help you to be open to new ideas and strong, capable people.

Try Exegeting Your Environment

Clergy training programs often imply that if we know the gospel, that will be enough for every setting where we will be sent by God to do ministry. I am not sure anyone fully believes that idea, but we often act like we do in our efforts to prepare clergy.

To get a clear idea of what God wants done in a new place, exegete your environment. This means examining your overlapping environments with the same thoroughness you would examine a passage of Scripture before preaching it.

Here are the five environments with key questions to help you start:

1. *Exegete your culture.* How are people different today than they have ever been before? What is the message from the gospel they would like to hear? What kind of outreach is most likely to get their attention?

2. *Exegete your town or city.* What are the demographics? Who lives near your church? Who are the unreached people groups in your town? What part of the demographic picture best fits your church's ministry and talent pool?

3. *Exegete your denomination or family of churches.* What is the most important fact about your denomination? Why are you part of this group? How committed is your congregation to the purposes of this group?

4. *Exegete the congregation you serve.* Why was it started? When was it started? Who sacrificed to be sure the church was planted in your location? What kind of people go there? Do they believe in you? Do you believe in them?

5. *Exegete yourself.* What are your strengths? Your weaknesses? What did the Lord have in mind when He called you? When He sent you to your present assignment? What kind of Christian are you? What about your family? Your marriage? Your extended family? A fun question is: How did I get to be me?

Now is a good time to push through the fog of frustration or self-doubt to a new beginning. Stop waiting and start blooming where God has planted you.

Today is all we have, but today is enough. Start tomorrow's longed-for supernatural achievement today. Treasure the present and use it well. Cultivate your spirituality, stability and strength to bloom a Christ-exalting ministry in your present assignment.

THINK STRAIGHT ABOUT TECHNOLOGY

Technology must be viewed as a tool for doing the work of the gospel. Like buildings and books and parking lots and chairs, it is for the purpose of helping persons come to faith—not just another gadget to impress someone or to consume the pastor's time.

Technology as a Tool

The other Sunday while waiting for worship to begin, I (Neil) mused about the use of technology in church. I snickered a bit when I thought about John Wesley preaching to thousands without sound equipment. It must have been hard to hear in those great out-of-door meetings.

But back to the present. As we entered the sanctuary, the usher gave me a computer-generated state-of-the-art four-color bulletin. That meant a computer, a printer and a folding machine were likely in the act somewhere. Then came the hymns and praise choruses beautifully displayed on the screens—the song texts were projected over mood-producing four-color photographs of sea, mountains and desert, too. And how the people sang.

I forgot to mention the pre-service communication. On the large screen, a flashing message requested that we turn off our cell phones, pagers, and any other electronic device. The screens also reminded us to pray for people who were ill or who had suffered a great loss during the week. A short video skit on the big screens reminded us of important ministries that needed our support during the following week.

On the walls of each side of the platform were two LED parental paging devices that simply flash a number to inform parents their child needs them in the church nursery.

To help worshipers get maximum good from the sermon, the main ideas, as well as the full text of the biblical passage, were displayed on the large screens using PowerPoint software. And somewhere in the sermon, the pastor told about the Bible software he used for research.

About midpoint in the sermon, I thought the pastor said something about the Scripture passage that I had never thought about before. I asked my wife to check the passage in her Palm—she has the whole Bible there. While she had the Palm open, I thought to ask where we were going for dinner that Sunday and with whom and at what time.

Today is all we have, but today is enough.

Communication to the masses, or even to a niche group of the congregation, is now possible with software that uses a combination of e-mail, text messaging and phones. Thus, it is possible to break main caller lists into members of the prayer chain, elders, deacons or even choir members. Churches are also using software to manage membership lists and addresses and to give records.

More and more churches are developing websites, which make it possible for them to announce time of services, list staff members, and provide a way for congregants to communicate by phone or e-mail. Many churches are sending their weekly newsletters by e-mail. Other churches are making the pastor's sermons available. And bloggers are developing creative strategies for use in churches.

With all this technology, it's easy to be overwhelmed with the possibilities—and more is always on the way.

There are four rules every pastor needs to use in relationship to purchase and use of technology in the church.

1. *Be master rather than slave to technology.* Computers were supposed to free up time, but we all know pastors who are mesmerized slaves of their computers.

2. *Keep people as the highest priority in your ministry.* Keep the human touch. Use the computer to put you in touch with the maximum number of people, but always keep in mind that a personal e-mail, phone call, handwritten note or personal contact can never be replaced by anything technology can do. Somebody needs your touch right now.

3. *Expenditures for technology should be carefully balanced against all other financial needs of a church.* It is possible to have state-of-the-art technology that is so expensive little money is left for mission.

4. *Evaluate advice from "techies."* Most congregations have at least one person with special interest in technology—they always

seem to know about the latest and best. Use these people as advisors, but resist buying the latest technology until you know it will serve you and your church well.

Technology as a Shaper of Faith

Although understanding the church's use of technology is significant—very significant—it is also important to understand how technology shapes the faith of Americans. Based on a Barna research study, David Kinnaman, vice president of the Barna Group, explains, "It is not just that younger adults own more digital devices—they use and experience technology in a way that is very different from their parents. This is important because it means that each generation actually lives in a different 'bubble' when it comes to the rapid advancement of the digital age."[4]

Kinnaman also comments, "Families should pay particular attention to how they use technology and how it shapes their children's lifestyles and attitudes. Congregational leaders should strive to integrate media and technology into the efforts of the church—but within the boundaries of their ministry vision and values."[5]

Once again, the contemporary pastor is faced with leading the congregation to asking and answering its own questions of mission and vision and the need for a crystal-clear awareness concerning their church's ministry target audience.

BECOME THE CHANGE YOU WOULD LIKE TO HAPPEN

Many recognize that contemporary pastors face confusion on many levels of modern life. Meanwhile, Christianity seems stalled in dazed disarray concerning mission, vision, priorities and strategies. No one knows what to expect next. Here are several first steps.

Question Your Frustrations

A newly married couple started their first church in a small Midwest town. After about six months, the young wife said to her overly serious husband,

"All you seem to think about or do is deal with what the church doesn't have, and it doesn't look like you're enjoying it much. All of this seems boring to me."

No pastoral assignment is made up of all satisfactions or all frustrations. Every pastorate has a good supply of both.

Although Old Testament Joseph never conceded that his brothers did right, the mind-set through which he viewed frustrations made a colossal difference in the quality of his life and the results of his work, especially during his years in Egypt. As an overcomer, Joseph enjoyed usefulness and serenity even during his tough years of adversity. Jubilant victory finally came.

To challenge your frustrations, try this: Question and attempt to eliminate at least one frustration every day. Ask yourself about your frustrations:

- Are they real?
- Do they matter in light of the big picture of my ministry?
- Who or what causes them?
- Do they flourish in some climates I create?
- How can I minimize my smoldering stress points?

A realistic response to this process can give pastors a more accurate perspective. It can unlock self-understanding and encourage increased productivity. In the effort, a pastor uncovers internal and external resources that he never knew existed. And he learns ways to change his conduct and attitudes to minimize or even eliminate frustrations.

Every pastorate has a good supply of both satisfactions and frustrations.

Challenge Your Worries

Challenge your worries about money, burnout, your family or your church members. Sort the facts from the fiction. The payoff will be spiritual fitness and emotional wellness.

Sure, this requires work. But similar to the "no pain, no gain" in physical conditioning, effective ministry develops through facing your frustrations and dealing with them. Such a strategy can also assist you in identifying possibilities in the midst of difficulties.

Why not commit to the reality that something significant can be accomplished for God in every setting. When you live by God's priorities and overcome your frustrations, the odds for such achievement are always on your side.

Do Some Serious Stretching

The approval and admiration of those we serve can be humbling. Many of those we lead believe we preach better than we do. They believe we pray more than we do. They assume we study more than we do. Many imagine we are better pastors than we know ourselves to be.

A peasant woman stretched St. Francis of Assisi's soul when she said, "We pray that you are as good as we think you are." Similar stretching capabilities come to us through our church members' affirmations.

Why not let God enable you to become what your church members believe you to be. Some of the most extraordinary pastors in Church history were loved into greatness by their congregations. This exercise also provides an antidote to the human tendency to infallibility in which an overblown ego needs more applause, requires more good news, and denies any hint that something might be wrong.

ABOVE EVERYTHING ELSE GIVE THEM CHRIST

From beginning to end, the Church is about Christ. The people worship Him. The pastor works to please Him. He is Founder and Owner of the Church. He is our Enabler, Healer, Redeemer, Leader and coming King. Jesus is the Lord of the ages, Lord of eternity, and Lord of the Church. He promised to be with us always until the end of the age.

And the work of the Church is to help people become transformed into His likeness. That means a life of purpose and focus—an adventuresome, abundant life. It is a way of love, joy, forgiveness, peace, grace, fairness, greatness, wellness, nobility and holy wholeness. Dallas Willard describes the Church as "just some ordinary people who are His apprentices, gathered in the name of Jesus and immersed in His presence, and taking steps of inward transformation as they put on the character of Christ."[6]

Ordinary people immersed in His presence—and you as pastor get to be in the middle of action like that. Keep the church centered on Christ and you will be amazed at what He will do. Watch the people grow. Watch outsiders become attracted to the community of faith. And watch yourself develop and grow as a Christ follower.

CONTEMPORARY CHALLENGE

How to Live in the Present

- Don't squander present opportunities.
- Learn to live in the present informed by the past.
- Crumbling securities provide spiritual opportunities.
- Learn from the emerging church movement.
- Find a cause that breaks your heart and then accept God's challenge to change it.
- Exegeting your environment gives amazing insight.
- Understand the two impacts of technology.
- Challenge your worries.
- Center your ministry on Christ.
- Become the change you want to see happen.

How wonderful it is that nobody need wait a single moment before starting to improve the world. —Anne Frank[7]

When the Mountain Blows

Musings from H. B. London, Jr.

It was a Sunday morning, and I greeted that day to see the yard and car covered with thick sticky ash. I had not realized then, but in one tremendous blast, 1,314 feet of Mount St. Helens had been obliterated. The explosion was heard 690 miles away and spewed ash that could be measured in 11 states that would soon circle the earth. I was in Salem, Oregon, at the time. Like millions of others, I bore witness to the most destructive volcanic eruption in U.S. history.

I will not soon forget that day, because I was aware that something had happened that no one could control nor stand in its path. Its force was unimaginable.

Although not every ministry is greeted with a volcanic eruption, all of us at some point will be faced with the unimaginable and the uncontrollable. These are the events that will test us and try our faith—situations so complex we can only shake our heads in disbelief. Perhaps this is what the psalmist was facing when he wrote, "God is our refuge and strength . . . therefore we will not fear, though the earth give away and the mountains fall into the heart of the sea" (Ps. 46:1-2).

Today, life has returned to Mount St. Helens. Trees were re-planted, and now some stand 70 feet high. That which was so devastated is now alive. The same is true with you, my friend. That which may appear to be the end could, with time, patience and faith, become a new beginning. Take heart! What we cannot control—God can!

CHAPTER 5

ENERGIZED BY
A DREAM

Keeper of Eternity and Molder of Dreams,
Fulfill Your promise this day
here and now.
Enable young pastors to see visions.
Empower older pastors to dream dreams.
Shock Your Church with
a new awareness of her potential.
Amen.

> # YOUR YOUNG MEN
> # WILL SEE VISIONS,
> # YOUR OLD MEN WILL
> # DREAM DREAMS.
>
> ACTS 2:17

DREAMS—SEEDS OF ACHIEVEMENT

Dreams are the raw materials of adventure and achievement. They stir people's blood and make them believe that they can move mountains. Nearly every advance in Christian history began as someone's dream.

Martin Luther King, Jr.'s "I Have a Dream" speech helped reshape human rights across America and around the world.

Irish dramatist George Bernard Shaw's visionary words inspire the masses whenever they are quoted: "You see things; and you say, 'Why?' But I dream things that never were; and I say, 'Why not?'"[1]

The musical lyrics from *Man of La Mancha* by Joe Darion and Mitch Leigh, "To dream the impossible dream, to fight the unbeatable foe, to bear with unbearable sorrow, to run where the brave dare not go," move us and have added vitality to thousands of sermons.[2]

A wise old preacher was right when he told two seminary students who came to visit him in his retirement home, "A pastor never achieves more than his dreams." That's an important perspective for effective ministry anywhere. Every pastor needs dreams focused passionately on the gospel.

Sadly, it is not always the case. "I can't go on. Our church services feel like we are tossing prayers into a wishing well. My dream is dead." Those dark, despairing comments from a conscientious Midwest pastor are too common. But we can't give up. Too much depends on our making the dreams come true.

Think of the possibilities for the gospel of thousands of dream-inspired pastors setting direction, restoring purpose and calling the country to God.

Think of the impact this would have on perplexed persons, dysfunctional families, indifferent churches, deteriorating neighborhoods and a Christ-needy society.

It's mind-boggling, isn't it, to imagine what could happen if pastors everywhere opened their minds to God's lofty, imaginative dreams for our times. Nothing could stop such a groundswell for renewed righteousness.

Think of what pastors have to offer the world. Compared to Jesus, no one on any playing field in the world offers a better remedy for our moral chaos. Nothing but genuine Christianity can save the souls of

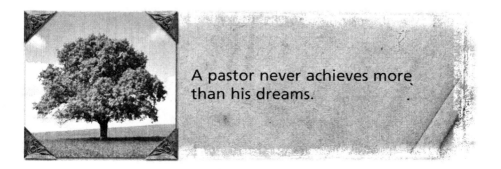

A pastor never achieves more than his dreams.

our cities, provide something immensely better than our destructive self-indulgence, or refocus our churches on God's mission for them. But God can.

What a time to dream. What a time to become spiritual change agents.

Be reminded again and again: Dreams are the seeds of achievements. Plant them. Water them. Watch them grow.

WHERE DID THE DREAMERS GO?

Where have the dreamers gone? Are they asleep or comatose? Did someone murder hope? What choked the creativity, imagination and daring out of our minds and ministries?

The Church needs more and better dreamers. Why not become the dreamers-in-residence for your church? God stands ready to inspire your dream and help you make the dream come true.

Let's remember that every ministry started as someone's dream. Every church, parachurch ministry, church college, Christian publisher and missionary organization started as a dream that God gave to someone. That's the reason I (H. B.) love to dream about my part in the ministry of Jesus in the world. It is exciting to think that right this minute, the Holy Spirit may be igniting a fantastic new expression of ministry in my heart or in someone I know.

Dreams That Never Die

My soul is stretched for dreaming by a variety of sources. I remember my dreams being resourced by the lyrics of a song that still sings its way into my ministry: "The dream never dies, just the dreamer."

Let me explain the occasion and the impact it had on me. Our church in Salem, Oregon, sometimes sponsored a summer series called "August Alive." The uncomplicated plan called for a different musical group to sing every Sunday night during August.

The Regenerations were among the best loved of all singing groups that came to our church. The leader, Derric Johnson, was a master at creating "aha" moments in the continuity between songs. In one service, he described people whose dreams had died and whose hopes had been crucified—people who had stopped singing, quit dreaming and accepted what they thought was inevitable. Then the band sang:

> The dream never dies, just the dreamer.
> So come on everybody, dream along.
> The song never stops, just the singer.
> So come on everybody, sing along.

In the same concert, Johnson told about pastors who stop dreaming for their churches. He described how they gasp for spiritual breath because the passion of their calling has leaked out of their expectations and priorities. They mark time in assignments that bore them, although they remember how it used to be. Hope has reached a low tide for them. Their vision is overcast and dark. Like the character in Li'l Abner, they walk around with a cloud over their heads.

Whatever we do, we can't let our dreams die.

Broken Dreams Sap Energy

Such a loss of dreaming produces personal pain. The agony showed in the face and voice of a pastor I know. He tried to plant a church that did not survive. He confessed, "Something in my heart died in that last service that I cannot describe. Oh, how it hurts!" Such grief for a dead dream depletes spiritual energy. Like the psalmist, we wonder how we can sing the Lord's song in such a strange land (see Ps. 137:4).

Then, in the process, a dreadful reality increases our torment: We cannot forget how things were *supposed* to be. Few people are more

Few people are more spiritually fragile than a once-fired-up Christ follower who stops singing and quits dreaming.

emotionally and spiritually fragile than a once-fired-up Christ follower who stops singing and quits dreaming.

Never forget the message from the Regenerations's song: "The dream never dies, just the dreamer." That's an encouraging message for every disillusioned pastor.

Dream again and sing along. God, the giver of dreams, wants you to know a new dream is the first step to conquering your fear of future failure. Our Father wants to ignite new dreams in you. He wants to reenergize great hope in you. He wants to renew your ability to imagine, anticipate and expect.

To start dreaming again, try singing Phil Johnson's inspiring song:

Give them all, give them all to Jesus,
Shattered dreams, wounded hearts, and broken toys;
Give them all, give them all to Jesus,
And he will turn your sorrows into joys.[3]

Most of us have more reasons for dreaming than we like to admit—a call, a cause, a commitment, a congregation, and a world that needs us. In the event that these assets for dreams are not enough, we have Christ, who indwells us, and the Bible to guide us.

Try Dreaming God's Dream Again

The contemporary Church is experiencing a frightening emergency caused by an acquiescence to evil and sin. The front lines, like the battle lines in Iraq, are sometimes difficult to identify. And although the weapons may not kill, they often maim ministers emotionally and spiritually for life. As a result, pastors' dreams are waning or burning out. This crisis shows in many ways.

My (H. B.) letters and phone calls provide me with a front-line seat in which I see placid acceptance of the way things are. What can be done? To start a turnaround, every pastor needs to ask how God wants things to be rather than simply accepting the current situation as inevitable.

Pastors who visit and write to me at Focus on the Family talk openly about shattered dreams. Their dying dreams show in their weary faces and tired voices. In their churches, the symptoms show in hackneyed religious phrases mumbled from hundreds of pulpits—words that have lost their meaning and passion long ago.

All over North America you can meet pastors and spouses who have abandoned their Kingdom dreams. Most are good-as-gold ministers who no longer dream or sing. The quicksand of lost aspirations and frustrated hope has them trapped in a survival mode. They are desperately trying to keep their faith, their dignity and their means of making a living. All of this desperation undermines their self-esteem, their marriages, their parenting skills and their relationships with the people in their churches and communities.

These pastors believe that they have valid reasons for settling in, coasting or giving up. They speak about church controllers who cannot see beyond the next dollar. For others, optimism has been dashed to bits by denominational leaders who advised them to be realistic—whatever that means.

Still others have had their high hopes stifled by church members who were unwilling to pay the price for spiritual greatness—they did not see the point. Judgmental people have murdered the dreams of others.

The consequences should not surprise us. These churches shrivel. Attendance dwindles a little more each year. And pastors die by inches as they mark time or quit.

Something must be done. Refuse to allow the incredible energy of Christianity to be squandered for such absurdities. Seek a new vision for what God wants to do through you. Get serious. Get desperate. Get hungry and thirsty. Pay any price for a genuine breakthrough.

DREAM A NEW DREAM

Go back to Jesus. Invite Him into your situation. Listen carefully again to our Lord's strong affirmation as if you were the only one to hear: "With man this is impossible, but not with God; all things are possible with God" (Mark 10:27).

This incredible, bigger-than-any-of-your-problems message was first spoken when Jesus and His disciples met a handsome, gifted, outwardly religious young Pharisee. Any pastor would welcome such a promising prospect. The young ruler, like seekers in every generation, wanted to make sense of his life. So he opened his heart to Jesus. Sadly, the man turned away from his only hope for meaning when Jesus explained that the cost of discipleship was not much—just everything.

The disciples were amazed at the conversation and its results. They questioned Jesus as they watched this impressive prospect walk away from the Kingdom. They asked the Master, "If this man can't get in, how can ordinary people like us inherit the kingdom of God? Who can, then, be saved?"

Jesus' answer speaks to every ministry problem anywhere: "All things are possible with God." This means God delights to use ordinary people who will become fully committed to His cause. He uses run-of-the-mill folks as well as superstars.

All Things Are Possible

"All things are possible with God" brings hope to dreamers who feel abandoned by God. "All things are possible with God" blesses those who serve in unknown outposts with limited resources. "All things are possible"— these are God's words even to pastors who told their spouses last week, "God has forsaken this place. We're wasting our time. I'm sorry God allows us to squander our lives in this backwater place." Jesus challenges us to dream again.

A near-identical message of hope appears in the biblical account of the young boy in Mark 9 who was thrown into the water and fire by an evil spirit. The pained father was sure nothing could be done. So out of his own frustration of powerlessness, the father told Jesus, "I've done everything. I've exhausted every solution. I believe it will always be this way. But do something if You can." The father added, as we might, "Is there anything You can do for my miserable despair?"

Then Jesus—Immanuel, God with us—answered as He always does, "Can I? You know I can. Everything is possible for anyone who believes."

Broken Dreams Can Be Mended

To repair your broken dreams, apply Jesus' words to your situation: "Everything is possible for anyone who believes."

A dead dream drops its burial garments and moves from the tomb to Main Street when one really hears these words. These words from the Lord of life make broken dreams spring into bloom. His assurance can help you clear your muddled thoughts and your toughest hurdles. Attention, disheartened dreamers. Give Jesus your full concentration. He wants you to hear some important old words. Listen with your heart to two affirmations from the Lord: "Everything is possible for one who believes" and "With God all things are possible."

Did you hear? He really said it. Christ promises divine enablement so that we can win over every defeat. Hope is then reborn as Jesus' words ring in our souls: "Can I do something? Are you kidding? Everything is possible with God."

MAGNETIC POWER OF A GREAT DREAM

Everyone gains when a pastor revitalizes his dreams. The pastor gains. His family gains. His church gains. His world gains. Start by taking Jesus' "everything" into your beat-up hopes. Dust off your unused opportunities with the life-giving words "All things are possible with God." Then ask God to help you see your assignment as He sees it. He placed you there because He wants something magnificent to happen in that place.

Every Congregation Needs a Pastor Who Dreams

What does God want accomplished in your situation? Why have you been placed in that setting at this specific time? Why not return in your memory to your original call?

Can you remember the time when God asked you to fulfill impossible dreams in partnership with Him? Is it possible that your initial call included achieving something magnificent in your current setting? It's serious, soul-searching business to think that God wants to use you to fulfill His dream for your present assignment.

Let me (Neil) introduce you to some of God's unheralded dreamers. I have in mind a young pastor friend in his middle 20s who started a church for street people in a Los Angeles warehouse. He serves people who find spiritual and social rehabilitation at the Los Angeles Mission, but who have no church to attend after they leave the mission. As might be expected, the church and the pastor's family face severe money problems every week. But he dreams about the power of these resurrected lives in the future of the Kingdom.

I know a middle-aged Filipino woman in San Francisco who started a church for Chinese immigrants from the Philippines. She borrows a fellowship hall every Sunday from an established church in the Bay Area. She believes that God placed her there and that the future of the church is secure. Her dream is being fulfilled by the people who come to Christ through her ministry.

I know a beginning pastor who serves a church of retirees in central Florida. In addition to all of his other pastoral duties, in five years he has won 15 young husbands/fathers through personal evangelism efforts. Recently, he was invited to serve a larger church, but he declined because he felt that he could not desert the converts. His dream is being fulfilled as these men make their homes truly Christian.

I know a pastor in his 60s who served a small church on the Navajo Indian Reservation. He earns his living by raising sheep. He serves on the tribal council of the Navajo Nation. His dream is to meet the spiritual needs of Native Americans.

I know a 35-year-old factory worker from the Indianapolis area who, after graduating from a Bible college, planted a church 50 miles northeast of San Diego. His congregation meets in a school. He believes that God gave him a dream to build a great church in Southern California.

God has revolutionary strategies waiting to be implemented at rural crossroads, in broken-down ghettos and in well-heeled suburbs.

I know a woman pastor in her early 60s who serves a tiny rural congregation in Southern Missouri. After her husband died and her children were grown, in her late 50s she returned to school and graduated from a Bible college. When this rural church invited her to become its pastor, she shared her dream that she planned to stay as the pastor until retirement. Her dream is a church family to love for the rest of her working life.

God always has a plan for every community if He finds a person to fulfill it. The living Christ has redemptive dreams for Peoria, Phoenix, Parkersburg, Philadelphia, Portland—and all points in between. He has revolutionary strategies waiting to be implemented at rural crossroads, in broken-down ghettos and in well-heeled suburbs.

Let's celebrate and cherish the reality that Jesus is the Lord of vital ministry for every setting. Resurrecting churches is His specialty. He wants to revive weak, sickly church members. He wants to reenergize pastors. He wants pastors' spouses and children to have good reasons to laugh and sing.

The Lord of the Church stands ready to transform the dreams He gave you for His Church into reality. The challenge is to dream God's new dream for your setting. Every place has possibilities from God's point of view. Take hope from Paul, the dreamer, who broke into ecstasies of praise when he recalled how God turned his dreams into spectacular accomplishments. God helped Paul in so many ways, at so many different times, and in so many impossible situations.

Paul knew from personal experience how God rekindles hope and energizes dreams so that ordinary folks can accomplish unbelievable achievements in unexpected ways and in tough places. The apostle almost sings as he writes to the Ephesians: "God can do anything, you know—far more than you could ever imagine or guess or request in your wildest dreams!" Then his pen dances across the parchment as he exclaims, "He does it not by pushing us around but by working within us, His Spirit deeply and gently working within us" (3:20, *THE MESSAGE*).

What a source of incredible energy for reviving dreams and restoring our songs—His Spirit working through us.

Dreaming and Believing Belong Together

I (H. B.) always have been a dreamer. I love to see God do impossible things. I have dreamed about battle-fatigued Christians, and I have seen God give them pulsating New Testament energy. I've grieved over split churches only to see God unify them in amazing ways. I've met hurting pastors and watched God renew them with nobility and vision.

Ministry for me has been a lifelong process of dreaming and believing. What an unbeatable combination. Dreaming of achievement, however, requires divine enablement; this is exciting and encouraging, sometimes miraculous. Along with you, I know that I cannot do much in my own strength. But God is able to do more than we can think or ask or imagine. With God as the senior partner, a dreamer becomes an invincible force for righteousness, wherever he may be.

First Steps Toward Miracles

Christopher Columbus dreamed a dream and discovered a continent. Beethoven dreamed how his symphonies would sound as he walked through forests and villages, and when he wrote the music, it sounded exactly as he dreamed it would. Columbus and Beethoven can teach pastors lessons about envisioning the way things can be in ministry.

Why not dream something as stupendous for your church as Columbus dreamed or something as beautiful as Beethoven dreamed? Why not dream about taking the gospel to the cutting edge of human needs—way out to the parts of society where the gospel seldom reaches? The world needs us there. The Church needs us there. That kind of achievement will enrich your life.

Einstein's development of the theory of relativity can help us with positive doubting. When Einstein was asked how he discovered the theory of relativity, he answered, "I questioned the axioms." His dream started when he questioned the way things were. He kept asking, "Why not?" Such positive doubting for Einstein became a seedbed for achievable dreams. The pattern that worked for Columbus, Beethoven and Einstein might help us renew our ministry to serve in our present opportunity.

Similar advancement can be seen in technology, transportation and athletics. Someone tests borders. Records are broken. New methods are advanced. Old ways are scrapped. People are retrained and morale is accelerated. Why not test musty old ways of doing ministry? Try performing ministry in innovative ways that will effectively have an impact on today's world. Emphasize God's eternal newness.

Resist Dream Destroyers

Strange and shocking forces both inside and outside of the church strangle our dreams for the Kingdom. Dreams for righteousness can die easily in a civilization that is bent on dismantling morals and subsidizing behaviors that contradict our basic values.

Secular Dream Destroyers

Overdosing on sin, secularism and sex has almost destroyed our society. The list of dream destroyers in our society is frighteningly long—murder, rape, violent crimes, abortion, divorce, out-of-wedlock births, filthy television, vulgar coarseness, coldhearted callousness, suspicious cynicism and shallow banality. It's enough to make pastors withdraw in absolute despair, frustration, and even panic.

How can anyone dream God's dream in a society that deifies complex technology, cultural sophistication and social chaos while allowing itself to be governed by moral pygmies? Greedy materialism, secular humanism and godless paganism try to make us believe that the world can be reformed without God's help. But strong evidence on every hand shows that this proposition is ludicrous.

Americans have been conditioned by so many disappointments that we often look right past the possibilities. Our culture seems infected by a morbid malaise of hopelessness. Millions fret about their jobs, pensions, old age and family, as well as their health.

Because of this, masses of people, including Christians, settle for a way of thinking that assumes the future will be worse than the present. Half-truths are tolerated in the media and compromise is accepted in the Church. We tolerate schools that do not educate, we pay for medical services that do not heal, and we endure government that does not work.

As we adjust to this corruption in society, we begin to accept criminality, violence, illegitimacy and family breakdown to be normal and expected.

Church Dream Destroyers

Subtle dream destroyers lurk inside the church walls, too. In churches, dreams are easily destroyed by self-sovereignty in the pastor or lay leaders who allow themselves to believe that anything goes as long as it sounds somewhat religious. Phony image building and doublespeak have become surprisingly common. Some pastors would rather try anything than do parish ministry and preach the Word of God.

Because we sometimes give up too easily on the centrality of Christ in our churches, we run our congregations like a democratic service club where everyone has a vote, where no faith commitments are required, and where everyone does as he pleases. So much of what happens in the Church these days has nothing to do with what the Church is supposed to be.

Self-Sufficient Dream Destroyers

Dreams always burn low when we try to do ministry in our own strength. Os Guinness, in his book *No God But God*, says we can build a big-attendance church without much help from God.

He is right. Almost anyone, from a human point of view, can do the right things, and people will be attracted to a church. It is possible to grow a church numerically without God's empowerment and have many people attend. If we succeed in our own strength, however, our church will be a shallow, misguided, self-indulgent, muddled crowd that only faintly resembles God's dream for His Church or for our ministry.

By depending on their own strength, experience, competence and wit, many ministers undermine their dreams of accomplishing magnificent achievements for God. They forget that God seldom blesses self-sufficient disciples. All effort to do God's work in their own strength turns into bleak, discouraging struggles. Without God's empowerment, they become disillusioned. And they prove that Hebrews 11:6 is right: "Without faith it is impossible to please God."

Superficial results can also wreck our dreams. Pastors and church leaders generally agree that the ministry is harder now than ever before.

This conclusion is accurate. Perplexing circumstances and low involvement by church members make the realities even worse.

A measure of the difficulty, however, may be rooted in ourselves. Maybe we do not give God opportunity to work miracles through us. Perhaps we have not allowed God to heal us on the inside so that we can be wholesome healers for others. Or maybe we are like my grandson at four who loved to say, "I can do it myself!"

HOW TO BEGIN DREAMING AGAIN

When will we say enough is enough and admit that we need more verve, virtue and vitality from God? Let's follow our dreams and bring back resurrection life, personal transformation and holy living—although they have been judged as being unrealistic for moderns in many places. Nonsense. History offers examples of many pastors who dared to dream that God would use the gospel through them to change people— and He did.

As a first step, we must dream God's dream again for our families, for our churches and for our world. Kingdom dreams start with imagination and hope. They are fueled by faith in an idea, people and a specific setting. They are sustained by the enabling power of the Holy Spirit. Let's begin.

Dream Past Your Pain

The City of Hope in Duarte, located in Southern California, is a great hospital. I (H. B.) went there as a pastor on a regular basis. I visited people and observed the devastating affects of cancer and chemotherapy. I tried to smile, hold the hands of patients and comfort them. But when I got into my car, tears would often stream from my eyes as I cried out in anguish, "Lord, it's not fair. These are good people. They love you. They are going to die. Why does it have to be this way?"

Please understand, I do not have all the answers for pain and suffering. But I know that our Lord says to the sick and afflicted and to us, "With man it is impossible, but all things are possible with God." His words revive hope and rekindle dreams.

When any kind of pain and suffering trouble us, we need to remember the Resurrection. After the scheming crucifiers did their worst, Jesus announced, "I am the resurrection and the life." This is a sure foundation for Kingdom dreams. We have Someone to count on who is absolutely trustworthy.

The kind of dreaming I envision is for us to rediscover the redemptive purpose that God has for every pastor and for the churches we serve. By this I mean a dream in which every pastor is consumed by a humanly impossible vision so that he is able to dream God's magnificent dream even in difficult assignments among unresponsive people.

The dream that I pray to be fulfilled is that every church will be saturated with resurrection power. I dream of a time when pastors will do ministry with indescribable gusto as they did in the New Testament.

This holy energy is undaunted by circumstances and comes from the full assurance that God is able to keep us from falling (see Jude 24), to guard what we have entrusted to the Father for safekeeping (see 2 Tim. 1:12), and to do immeasurably more than we ask or imagine according to His power that is at work in us (see Eph. 3:20).

Dream Past the Enemy's Lies

Satan wants to stop our dreams about ministry and personal spiritual growth. Our soul enemy, whom the Bible calls the "spoiler," will show us awful mental pictures of the worst possible thing that could happen to ourselves, our family and our ministry. He knows that ministry shuts down when he is able to persuade us to focus on problems rather than on possibilities.

He paints the worst scenario for our ministry and wants to make us believe it will happen. It won't.

He wants us to believe there is no help. He lies.

He wants us to assume that there is no hope for our children. Not true.

He wants us to suppose nothing can happen in our church. He lies.

He wants us to believe we cannot have fun in our marriage or adventure in our parenting. Not true.

Dr. Timothy George's strong words in a *Christianity Today* editorial put the issue in clear perspective: "In those times when we stumble for our footing in the awful swellings of the Jordan, and the Evil One whispers in our ear, 'Why did you ever decide to be a preacher anyway?' the right answer can only be, 'Cause I was called, you fool!'"[4] The enemy cannot be allowed to determine the intensity nor the outcome of our ministry.

We know the devil lies. He always does. So, because we know who he is and what he does, why do we have such audacity in the Church of Jesus Christ to allow his lies of materialism and secularism to make us compromise our God-given dreams? This is where we need to repent and cry out to God, "Renew my dreams. Reenergize my vision. Open my eyes to see beyond my circumstances to Your miraculous plans for me and the church I serve. Saturate my life and ministry with resurrection hope."

Such a renewed dream will transform us from sniffling weaklings to courageous achievers. A thousand difficulties may lie in our way, but God is able to bring us through. The devil may appear to have control of our culture and the human race may appear to be careening headlong to destruction. But the devil is no match for God. Beyond Satan's shackling control is the Savior's glorious sufficiency.

Dream Past the Church's Weaknesses

The Church is weaker than we wished it were, but it is not dead. The Church in all her history has never had to face such a huge number of messy sins all at once and with so many weary, discouraged disciples. But God wants the Church to be robust again. This will require dreamers and prophets in thousands of pulpits announcing the meaning of Scripture for our time.

I love the story of the duck hunter who told his adult son, "I'm the best duck hunter in the world. And I am ready to prove it." The son called his father's bluff, saying, "Okay, Dad. Let's prove your skills tomorrow morning."

So the father and son got up early on a freezing morning and went to the duck blind. It was wet. It was cold. Ice formed on their mustaches and their teeth chattered. The father urged patience, though no ducks were in sight.

Finally, one scrawny duck flew across the sky. It came closer and closer. The father took aim and pulled the trigger. An awful explosion followed. After the smoke and commotion cleared, the scrawny duck was still flying in the sky.

The father had to say something. So he said, "Son, you have just witnessed a miracle. There before your eyes flies a dead duck."

The contemporary Church is like the scrawny duck. She still has life, but she needs to be revived. She is tired, sick, anemic and confused by many evils that confront her. Yet even though she may be weak, she is still flying. She represents one of the world's last chances for survival. A winning formula for infusing the Church with mission is dream + passion + priority = accomplished purpose.

HIGH-PROFILE DREAMERS TEACH US HOW TO DREAM

Dreamers can be found on nearly every page of the Bible and in every generation of the Church's history. Often, they were unique in fitting ministry to a particular need of their time. But they had one thing in common: Modern and ancient dreamers all agreed that significant achievement for the Kingdom starts with a bigger-than-life dream of what God wants done—and then doing it.

Dreamers trust God to enable them to achieve supernatural exploits for the cause of Christ and for the people they serve. Seldom do they realize that they are doing anything unusual in their dreaming and doing.

Moses Dreamed of Freedom for His Nation

What would have been the consequences if Moses had failed to follow God's dream? Read the biblical account again and let your imagination be staggered as you consider God's dream for Moses the herdsman.

Exodus recounts that while Moses was tending his father-in-law's sheep on the backside of the desert, God interrupted Moses' entire pattern of life. The Almighty said, "Moses, you've done enough sheepherding. I want you to go lead several million people out of Egypt. I have it all prepared. I just want you to go and do it."

Like us, Moses asked absurd questions: "Well, Lord, aren't there mountains and water and sand that will complicate my life? Isn't it hot out there?" Moses never stopped to consider that everyone deals with mountains, water, sand and heat. Many issues we consider ministry difficulties are mere human problems that everyone faces.

God was patient with Moses and replied, "Yes, there will be obstacles, but we will overcome them together. I promise to guide you with a cloud by day and fire by night. I pledge I will be everything you need."

Moses minded God and led his people. Pharaoh was right behind them. The hindrances that he and the Israelites faced were bigger than any problem a contemporary pastor is likely to face on his most perplexing day. Moses probably would not have fulfilled the dream if he had tried to figure it all out first. But when God said it was going to be okay, that was enough for Moses. And it's enough for us.

The dream grew dim, however, as the children of Israel neared the Promised Land. Spies, who had never dreamed the dream, were sent to check out the land they were about to possess. The spies were better at fact finding than in faith believing. They looked the situation over and reported, "Oops! Something is wrong with the dream. We had better not go. We look like grasshoppers compared to those giants."

Can you imagine going through all the Israelites went through to get so close to the Promised Land? Can you image so many people being frustrated for the rest of their lives because the spies never saw the dream? Can you image waiting 40 years in the wilderness for the old generation to die so you could possess the land God wanted you to have in the first place?

The contemporary Church represents one of the world's last chances for survival.

To modern dreamers, this means that we should be careful who we choose as fact-finding spies. It means dreamers must be cautious about what they do with so-called "factual reports" prepared by those who never understand the dream.

We make the same mistakes when we let dreams grow dim or die. We go through the motions of having church without divine enablement, and then we wonder why it is so boring. We languish near the Promised Land and allow ourselves to be shackled by our excuses, prejudices and fears. Sad for us and destructive for the cause of Christ, we may be only one dream away from a breakthrough. Much of the time, we stand only a prayer away from supernatural accomplishment.

What adventure we miss and what defeat we experience when we are frightened away from a dream by an obstacle that seems larger than the promises of God. Then, too, as dreamers we must face the fact that every frustrated dream has eternal and negative consequences for someone we may never know.

Mother Teresa Dreamed of Compassion for the Destitute

Mother Teresa was a dreaming hero for contemporary Christians. She was a tiny, unassuming nun who grew weary of pointless activities for the Church. So she set out for Calcutta, India, where she dreamed of giving comfort, dignity and courage to homeless, lonely and dying people— not a pretty setting for ministry.

As an initial phase of fulfilling God's dream, Mother Teresa secured a small building in a pitiful area of Calcutta and opened the doors to dying and destitute people. Mother Teresa's first patient was a homeless old woman who was half eaten by rats and maggots. Mother Teresa helped this hopeless human being into her small center, where she loved her, bathed her and caressed her until she died. That woman—and thousands after her—died knowing that she was cared for and loved. Everyone needs that kind of love when they approach the shadow of death.

In describing her work, Mother Teresa said that the most dreadful disease in the world is not tuberculosis or cancer but loneliness and not knowing you are loved. This little nun gave her life to her God-given dream. Her dream miraculously multiplied so that now thousands of people around the world help fulfill Mother Teresa's dream. Some work in the centers, but thousands of others give their prayers, time and money to support the dream.

Think how Mother Teresa's dream affected those she served in their misery. Like ripples on a quiet pond, one obscure woman challenged the whole world with an active new definition of Christian compassion. As an incredible fringe benefit, her work among dying people has become a significant motivator to millions of others to encourage them to believe in their God-inspired dream.

Uncle Jimmy Dreamed of Healing for the Family

Let me (H. B.) tell you about an amazing dream that unfolds before my eyes every day at Focus on the Family. This dream astounds the secular world and inspires tens of thousands of Christians.

On the surface, the dream appears to have started in 1976 when Dr. James Dobson founded Focus on the Family. But this ministry is more than the work of James Dobson. It started earlier in the heart of an almost obscure minister, Uncle Jimmy, Jim's father and my uncle. Uncle Jimmy gave his life to ministry as a pastor of small churches and as an itinerant evangelist. Later in his life, he taught art at colleges in California and Kansas.

Two years before his death at age 67, Uncle Jimmy had a beyond-imagination dream that challenged and mystified him. Here's how James Dobson told the story on one of his radio programs:

"My father was in prayer for three days and three nights about his own health and about the health of his brother-in-law back in 1977. Both of them were ministers, and he was asking the Lord to allow him to have more time, time to preach the gospel and to win people to the Lord; he had a passion for the ministry.

"The Lord spoke to him early one morning and told him that He had heard his prayer and that He was going to answer it. He said that He was going to reach literally millions of people around the world, but it was not going to be through his brother-in-law, who had cancer. He said, 'It is not going to be through you either, but it is going to be through your son.'

"God revealed to Dad all that Focus on the Family has become, but my father had a massive heart attack the next day and was never able to tell me that story. My uncle died that very afternoon, so the story was not communicated to me until seven years later in 1985.

"My father had shared all of this with Alline Swann (his brother-in-law's sister), and she said she had wanted to tell me about it for seven years but the Lord had said, 'Not yet.' In 1985, when I was going through a really tough time (I was on the pornography commission, Focus on the Family was going through some financial difficulties, the burden of this ministry was so heavy), she said the Lord told her, 'This is the time.' So she wrote me and told me the story.

"Then I realized, for the first time, why the blessing of the Lord has been on this ministry. It doesn't have anything to do with me; my job is just 'not to mess it up.' The truth of the matter is, the Lord answered the prayer of my father, and that's why this ministry is here and why it is now a worldwide outreach to the family. It is a gift to my dad. And the last line of Alline Swann's letter said, 'The end is not yet.'"

Think of the faithfulness of God to Uncle Jimmy's prayers and dreams. Dr. James Dobson, the son, went to Pasadena College and then into the military reserves. Later, he completed a graduate program at the University of Southern California, earned his Ph.D., and served as a clinical psychologist on the medical staff at Children's Hospital in Los Angeles. He wrote a bestseller, *Dare to Discipline*, which helps families apply Christian principles to their child rearing. Then one day, this Focus on the Family idea clicked with Dobson.

Following God's dream, Dobson resigned his position at the hospital, rented a little office and began a modest ministry. His first radio broadcast was made in Chicago on the same day he had been beaten up emotionally and spiritually on the *Phil Donahue Show*. Just before Donahue and Dobson walked before the cameras, the host told Jim, "I want you to know that I disagree completely with everything you believe in, and I will do my best to prove it before this audience today."

After the television program, Dobson returned to his hotel room. He stood looking out the window and prayed, "Lord, I'm embarrassed.

I've been disgraced before a nation of people. I am discouraged. And I am supposed to go begin a radio ministry today. We have little money and very few radio stations."

At that moment, God gave Dobson a wake-up call that was more real than an audible voice: "Jim, remember what your dad prayed. Remember what your dad believed. Remember what your dad thought. The dream never dies; it is still alive in you."

That night, Dobson taped three radio programs and started a ministry that today reaches around the world. At the time of this writing, the broadcast is heard in more than 954 radio stations in the United States and Canada, plus 4,377 stations in 165 countries, and it is translated into 26 languages around the world. Uncle Jimmy dreamed for his son what he could not dream for himself. And the dream continues to bear unbelievable fruit.

Dream for Your Congregation

You, my friend, must dream for members of your congregation what they are incapable of dreaming for themselves.

Look in the mirror. You are the dreamer that God designated to get your church dreaming and doing. He wants to inspire you with the miraculous possibilities for your church. Maybe you had low attendance last Sunday, the offering was down, two more Sunday School teachers threatened to quit, a key family is moving to a new job, or the church facilities are run-down. Maybe the situation is extremely desperate and you don't know what to do.

Maybe God wants you to dream your impossible limitations into victorious achievements. Remember, impossibilities are His specialty. Why not ask God to transform your worst hindrances into the fulfillment of an impossible dream? That's the way it was with Moses, Mother Teresa and Uncle Jimmy.

Moses' countrymen needed a courageously committed leader to make a difference. Often, they had no intention of fulfilling what little they understood of the dream. But Moses persisted and succeeded in spite of their unbelief and stupidity. He took them to the edge of the Promised Land. On the way, Moses enjoyed seeing God's promise fulfilled: that every place Moses' foot touched would be given to him.

Although the demands where you now serve may be confusing and disappointing, consider how much God needs you there. Ask Him for wisdom to lead your church to the cutting edge of faith and achievement. Try relinquishing your fear of failure and giving your uncertainties to God. Ask Him to give you a dream for your people like He gave to Moses.

Mother Teresa's dream sent her to share the love of Christ with the dying destitute of India. God assigned her to people no one else wanted to serve. The excruciating pain and terminal illnesses of these people would thoroughly depress most Christian workers. Who would choose to serve dying people who could do nothing for the Church and who could never give a dime, attend a service, hear a sermon, serve on a committee, sing in the choir or do anything else "good" church members do? Mother Teresa did.

Uncle Jimmy's pattern for dreaming speaks to us as well. He saw a heartbreaking need developing in society. He saw homes falling apart and knew that God was the only answer. Our society needs 10,000 Uncle Jimmys to dream about how God wants the gospel applied to the moral decay that is causing so much havoc in our society.

God needs dreamers to weep and to pray about today's moral decay and dwindling churches. He is looking for faithful, loyal, listening disciples who open their hearts to Him and ask how to take the good news wherever human need abounds. He needs somebody to take ministry to AIDS hospital wards, to infiltrate gangs with the gospel, and to reach homeless families and other front lines of the war between good and evil.

What a collection of dreamers: Moses, Mother Teresa, Uncle Jimmy—James Dobson, Sr.—and you.

Dreams for Today's Pastors

Many other unheralded dreamers are doing magnificent things for God. We may never hear about them, because they serve in out-of-the-way places. But these dreamers are well known to God, and they impact many people with the gospel in incredibly significant ways. They depend on Jesus' promise that "all things are possible with God."

We, H. B. London, Jr. and Neil B. Wiseman, dream about helping pastors bloom where God plants them. We view the local parish the way Sue Bender describes Amish farmers: "They make a lifetime commitment to the land, and their religious beliefs even determine farming methods. Over the years they have learned that with patience and perseverance they can transform dry, harsh land into a workable field. They have devised innovative ways to improve God's land . . . rotation of crops, use of irrigation and natural fertilizers, and the planting of alfalfa and clover all help to revitalize the land."[5]

It's a big dream we have for contemporary ministry. Some believe the dream is too big. Others believe the need is not nearly as great as we know it to be.

This Kingdom dream is to cherish and affirm pastors who doubt that their work matters. Our dream is to encourage pastors with the reality that a supernatural breakthrough may be around the corner. Our dream is to inspire weary pastors to try again to make God's dream a reality in their churches. We dream about pastors rediscovering adventure in their calling so that they can enjoy making a redemptive difference in churches, communities, countries—everywhere.

We believe that God wants pastors to dream of saving the nation. We believe that God wants pastors to dream of loving thousands into God's kingdom. We believe that God wants pastors everywhere to dream of building spiritually sturdy churches.

Never desert your dreams. The old praise song, one still sung in youth camps, is still amazingly accurate: "God specializes in things thought impossible, and He can do what no other power can do."[6]

Allow your dreams to direct your ministry. Focus on what matters most. Get fired up by what can happen. Tie your commitments and your dreams together so you see new ways of doing ministry. Find strength in Daniel and Carol Ketchum's song "The Molder of Dreams":

The blind man dreams of seeing,
The crippled child dreams she runs a race,
The leper dreams of being clean
And the dying man dreams there is no grave.

Where do dreams like these reach fulfillment?
Where do dreams like these rise full view?
There's only One place, and that's in You, King Jesus,
Where dreams like these are destined to come true.
You're the King of the Ages,
Now a mystery unseen;
You're the Shaper of Destiny,
And the Molder of our Dreams.[7]

CONTEMPORARY CHALLENGE

God Wants to Make Your Dreams Come True

- Tough times require new dreams.
- Dreams always shape ministry.
- Dreamers find new ways to accomplish ministry.
- God starts every ministry from someone's dream.
- Faith, hope and curiosity are the raw materials for dreams.
- God's dream is that every church be saturated with resurrection power.
- Dreams are never achieved without someone's sacrifice.

For broken dreams the cure is, Dream again. —C. S. Lewis[8]

Handling Criticism

Musings from H. B. London, Jr.

Many of us in ministry have been severely criticized for something we said, didn't say, did or didn't do. Although we know criticism goes with the territory, it still hurts—and hurts a lot.

As pastors, how should we handle conflict and criticism? How should we react when people falsely accuse us or misinterpret our motives? Here are some suggestions:

1. **Accept personal responsibility for the situation.** It may not be our fault, but we must take the initiative for reconciliation.

2. **Make every effort to move toward the person or persons in the conflict.** Try the following approach: "I understand this was said. Do you have some time when we can sit down and discuss our differences? Perhaps we can find common ground."

3. **Confront the issue for the sake of the relationship.** If we fail to address the issue, there will always be unrest—maybe even anger—in the relationship.

I once received a scathing, critical letter. The person had been carrying his ill will for several years and just vented his feelings that day. Although he hurt me, it must have really been painful for him. I responded in love, but the pain does not go away.

I guess I need to take some elephant-skin pills. Do you have any?

"Get rid of all bitterness, rage and anger . . . along with every form of malice. Be kind and compassionate to one another, forgiving each other, just as in Christ God forgave you" (Eph. 4:31-32).

CHAPTER 6

FALL IN LOVE WITH YOUR CALL AGAIN

To the One who called me,
renew my love for ministry,
season my attitudes with grace,
and enable me to serve so others know that
Christianity is more
than a rule for life, but also a Person to love.
Amen.

> MAY THE LORD,
> THE GOD OF THE SPIRITS
> OF ALL MANKIND, APPOINT A
> MAN OVER THIS COMMUNITY TO
> GO OUT AND COME IN BEFORE
> THEM, ONE WHO WILL LEAD
> THEM OUT AND BRING THEM IN,
> SO THE LORD'S PEOPLE WILL
> NOT BE LIKE SHEEP WITHOUT
> A SHEPHERD.
>
> NUMBERS 27:16-17

REKINDLE AN OLD FLAME

"I have nothing more to prove in basketball," Michael Jordan said in 1993 during a press conference in which he announced his retirement from basketball at the age of 30. At the time, the NBA superstar was considered the greatest player of his time, perhaps of all time. After some time away from the game, Jordan came back to the Chicago Bulls for three more seasons. He retired in 1998, stayed away from basketball for two seasons, and then finished his unparalleled career with the Washington Wizards. Throughout his years in the NBA, he averaged more than 30 points per game—amazing.[1]

Jordan's withdrawal at the height of his career has many parallels for weary pastors. It is frighteningly simple for a parish minister to lose his fire.

Without frequent rekindling, passion for ministry may burn low, or it may die altogether. Problems quench the fire. Misplaced priorities and frequent disappointments dampen passion. Then, when the flame starts to flicker, many ministers quit, burn out or drift into cycles of low achievement.

When a basketball star like Jordan leaves the game, people are disappointed, but their lives are not ultimately affected. However, pastors deal with issues that ultimately count—issues such as truth, destiny, hope and faith. When pastors experience burnout and leave, congregants' lives are adversely affected.

Yet a pastor's fervent passion for ministry can be refired with new challenges, worthwhile opportunities, and a revitalized realization of his divine partnership with God. Essayist Frederick Buechner helps us rekindle that old flame of our original call to ministry: "The place God calls you to is the place where your deepest gladness and the world's deepest hungers meet." Relive your original call and rejoice in it.

A Call: Life Sentence or Bold Adventure?

A newspaper cartoon portrayed a large Angora cat as a presiding magistrate. As a frightened defendant kitten stood before him, the judge rendered his verdict: "Since you have been a bad kitty, I hereby sentence you to nine lives as a cat."

Ministry is sometimes seen as a sentence that lasts for nine lifetimes. Many people think of a call as a judgment that God uses to make pastors miserable, lock them into poverty and choke the fun out of their marriage, parenting and work.

Nonsense!

The problem may be that the call to serve has become musty, dim or far-fetched.

Why should ministry be viewed as anything less than an adventuresome way to live? Why do so many contemporary pastors long for something that might allow them to respectably leave pastoral service? Could it be that pastors themselves have lost faith in the importance of ministry?

The problem may be that the call to serve has become musty, dim or far-fetched. Could it be that a frightening weakness of contemporary Christianity is rooted in this disconnection from "divine sentness"? Apparently, some pastors lost this inner spring of motivation years ago but never missed it. Some have forgotten how insistent the call was when they heard it the first time. Still others question if the call they heard in their childhood or adolescence has relevance now. Most have forgotten the power that a few ordinary folks like them have to change the world—that's their God-given mission.

Caution! A low-intensity call always leads to arid deserts of unsatisfying service, whatever our season of ministry. A disconnection from our call damages ministry as much as shutting off oxygen damages the brain or as withholding nourishment weakens the body. Ministry disorientation invariably follows.

On the contrary, a robust, up-to-date call energizes all phases of ministry. A call invigorates us and makes us spiritually alive. It sharpens our focus on the meaning of our ministry. It makes us more noble and more in touch with God than we could have ever been without it. It vitalizes vision and fuels motivation. A call reserves a front-row seat for us at what resurrection life does for human beings.

The God-initiated summons takes us into life's main arena where people wrestle with ultimate issues such as birth, life, death, sickness, broken relationships, health and hope, as well as ambiguities and apprehension. This partnership with God takes us to private and public places and to sorrowful and cheerful places. It is our lifetime ticket to represent Jesus at weddings, hospital waiting rooms, grave sites, baptisms, Holy Communion and life-shaping questions that good people have reason to ask, such as "Where is God now?"

A call to ministry supplies a driving force for our ministry as it empowers our commitment to revolutionize the world for Christ. This

God-inspired energy takes us to people who do not want us and empowers us to stay until they cannot get along without us. It is the gospel dressed in our shoe leather.

A Call: Uniquely Personal

God's initial call to us to enter the ministry has very little to do with our abilities, skills or expertise. However, it has everything to do with our faith, devotion and glad embrace of His will. A call most often starts at the core of our being, where God affects our identity and self-worth, and then moves outward to the needs of the world or to a hurting person next door or across town. A call tends to clarify the meaning of our life and to give us a purpose for living.

A call combines supernatural and earthly dimensions. Those awesome words, "a call to the ministry," often conjure up images of burning bushes and lightning strikes, but they also produce mental images of privilege and of being willing love slaves to the purposes of God.

Henri Nouwen, an influential spiritual-formation writer, suggests that at the point of a call, a potential pastor "gets rid of the scaffolding: no friends to talk to, no phones to answer, no meetings to attend, no music to entertain, no books to distract—naked, vulnerable, weak, sinful, deprived, broken—nothing."[2]

This is a private meeting when God summons us to a special work that we never comprehend completely. The call often highlights our weaknesses or failures so that the enabling grace and empowerment of God stand out in bold relief in our whole scheme of living. In the calling process, we generally come to view how weak we are, how much more

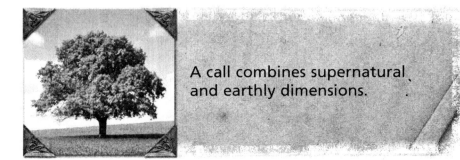

A call combines supernatural and earthly dimensions.

God intends us to become, and how the world and the Church need someone just like us for this work.

A call means being used to impact a part of God's world—that noble and eternal part. At the same time, a call means that we work where God sends us—in Fairbanks, Selma or Manhattan. That's the sweaty and earthy part of a call. It is a summons to unknown territory, but it always promises the company of the absolutely trustworthy God. It is realizing that it is more important to know who is leading than where we are going.

None of life's most lofty experiences for the called minister ever surpasses such a meeting with God. The called person can never forget the fact that he has been called. In a spiritual sense, his soul is indelibly branded forever. The Caller—God Himself—communicates a distinctly personal summons that can only be heard by the called, but he hears it like the thunder and generally for a lifetime.

A Call: A Love Connection to God

The love connection dimension of a call needs significantly more attention and visibility than it now has in most places. The ministry is love at work: love God shows to the pastor by trusting him; love the pastor shows for God by serving Him; love that God and the pastor show to human beings in need.

All the dreadful foreboding and enslavement verbiage so often heard about a call to ministry must be questioned and rejected for something better. Delight, gladness, pleasure, serenity, enchantment and also accomplishment of a mission must be highlighted more. Glorious, vigorous call-to-arms words such as "faith," "hope," "integrity," "credibility" and "service" must be stirred into the delightful recipe. The joy, romance and fun that God builds into every pastor's call need much more expression. Ministry is adventure.

I (Neil) once met a newly married student who fairly shouted at the opening of our conversation, "I love being married. It's great!" His wife loves that kind of talk, as well she should. I wonder what would happen in every congregation if a pastor declared with his wholehearted affection, "I love being your pastor!"

I once met a first-time father who overflowed with enthusiasm, "Having our baby girl depend on me is the greatest joy of my life." That attitude might work in church, too. Why not start a revolution of communicating such loving affection in your church? What if every pastor in every pulpit would say, "Having a part in your spiritual development is the most exciting thing in the world for me"? Think of the possibilities and spin-offs such a renewed love affair might cause.

A pastor friend of mine summarized ministry joyously and accurately: "I get to see more of what God does in one week than most people see in a lifetime." Our call always does that. If we are willing to see, it allows us to observe firsthand how people apply their faith to the worst and best in their lives.

Let's get our bearings again. Our call takes us in love to the middle of delightful spiritual action—our own and others! Ministry is not slavery but an *agape* love force for the spiritual recovery of self and society.

Unfortunately, many do not think being anointed is enough. They believe there is something better, bigger and more important. But in reality, the call is God's anointing. It does not get any better than that. What more would anyone want?

A Call: Not Unlike Country Doctoring

To appreciate the amazing potential wrapped up in our call, we should try viewing our ministry as a spiritual counterpart to an old-time country doctor. The seasoned practitioner delivered babies, saw children through their growing-up years, gave them preventative shots, cured their fevers, listened to their dreams, helped them through puberty and

The ministry is love at work.

pimples, taught them the facts of life, attended their weddings, delivered their children and then started the cycle again with the new generation.

"Old sawbones," as he was affectionately called, was frequently tired, frustrated by his failures, underpaid by his patients, poorly equipped by technology and not especially viewed as an important professional by his peers in big-city hospitals. But as he lived his life, he had the incredible joy of knowing that he saved Tom's life, brought Mary and her baby through difficult labor, sat up all night as Granny White changed worlds, and prescribed healing medicine to make Jim feel better in two days.

The minister has a similar impact on the spiritual development of those he serves. He is a general practitioner, father confessor, spiritual obstetrician and faith specialist. Pastors, however, should enjoy much greater exhilaration than the country doctor. They point people to Christ, enable others to make sense of life, preserve cracking marriages, teach faith to children, hold the hands of dying saints and share a holy partnership with Christ. The privileges and accomplishments are absolutely amazing.

THE REALISTIC ROMANCE OF MINISTRY

Falling in love again with your call may be an adolescent, illogical or even utopian return to what never was—something like your first puppy love for the little girl next door or a crush on your kindergarten teacher. On a more satisfying level, a rekindled realistic love for ministry may be more like listing on a legal pad reasons to be in love with your spouse after being married for a decade or even half a century.

Veterans of mature love in marriage and ministry say that it is as fully satisfying as beginning love—and maybe even more so. And though some ministries and marriages endure without love, they are more enjoyable and more useful when fueled by affection, fidelity and shared dreams.

To fall in love again with your calling requires a return to the basic anchors of ministry. The pressing questions are:

• Who called you?
• Who started you in this work?

- How does love leak out of ministry?
- What will it take to make love your most compelling motivation again?
- Has secular culture strangled significance out of Christian service for you?

Love is the fascinating incentive for ministry—the exciting faith dimension that keeps a pastor's ministry personal and fresh and intimate. Any other motive eventually frustrates and short-circuits ministry. Love also provides a personal safeguard. Without love for Christ and people, ministry easily turns into uncontrolled ego gratification and a grasping need for prominence and control. When this occurs, a pastor is in danger of becoming a pontificating religious quack. Love for Christ, however, keeps the pastor focused on what really counts.

Christ-closeness nourishes ministry. When we allow love for the Lord to grow dim, we become dumfounded by the needs around us. The needs are too vast and the resources too small. At times such as these, it is easy to feel rejected by those we serve and frustrated over their slow spiritual progress.

On the contrary, if we keep focused on our love motivation, we are able to see God working in even the most trying circumstances. We can then relish our relationship to our Senior Partner who carries most of the load and directs our next move.

Our intentions and motivations are among the most important issues in ministry. Although pastors may be driven by many mixed motives, an authentic call must be rooted in a forthright commitment to serve God

Christ-closeness nourishes ministry.

and a sincere yearning to care for hurting, sinful and broken people in Jesus' name. The bedrock foundation is a passion for truth, for pleasing God and for useful service.

Our task is to rekindle or to recapture the adventuresome love affair with our call that we knew at the start when God's direction was fresh as the morning dew.

Act As Though You Love Ministry

A middle-aged woman wrote to a syndicated personal advice columnist to report that after 25 years of marriage, she was falling out of love with her husband. She said the spark was gone, the glow dead; he snored and had gained 30 pounds. The old magic feeling had disappeared, and she no longer heard bells or whistles. The children had grown and left home, so she lived in a lonely, empty nest. She asked for advice on how to desert, divorce and start again.

The columnist advised: Stay where you are. Start acting as if you are in love. Do loving deeds. Quit pitying yourself. Show love until warm feelings start growing again—they will. In this process, you might learn to love your husband more than you did when you counted on magic in place of authentic relationship, enduring faith and continuous loyalty.

Let's try taking that advice into ministry. Perhaps we could create an exciting, positive, self-fulfilling prophecy for ourselves.

During an area ministerial association meeting, a novice minister shared his dreams as a newcomer. He told how he began his first assignment with extraordinary fervor in a place that no one else wanted. He told about the futility he felt in his former occupation as a stockbroker. To anyone with a speck of spiritual savvy, his sense of call had the same electricity as Paul's vibrant phrase, "The hope to which he has called you" (Eph. 1:18).

Sadly, several seasoned pastors in the group responded with discouraging grousing about the monotonies of modern ministry. Their excitement had died; their focus had shifted to dreadful chores they detested. They whined about lackluster meetings, humdrum paper shuffling, fussy parishioners and self-inflicted coercion to succeed in a worldly way.

Understandably, God seemed far away from them and the people they served. They were spiritually depleted and felt that no one received much help when they preached. Ministry was miserable, hard work for them.

The discrepancy between these two radically different perspectives is startling. The beginner is probably overly idealistic, and the veterans are much too gloomy. But the novice and the old hands need a mature love for ministry that can grow throughout a lifetime of service. Effective ministry cannot continue for long without it.

For many unfortunate reasons, thousands of pastors have lost faith in themselves and their calling. If they are to again serve adequately and happily in their ministry, something supernatural has to happen to them. For their own wellbeing, for the good of the Church, and for the salvation of the lost, something has to change.

Glory, privilege, joy and fulfillment have to be recaptured. The dying spark has to be stirred into a red-hot fire. Duty has to become delight. Excitement has to be revived. Love has to be reborn. Imagination, intensity and anticipation have to flourish again. The first step, of course, is to act as though they love ministry as much as they did when they started.

Personalize Ministry Renewal

Every pastor has had a counseling experience with a couple that seemed more interested in seeking a new love than in restoring an old one. The energy the husband and wife are prepared to invest in a new relationship could easily rekindle meaning in their existing one. The same thing needs to happen in faltering ministries. When such a renewal takes place, we will never consider quitting to sell used cars, become a social worker, take up carpentry or become a king.

We need to give ourselves a reality check. We might already have more meaning than we realize. No occupational fulfillment in the whole world compares with the satisfaction enjoyed by a pastor who loves God, loves his call and shows love for the people he serves. Few experiences are more fun than serving a congregation when things are going well. Nothing produces as much meaning as being needed. No other vocation allows a person to get so close to so many people in such life-changing ways.

Renewing love for our calling takes effort, time and closeness. We all know that meaningful courtship always demands all of us—heart, mind, will and body. And this renewed love affair needs our all-out effort as well.

Remember that ministry is more than an honorable profession, a praiseworthy dedication or even a commendable way of life. Rather, it is a tender, life-giving relationship between the Savior and a shepherd.

Sometimes pastors believe ministry would be more effective and more enjoyable if systems, denominations, parachurch organizations or local congregations were reformed. Admittedly, some of these entities desperately need renewal. However, motivation for contemporary pastors will more likely come from persons than from organizations, from individual manifestations of ministry than from revitalized systems, and from our hearts than from our brains.

Love for ministry must be renewed. Treat yourself to new romance in your work for God.

Contemporize Your Message

"How could I be bored with my assignment when I look out on the congregation and count 25 baby Christians that I had a part in leading to Christ?" This is the way one pastor described his firsthand experience of this love lesson. He had moved beyond merely satisfying the saints into transforming troubled people. He quickly discovered that incredible satisfaction comes from ministries that reach contemporary people.

Each new generation must experience for itself the incredible joy of introducing its own generation to the gospel of Christ. Each generation must see this task as something much more than a drab and dismal exercise of conserving ancestral piety. Each generation must realize that God summons new ministers to revitalize, renew, revive, remake and reform themselves, their churches, their communities and their cultures. Whatever its sin or secularism, each new age needs what the Christian gospel offers. When has the challenge to rediscover the gospel been greater than it is today?

The joy of communicating the gospel in terms that contemporary people understand will stretch our understanding of Scripture, our awareness of the moral bankruptcy of society, and our speaking and writing skills. It has to be done. And the excitement of pointing secular-ized people to Christ brings new fulfillment and authenticity to our ministry.

Grow Past the Honeymoon

After the honeymoon ends, the house has to be cleaned, the garbage has to be taken out, routines have to be established, mortgage payments have to be made, and the broken-down car has to be repaired.

No honeymoon lasts forever, but love can be tended into a signifi-cant lifetime experience. And even though mature married love is not better than the first blush and rushing emotions of the first year of mar-riage, it is satisfying in different ways and is more enduring. It is not a denial of the joy of the beginning, nor is it inferior to the honeymoon period. Beginning and ripening produce their own unique satisfactions.

A similar developmental growth should be expected in ministry. After an exhilarating beginning when the pastor meets new people and feels the excitement of his education, ordination and installation, ser-mons must be prepared, sinners must be led to Christ, shut-ins must be visited, crises must be faced, believers must be trained, relationships must be established, and money must be raised. The beginning and the continuing are meant to be important phases of the living out of min-istry among the people of God. The excitement at the beginning was designed to be an important first step in the happy process of maturing of ministry.

Even though renewing love for ministry and shaping it into a mature relationship requires energy and imagination, it requires much less effort

God summons new ministers to revitalize, renew, revive, remake and reform themselves, their churches, their communities and their cultures.

than starting over in a new parish. This ripening relationship, like a maturing marriage, provides an additional payoff of a congregation of best friends who give strength to each other in ways that short-term or superficial relationships simply cannot provide.

Like love in marriage, a ministry call often needs rejuvenation. One church leader I know believes that ordination services accomplish that purpose. He calls these services "a time when veterans get to hear the recruitment speech again." He is right, but there are other ways to rejuvenate ministry.

Why not search for maturing growth at every conceivable event and relationship in your pastorate? Cherish every affirmation parishioners give you. Look for it in every expression of service. Pay whatever price it takes to find lasting satisfaction in your work for God. The resulting awareness of being on a momentous assignment for Him rekindles vigor, zest, mission, focus, dependence on God and affection for the work. It will also strengthen your personal spiritual stamina.

Nurture Your Call

Ministry is tomfoolery without a sacred summons. It is sheer madness to tackle ministry without God's empowerment. But divine enablement is promised, and we need to keep plugged into it. In the process, greatness will be etched onto our souls.

Personal intimacy with Christ is our essential source for ministry. Devotion to God is the fertile soil in which a ministry is rooted and grows to maturity. Without this basic bond, the call will be fuzzy. Thus, the call always gets out of focus when our relationship with Jesus is allowed to become ceremonial or superficial. On the contrary, closeness to Christ creates strong character and takes us to the center of God's redemptive activity among His people.

Ability to preach, knowledge of the Bible and theology, and even ministerial experience are not sufficient. The founder of Methodism, John Wesley, raised three questions prior to asking about a potential candidate's gifts for the work: "Does he know God? Does he desire and seek nothing but God? Has he the love of God abiding in him?"[3] John Wesley's first concern for a pastor's intimate friendship with God should be ours as well.

A call to ministry can accomplish incredible achievement beyond our wildest dreams because of such a personal relationship between God and a pastor.

Although a call has far-reaching congregational and social dimensions, it begins as a private dialogue—an alive, life-changing encounter between God and the minister-to-be. Even though it may be later identified with a time and a place dimension where God met the prospective pastor, the call is really a holy meeting, an adventure with deity, an "aha" moment, an insistent urgency, a summons to active duty and an extravagant invitation combined.

One minister called it a "spiritual showdown." He explained, "After being called, I felt like a marked man—no one else could see the mark but God and me. And I have been trying to work out the meaning of that meeting for a lifetime."

In the rough and tumble world of ministry, every day brings some confusing events, disturbing ambiguities, wild fantasies or strange affiliations that team up to cause us to question our adequacy, our commitment and our effectiveness. Regardless of the fact that each new struggle may be slightly different, it is a struggle nonetheless. It is precisely in the midst of these questions and change points—whether they are personal, family or professional—that our Lord comes and reminds us, "I have special need of you for a unique task, even when you are at a high noon in these struggles."

Transform Concepts to Specifics

For some unknown reason, it is easy for the Christian faith to become a high-level academic pursuit similar to the study of biology or physics—conceptual but not specific in its application to life. But in moments of intimate communication with our Lord, He often brings clarity and concreteness to our attention. Then, faith moves from the realm of abstractions and nebulous concepts to specifics and particulars. Artificial walls between the secular and the sacred tumble down. Radiant ministry flows from the heart and mind of the God-called minister who, in the quiet place, has received orders from the Commander-in-Chief.

The results: Ministry is clarified and prioritized so that we can work with the strange notions, confusing backgrounds and infantile beliefs of real persons with specific needs. In this process, God helps us separate pastoral chaff from ministry wheat so that we are able to sort out which of our ministerial priorities and activities are for the glory of God and which are for the aggrandizement of our lofty intellect or conniving self-interest. Love energizes this give-and-take with deity that enables us to make ministry specific for Jim and Mary, Tom and Sally, Mark and Susan.

Allow the Right People to Reenergize Your Call

In pastoral ministry, it is possible to spend too much time with the wrong people (for example, negative long-term lay leaders who seem content to control the church without changing it). It is also possible to spend so much time with new people that the established folks organize a pity party for themselves—and that's no party for the pastor.

In his book *Your Ministry's Next Chapter*, Gary Fenton offers advice on this point: "The best way for me to reenergize my call is to spend time with non-Christians who are searching for God in all the wrong places, new Christians enthusiastically throwing themselves into the life of the church, or hurting Christians who desperately want to find their way back into the fellowship of Christ and his people."[4]

Ask God for Visionary Bigness

Every congregation needs a pastor to pray, "O God, our Father, let us not be content to wait and see what will happen, but give us the determination to make the right things happen."[5]

God wants such a growing edge on every pastor's call—a kind of fresh hope, a new beginning, and a visionary bigness that sees beyond every limitation, whether it is real or imagined. A pastor's call is related to a breakout spirit for every achievement for God, and it is the only hope in many dying or dormant situations. In revitalizing his call, God helps the pastor see what others might consider to be a lofty illusion as an unfinished reality of what God wants done in that setting.

This experience is similar to what a pastor experiences in his initial call when God shows him the needs of the whole world. Although it boggles his imagination and his self-concept, the novice is forever changed by a vision of global needs that someone must meet in Jesus' name.

This is exactly the situation in many struggling, tough church settings today. Something great needs to be done, but the only hope for supernatural achievement in that place is for the called one to believe that God is already working and will bring significant achievement to pass. This visionary bigness helps a pastor develop a clear, sharp vision for a given church so that he can see possibilities in a situation that no one else sees.

This is how Thomas Wise was fired up to start his ministry. After finishing Bible college, his call to ministry inspired him to plant a church among people he did not know, where the demographics were largely unfavorable and economic opportunities were stagnant. He began working part-time as a grocery store bag boy in a tiny Oregon coastal town and made contacts with residents of the community.

Six years later, mostly through loving people and after-school Bible clubs for children, he had developed a congregation made up mostly of new converts, had helped construct a church building on a five-acre tract of land, and had won the affection of an entire community. No one else saw what he saw. He responded to what he believed to be God's specific assignment.

Welcome God's Challenge

At one point in their training, Peace Corps volunteers in one location were assigned a 24-hour survival stint alone in the jungle. One young man came away from the experience visibly shaken: "You know, as soon as I found some running water and got my hammock slung where I figured no tarantula would get me, I knew I'd be all right. But then it suddenly hit me: For the next 24 hours I'd have to pay a call on myself, and I wasn't sure I'd find anyone home."[6]

A call always stretches us to be more than we believe we can be. The invitation to ministry is a call to become fully like Christ as much as it is to do ministry. It keeps us remembering who we are and Whose we have become. If we allow it, this process will stretch us into the image of God's own dear Son and will pack significant meaning into our lives. It may make us willing or even comfortable to be at home with who we have become.

The call of God pushes us to get to know ourselves. One college chapel speaker was strong on this point and urged students to heed this advice:

"Know yourself. You size up professors, fellow students, girl and boy friends; why not look at yourself? Meet yourself on campus and ask, 'Why am I here? What am I here for? What do I want? Where am I going?'" As the speaker paused for a breath, a student in the balcony was heard to say in a stage whisper, "If that guy ever meets himself on this campus, we are going to observe the worst dog fight this school has ever seen."[7]

Maybe the student was right about that particular speaker, but pastors need to learn who they are and how God can uniquely use them. The reality is that because we never lead people to heights we have not climbed, a lived-out ministry call constantly stretches us to be more like the Master for whom we minister. This issue became clear in the life of a young minister. As he was coming away from the gravesite of a teenage boy he had just buried, the youth's father said, "I don't know if I believe everything you said back there at my son's grave. But it means more than you can imagine for me to know that you believe it."[8]

This is the kind of stretching of heart and soul a call to ministry has on our faith and character development. God's stretching makes us better, purer and more like the Savior. The process reminds us of one pastor's comment: "God called me into ministry because that was the only way I would become like Him."

In the book *A Diary of Private Prayer,* John Baillie, famous preacher from another generation, lists a number of personal stretch points to help us become more like Christ:

My failure to be true even to my own accepted standards;
My self-deception in face of temptation;
My choosing of the worst when I know the better;
My failure to apply to myself the standards of conduct I demand of others;
My blindness to the suffering of others and my slowness to be taught by my own;
My complacence toward wrongs that do not touch my own case and my over-sensitiveness to those that do;
My slowness to see the good in my fellows and to see the evil in myself;

My hardness of heart toward my neighbors' faults and my
readiness to make allowance for my own; and
My unwillingness to believe God has called me to a small work
and my brother to a great one.[9]

YOU CAN FALL IN LOVE AGAIN

Believe in your heart that your ministry equips people to live a Christ-quality life. When you love ministry and demonstrate that love, your expressions of ministry will affect people more than you can imagine. You will help people grow. At times, you will swing from tender pastor to fiery prophet to pleading priest. You will enrich your life. You will stand taller and nobler. You will be more spiritual and less secular. You will have a cause to live for, to fight for and to die for. You will feel a sense of purpose, of making a difference and of recovered self-worth. So wrap your arms around your ministry. It will love you back in ways beyond your loftiest dreams.

CONTEMPORARY CHALLENGE

Ways to Fall in Love with Your Ministry

- Act as though you love ministry.
- Personalize your ministry renewal.
- Contemporize your message.
- Grow beyond your honeymoon.
- Nurture your call.
- Allow God to make ministry specific.
- Ask God for a visionary bigness.
- Welcome God's stretching.

The minister of the gospel is frightened by the magnitude of his assignment until he discovers the Presence at his side. —Milo Arnold[10]

Peace—to You!

Musings from H. B. London, Jr.

My hope is that you live in an atmosphere of peace. Jesus said to his disciples, "Peace I leave with you; my peace I give you. I do not give to you as the world gives. Do not let your hearts be troubled and do not be afraid" (John 14:27).

How many times have you prayed with a hospital patient or someone who has lost a loved one that they might have peace? You were praying that as they surrendered there would be a lifting of heaviness and a realization that a divine presence had entered their personal world.

As I travel to do ministry, I have encountered many of you who are struggling with a prodigal child or a troubled marriage. I have talked with those of you who were uncertain as to your call—and unhappy in your assignment. I have prayed with you over an issue of addiction or moral failure. I have listened as you spoke of a contentious church. For some of you, the situation ended in a loss of ministry. I know about your troubles, because as a pastor I have experienced some of your similar challenges.

Yet in all of this, there is the assurance from Deuteronomy 31:6 that is echoed in Hebrews 13:5: "Never will I leave you; never will I forsake you." That is the atmosphere of peace that I pray you have—the assurance of His love, His presence, His direction and His understanding of your situation.

The challenge is your surrender, isn't it? It is in the letting go. Peace to you, my friend.

CHAPTER 7

PERKS ONLY PASTORS ENJOY

Lord, I need help
to better recognize satisfactions in service,
to enjoy partnership with You,
to delight
in studying, seeking and speaking for You.
Rescue me from the prison of merely doing my duty.
Amen.

A pastor's unmatched fringe benefits are rooted in ministries given, in kindnesses received, and in gratifying results. Ministry given includes preaching, pastoral care, outreach evangelism, administrative leadership, and counseling. Kindnesses received has to do with those generous gestures of love people give us, often because we served them in some helpful way. Gratifying results are the happy outcomes in people's lives that are sometimes unknown until months or even years after the actual ministry is given. When I think about perks we enjoy in ministry, I am always drawn to Gene Fowler's great sentence, "Love and memory will endure even after the game is called because of darkness."[1]

Lasting meaning—the best of perks—comes from doing ministry well, as unto Christ and for His glory. As you read this chapter, total your list of satisfying perks and you will feel like singing, "Count your blessings . . . and it will surprise you what the Lord has done."

Unmatched Fringe Benefits

Just now, the sound and smell and suffering of a hospital returns to my memory from an Easter Sunday dawn from my past. That Easter morning, before I (Neil) went to preach the joyous resurrection gospel to the people of God, the Father gave me opportunity as pastor to be His spokesman to a grieving family whose teenage boy had been gravely injured in a car wreck the night before.

What soul-stretching confusion between the brokenness, despair and bewilderment at that hospital and the wholeness, faith and hope in the New Testament account of the Resurrection.

God's words for that family communicated through me brought them promise and strength—words I was incapable of speaking either spiritually or professionally.

I was enriched by the perks of usefulness both from pastoral care and later from preaching.

I recall another time when anguish started to lift from a mother's countenance as she met me at her front door. I was there within minutes after she received word her youngest son had been killed in a military accident. Although she seemed glad to have me there, it was the One I represented that sustained her. I simply said, "I've come to cry with you." Both of us were strengthened. I remember how wonderful it felt to be used by God.

I love the privilege of living at the front lines of life where grace works. I love being present when God and broken people sign reconciliation treaties. As flawed and frail as I know myself to be, I am privileged as a pastor to represent Christ at main events of people's lives.

Thousands of memories flood my mind when I reflect on the essence of ministry. I think of the incredible perks I have received while representing Christ.

I intend to stay in ministry for a lifetime to continue enjoying these amazing fringe benefits.

Outrageous Joys of Ministry

Unlike many church vocations, secular corporations often offer employees generous fringe benefits that sometimes cost as much as 40 percent over base salary. Such perks are costly to the business and wonderfully helpful to workers.

In the business sector, labor and management leaders enjoy debating over who deserves credit for perks. Management claims fringes started when businesses volunteered to share profits with employees. Labor insists perks became a reality only when they helped workers demand them. Whoever started fringe benefits, the list often includes medical and life insurance, vacation pay, shorter workweeks, paid holidays, sick leave and retirement benefits.

Although pastors often receive some of these same fringe benefits, their richest perks can never be enjoyed by those who work in corporate boardrooms, hospital critical-care units, courtrooms or auto-manufacturing plans. Unique perks, like beautiful spring wildflowers, surround pastors in rich profusion all along the ministry pilgrimage.

The possibilities sparkle in these sentences from C. S. Lewis: "Indeed, if we consider the unblushing promises of reward and the staggering nature of the rewards promised in the Gospel, it would seem that our Lord finds our desires not too strong, but too weak. We are half-hearted creatures, fooling about with drink and sex and ambition when infinite joy is offered us. *We are like an ignorant child who wants to go on making mud pies in a slum because he cannot imagine what is meant by the offer of a holiday at the sea.*"[2]

Those noble words make us wonder why anyone would settle to be a king if he could be a pastor.

Seeing How Faith Really Works

Some time ago, I led a funeral celebration for a 94-year-old jubilant Christian. Until a few weeks before her death, she played hymns she had known since childhood, though she could not remember her name and seldom recognized her grown children.

I was once her pastor, though we had been out of touch for nearly 25 years. She had outlived her friends and siblings and spouse. Severe problems of aging had kept her from church for years. But I was deeply moved by the imprint songs of faith had made on her soul. I was glad to hear her children and grandchildren and great-grandchildren talk about the power of a song, a touch, a gentle word, a kind affirmation, a listening ear or an assuring prayer.

It's a great perk for a pastor to see what grace does in a long, holy life.

This woman's family gave me another perk when they spoke kindly about my influence in their lives. One grandson even spoke of the positive impact that went across generations.

Another serendipity increased my perks that day: Would you believe a woman attending that funeral was a church member I had loaded into my car on a snowy wintry night (about 2:00 A.M., as I recall) to take to an emergency room because she had overdosed? The doctor pumped her stomach and kept her at the hospital overnight. There she was, 25 years later, enjoying life, visiting with friends, following the funeral and showing pictures of her grandchildren and great-grandchildren.

What a day for perks—a memory of a life lived in faith for so many years, three generations expressing thanks for ministry, and meeting one whose life I had saved. Who but a pastor has fringe benefits like that?

A Renewed Focus on What Matters

Many pastors these days are taking a novel new look—or is it a serious old look?—at genuine pastoral perks. More and more ministers are rethinking what they consider the most significant segments of ministry. It's a healthy trend. Increasing fulfillment is being found in imaginative, life-changing preaching and in helping believers find a vibrant intimacy with Christ.

This trend means more ministers have decided to ignore trivia and to pay less attention to unimportant expectations from outside sources.

Sustained satisfaction starts by recognizing the incredible perks God has planted in every pastoral assignment.

They want to concentrate on essentials. This new breed finds enormous contentment in making a life-transforming impact on people near them. In the process, their ministry focus becomes more local than global—more tangible and less theoretical. Many say they discover incredible contentment in developing the spirituality of others and in ripening their own faith.

Sustained satisfaction starts by recognizing the incredible perks God has planted in every pastoral assignment. Fulfillment can be found any place people need ministry. And being a pastor means God sends us to those places often.

SATISFACTION 1: PRACTICE AND PERFECT YOUR SPECIALTY

It is difficult to fathom why any minister would be shy about discussing the most important specialty in the world—the power of the gospel to transform people and provide quality of life.

Did Edison consider keeping electricity to himself? Did Alexander Graham Bell keep the telephone locked up in his creative imagination? How would a resourceful medical researcher be judged who did not share a newly discovered cancer cure? Or what about a cardiologist who declined to treat heart disease?

Neither can we keep God's good news to ourselves. It's time to overcome timidity and take our healing specialty to the street.

It Worked for Ruby Bridges

Dr. Robert Coles recounted Ruby's story during his keynote address in the mid-1990s to the Provident Counseling Annual Conference in St. Louis, Missouri. Eight hundred professionals—including educators, social workers and mental-health therapists—attended the event.

Dr. Coles, a Harvard professor and Pulitzer Prize-winning author, spoke of the potential vitality of faith as he recalled how six-year-old Ruby Bridges's resilience surprised him like nothing else in his professional practice had ever done.

You may remember that Ruby was the first black child to attend New Orleans's white Frantz School in 1960 when the courts ordered desegregation. Although social scientists expected little Ruby to be plagued by eating and sleep disorders, she appeared to suffer no difficulties. The reason—the robust religious convictions learned from her devoted Christian parents bolstered her. She learned from them to pray, "Please, God, forgive them, because they don't know what they are doing."

Coles continued, "Ruby told me her mother and grandmother instructed her that was a fitting prayer. Amazingly, her petition connected her with something that happened a couple of thousand years before in a distant land with the life of an itinerant preacher whose name was Jesus."

When other professionals interviewed the girl, they were surprised to find inner spiritual sources had strengthened her and kept her emotionally fit, even at her young age.

Later, while discussing what every pastor knows to be spiritual empowerment, Coles urged conferees when counseling clients to "look within every life for the moral possibilities, rather than emphasizing dysfunction." Other conference speakers picked up the idea and suggested a valuing of "resilience and sustenance in individuals"—especially by those who have been toughened by trauma.

Conferees were challenged to start using a new vocabulary of strength in place of depressing conversations about dysfunctional emotional illnesses.[3]

These insights shared among family therapists at the conference sound surprisingly like the teachings of Jesus and Paul. But as pastors, we sometimes forget to speak up about our specialty and to tell people we serve that God builds strength, resilience and fulfillment in those who take spiritual fitness seriously.

Can you imagine the perks Ruby Bridges's pastor must have felt in those early years of the civil rights movement? And since?

SATISFACTION 2: STRONG MARRIAGES ENERGIZE MINISTRY

Marriage provides an ideal relationship for a pastor to receive and give personal fulfillment and emotional strength. Of course, ministry couples do not build a strong marriage just to make ministry more credible, but to make themselves more whole persons.

When you strengthen your marriage, you provide perks for yourself, your spouse, your family, your congregation and your community.

Beginners Find Help

I know a delightfully devoted young ministry couple who had a common, though mostly undiscussed, handicap that hindered their happiness and short-circuited their ministry. They came from broken family backgrounds, so their models for marriage were grossly flawed. To protect their identity, let's call them Sally and Sam.

Sally and Sam were two thoroughly converted human beings who met at a Christian college and married in their early 20s. When they married, they dedicated their future to serving together in ministry. As they accepted their first church, they looked forward to introducing people to Christ and helping others nourish their faith. However, although they didn't realize it, they were emotional cripples because of their turbulently dysfunctional family backgrounds.

They realized almost immediately in their new church setting that making their marriage strong had to take place before they could help others. So they took an emotional three-month timeout. They continued their ministry part-time, but their primary focus was to find resources to strengthen their marriage.

Sally and Sam gave their marriage the same priority a family devotes to a medical emergency. During that time, they sought help from counselors, read books together, instituted a mentoring relationship with a mature clergy couple in a nearby town, and attended marriage work-

Marriage provides an ideal relationship for a pastor to receive and give personal fulfillment and emotional strength.

shops. Eventually, their much better adjusted marriage contributed to a sense of wholeness and well-being.

Sally and Sam started growing their marriage by leaps and bounds when they realized that a meaningful relationship requires persevering commitment, determined faith, soul friendship and selfless love—*agape* as well as *eros*. In the long term, their mended brokenness enhanced the joy of their marriage, increased the effectiveness of their ministry to other hurting people, and served as a model for healthy marriages.

Their perk—awareness that they had become authentic wounded healers.

A Couple Makes Home a Sanctuary

Another ministry couple used their home as a setting for a satisfying perk pastors often overlook—a place of retreat, togetherness and solid spirituality where they could recharge their emotional batteries and refocus their perspectives about ministry.

As a starting point for bolstering marriage and for increasing ministry satisfaction, this couple turned their home into a sanctuary.

Both were involved in highly demanding professions—she as a high school counselor and he as a pastor. Both jobs required immense psychological, spiritual and physical energy

The effort paid off. They made their marriage a source of joy and fun. They are quality people, mostly because they have a quality marriage.

That's a perk they gave themselves, and in the process they helped their church.

SATISFACTION 3: FOCUS ON
FAMILY FULFILLMENTS

"Family feeds and complicates ministry," was a veteran pastor's summary in a series of family-life lectures to seminarians. This is an interesting way of saying that God designed the family as a remarkable source of well-being but that we sometimes allow it to become a bewildering or even clinical jigsaw puzzle.

Simply stated, a strong stable family is built on a balance of doing for, doing with and getting the family to do for each other. Since the family of God at church and the family at home have much in common, working through personal family issues is a good gift a ministry couple can give the congregation and a special perk they can give their family.

Family Need Not Be a Runner-Up

A winning formula for family and church is for the pastor's family to enrich and enable ministry. Paul Pearsall, a family specialist, underscores the benefits of family: "Being a part of any family can be the most important privilege of being human, the most healing experience of being alive and the source of lifelong and evolving understanding of what it really means to live."[4]

He adds an introspective admonition: "But first we must learn to raise our families instead of our children."[5] To make this idea operational, every pastor must provide spiritual and emotional strength for all members of his family.

The task of parenting runs the gamut of experiences: from the hospital delivery room, to changing diapers, caring for sick children, keeping track of Little League schedules, corralling children for Sunday School classes, family vacations, first dates, rebellious teens, college goodbyes, weddings, grown children, and the arrival of grandchildren. This partial list of parenting experiences shapes a pastor's perspective about his leadership in the family of God.

Living and enjoying the rough-and-tumble of family life molds a pastor into an authentic human being who better understands the dynamics of the family of God. For example, it is almost impossible for a pastor to get lost in his work when an eight-year-old Little Leaguer keeps pushing into his office with demanding questions about the next game, especially when the caller looks a lot like the pastor looked at that age.

A Microcosm of the Family of God

Family, home and marriage should be valued as the most authentic relationships in a pastor's life and at the same time his greatest teachers. These ties provide him with a close-up relationship laboratory that helps shape the pastor's understanding of his own family and how the family of God at church functions. Therefore, no one should ever consider a pastor's family to be a pesky intrusion on ministry activities when they may in fact be teaching him how to do ministry in the family of God.

SATISFACTION 4: LOVE IS A TWO-WAY STREET

Healthy, loving relationship between pastor and people is one of a congregation's deepest longings and a pastor's greatest hunger. Sadly, congregations that treasure brothers and sisters seem to be in short supply these days. This is sometimes even evident in groups of believers who talk the most about love, fellowship and community.

Although many contemporary pastors preach about love and fellowship, they often do not view developing friendships with fellow believers as an important part of their work. Many even try to keep parishioners at a professional arm's length as a physician does with patients or a lawyer does with clients.

When this occurs, a cut-flower kind of Christianity results in the church and in the pastor's soul. Such shallow connections may make a fine appearance but have no roots for emotional and spiritual nourishment. As a result, a pastor may become lonely and alienated. He forgets to apply to himself what he preaches about nourishing relationships being an essential ingredient for spiritual health.

When locked into this misconception, the pastor feels isolated in a crowd and friendless at church and wonders why. Then he misses the energy and support that wholesome bonds with other Christians provide.

More Than a Business Relationship

Unfortunately, in many situations the church has a significantly different focus from that of an extended family. It appears that the church is now starting to reap a gloomy harvest from a popular notion that every church would flourish if the pastor were a CEO or president of the church corporation.

This assumption, copied from the secular world of business, theorizes that pastors must be skilled managers with diagnostic skills and business shrewdness. Notice these characteristics are not high priorities in Scripture. In this ensuing attraction to secular management, the church tends to borrow too heavily from corporate strategies and government practices.

Without thinking it through, lay leaders pick up the theme and shout to everyone who will listen, "The church should be run like a business." The concept sounds so reasonable that it has been put in motion on many levels of church life.

Of course, no one wants to argue against solid organization, fiscal soundness and competence in the church. But more is needed to make the church work according to God's plan.

The main difficulties come from the fact that the Church's mission is so diametrically different from commercial enterprises and civic organizations. Churches must spiritually develop people, while businesses must earn profits.

These differences are staggering. Businesses create products, offer services and engage in competition. Government, though frequently off course, is intended to assist its citizens and not make money.

In contrast, the Almighty God is the supreme authority of the Church. Pleasing God and introducing people to Christ are the Church's main reasons for being. Contrary to standard practices in some places, the Church has nothing to sell and no special interests to promote. The people the Church wants to win are looking for something different from what they see in the marketplace or in government.

Believers Bonded by Family Ties

To make the contrast between business and Church even more distinct, God calls the Church to be His holy family. He wants this family to exist in a love relationship with Him and with each other. This love is not merely gushy or sentimental, but an abiding affection for God and for each other. With this focus, a church keeps expanding its influence. This kind of love makes a church magnetic, especially to the lonely and broken. Surprisingly, relational connections in a church are often deepened at the moment a pastor relinquishes his management mentality and starts loving people for who they can become by grace.

This challenge does not require a pastor to abandon good management practices but to infuse administrative tasks with *agape* and soul and grace. To realize this purpose, a pastor must see himself as the head of an extended clan—something different from a CEO of an ecclesiastical enterprise.

In this design, a pastor heads a clan of Christians who become semi-fanatics in their love for each other and in pursuing the mission of Christ in the world. New believers then want to be adopted into this branch of God's family. And they are welcomed with open arms.

They become family—much more than customers or newcomers or clients. Precious babes in Christ are accepted into the church with the same tender affection as one welcomes a new infant into a human family. The church then becomes a family of faith tied together by fascinating love for the Master and for each other.

Jesus Showed Power of Love

This plan to be a soul family to the friends of Christ is as old as the first century, when Jesus loved His disciples into the kingdom of God and showed them how to love others. They were as close, or closer, to Him than family. He demonstrated before the critical eyes of established religionists and a surprised world that love is more important than organizational flow charts, parliamentary procedures or secularized strategies—and that it has more appeal, too.

Relational ties attract people who have little love in their lives from other sources, and this includes most of us. Love, acceptance, faith and hope were the glue that held the Early Church together. Their trademark

Pleasing God and introducing people to Christ are the Church's main reasons for being.

was, "Behold how they love one another." Love for Christ sent them out to accomplish the most productive soul-winning achievements and church-planting effectiveness the world has ever experienced. God still intends for love to be a dominant source of sustained satisfaction for us.

SATISFACTION 5: SPEAK UP FOR RIGHT

Refuse to allow moral compromise or even the pastoral nitty-gritty to short-circuit your ideals. Resist relationships that hint of thwarting your vision or of undermining your awareness of God.

At the Bible college where I (Neil) taught for years, we frequently invited pastors to speak to the students in chapel. A visiting pastor offered this challenge: "As pastors, you are the resident representative of the King of Glory. Plead His cause often and well. Walk your talk. Allow the strength of your personal faith to direct the details of ministry for you. An imposter subverts the credibility of us all. And remember, a pastor cannot sustain satisfaction in this work if he is only a play actor." This pastor was exactly right. Genuine authenticity and honesty form the bedrock foundations for every phase of ministry.

Authenticity Comes from Christ

Degrees, ordination credentials and trappings of ministry, as important as they seem to us, do not make ministry spiritually authentic. The necessity of our Christ-saturated intimacy shines through these insightful words from author Richard Lovelace:

> The instruments through which God works in the church are human beings, especially pastors. If our hearts and minds are not properly transformed, we are like musicians playing untuned instruments, or engineers working with broken and ill-programmed computers. The attunement of the heart is essential to the outflow of grace.[6]

You might want to add an enthusiastic "amen" while strengthening your own intimacy with the Savior.

Believability Enhances Ministry

Believability escalates when a pastor lives an exemplary Christ-centered life. It becomes a silent statement made with his life that he is committed to more than the minimum requirements of his ordination vows and lives beyond the minimal standards of respectable behavior. It is a super vow to God and himself that every expression of ministry will have the highest possible spiritual authenticity and professional quality.

The impact is the exact opposite of what happens when prominent TV evangelists bite the moral dust. Then everyone—clergy in ministry, individuals on the street, and believers in the pew—suffer the shock caused by these fake charlatans.

Christ-centered living in the pastor helps everyone believe that holy character and integrity are possible and attractive. The power of lived ideals shows in an unsigned letter in the opinion section of the *Denver Post*: "Knowing my priest is holy attracts me to the church and makes me believe I, too, can live a pure life." There is power in living out our ideals.

Self-Evaluation Is Needed

Pastors who desire sustained satisfactions must initiate regular self-evaluation. Such self-evaluation provides opportunities to ascertain the quality of his life and ministry. As a starting point, ask yourself:

- Is my handling of church money squeaky clean?
- Is my use of time ethically authentic?
- Is there disparity between my beliefs and the quality of the sermons I preach or the pastoral care I provide?
- Is my marriage as enjoyable and fulfilling as God intended?
- Do the people I lead believe me to be unequivocally trustworthy?
- Do I deceive myself with self-deception?
- Do my wife and children compete with my ministry?
- Do I accept my part in failures in my life and church?
- Do I flirt with potentially destructive relationships?
- Do I tell half-truths and exaggerate my successes?
- Is my ministry consistent with what I really believe God wants my life to be?

Sterling Behavior Is Rewarded

For a pastor, sterling behavior means more than living up to a vocational public-image requirement. God plans for Christ-pleasing living to help us enjoy truth, love and wholeness, a fascinating way to live that provides energy for meaningful ministry.

Such a lifestyle takes a pastor miles beyond suffocating duty into the grandeur of noble living. It is written into the moral genetic code of human beings that love feels better than hate, honesty better than chicanery, honor better than corruption, and faith better than hopelessness. Expand the list if you wish, but you will discover that godliness always outranks the profane.

Two pastor friends near middle age discussed difficult ethical decisions in their churches. When one expressed hope despite extreme difficulty, the other joked, "I'm surprised your idealism isn't more corroded after living this long." His comment is more than a joke—corroded ideals have created immense levels of skepticism in some pastors and in even more laypersons.

On the contrary, a minister who lives his ideals while resisting the flood tide of broken promises and flagrant cynicism enjoys sustained satisfactions. He resists the permissiveness he sees in others. He refuses to take moral shortcuts. He allows himself no white lies, no manipulation, no sexual compromise, no financial exploitation and no negotiation of enduring values. He resists shaping his conduct and character by what others do.

A PERSONAL WORD ABOUT PERKS

I (Neil) would like to add a personal word about perks. Nearly everyone knows being a pastor is hard work with long hours and often low pay. In this book and in many other settings, H. B. and I have championed the idea that people are the Church's main reason for being and that the intricate relational ties built into ministry have immense potential for misunderstanding. However, the converse is also true—the minister's close connections with people have potential for some of life's greatest perks.

I'd like to suggest my favorite top 10:

1. **Front seat at the spiritual action.** A pastor has the perk of seeing people come to faith and then seeing them develop in their relationship to God. He has a front-row seat at transformations, and he gets to see how faith works in crises.

2. **Instant friends.** When a pastor moves to a new setting, there is already a group of people waiting to welcome him and his family. Often these new friends are there on moving day, and they stand ready to help with the adjustments of relocation.

3. **Extended family.** In our day of mobility, few people have the help and support of an extended family that includes several generations who care for each other. But that is what the congregation provides for a pastor and his family from the first day.

4. **Confidence.** With few exceptions, churches stand ready to believe in their new minister from the first Sunday. Such acceptance would take months or years to develop in most other occupations.

5. **Support for children.** Although shocking war stories are sometimes heard about the ways congregations treat a pastor's children, for the most part, the congregations love and affirm his kids.

6. **Housing.** Although many pastors own their own homes these days, the congregation is likely to feel responsible for helping a pastor find a place to live when the family first moves to a new assignment.

7. **Flextime.** Most pastors live with tight schedules, yet often they have control of their schedule so they can flex their time to be at important family events like Little League and Parent-Teacher Day.

8. **Family service.** Because the pastor is involved in many decisions about personnel for Christian service, it is often possible for the minister's family to choose some form of service they can do together.

9. **The "more" reality.** Parishioners may not express it adequately, but in most congregations more people love you than you think. More people pray for you than you think. And more people believe in you than you think.

10. **Love affirmations.** This category is hard to define but easy to describe. It's four saints who promise the pastor to intercede for him and his family. It's the chicken casserole or apple pie someone brings to your front door. It's the hug from the four-year-old child who whispers, "I love you." And it's the sweet encouragement that comes from someone saying, "Your sermon helped me this morning" or "You showed me the spirit of Jesus when I called your office this week."

And what can I say about those personal perks that flowed from the people of God to make me rich? With an astounding sense of debt, I relive priceless experiences when ministry became a boomerang given back to me by the ones I served.

From parishioners, I learned new ways to trust my weary soul to the grace of God as I saw them live out their faith in the midst of overwhelming tragedies.

When my failures embarrassed or humiliated me, I cherished the love words I received from the people of God who believed in me.

When my family was up against it in medical crises and tough financial times, I remember the kindness and generosity from those who stood by us in our time of need.

You can tell how much gratitude I feel for those who bore burdens with me in long-ago pastorates. I rejoice over victories we celebrated together. Although many people might believe I have forgotten their kindnesses over the years, much of it is as fresh as this morning's sunrise.

It's true—love and memory endure.

ENJOY THE PERKS TO THE MAXIMUM

Opportunities of satisfying perks surround every pastor. Rejoice in the benefits God has planted on Main Street as well as in the quiet corners of pastoral routine. Cherish the adventures that flow from a Christ-saturated ministry. Maximize your perks.

Many pastoral perks reward the pastor immediately. Others are paid in installments across a lifetime. Some sneak up on us from ministry given half a lifetime ago. And others are yet to come when the Father says, "Well done!"

Savor your satisfactions. Allow them to cultivate an exciting marriage, to rear outstanding children, and to build an effective church in a place where they said it couldn't be done. And as you do, allow ministry to help you grow a life that is honorable, authentic and useful to God and those you serve.

CONTEMPORARY CHALLENGE

Your Perks Make You Spiritually Rich

- You represent Christ at life's main events.
- You enjoy a front-row seat at grace happenings.
- You have a partnership with omnipotence.
- Your congregation loves you.
- Your marriage and ministry can nourish each other.
- Your church wants to affirm your children.
- Your spiritual development is a serendipity of effective ministry.
- Your home can be an emotional sanctuary.
- Your ministry allows you to turn vision into achievements.
- Your specialty helps people cope with life.

Every person carries in his heart a blueprint of the One he loves.
—Fulton Sheen[7]

What to Do When You Shoot Someone

Musings from H. B. London, Jr.

When James Dobson and I were kids, I almost shot him twice. The first time, we were squirrel hunting and I didn't know if the safety on the gun was on or off. It was off, and I whistled a shot close to his ear. I would not soon forget that day—and neither would he. The second time, we were bird hunting. As I was walking across a gully on a log, I lost my footing, fell from the log, and the shotgun went off. It was another close call.

What do you do when you almost shoot someone?

You apologize like crazy!

Now to the point. So often, pastors shoot one another. We do not use guns but words as our firearms. We do irreparable damage to another by accusations, innuendos, gossip and idle conversation. Every one of us has been "shot at" by a colleague or parishioner. It always hurts, and it can result in permanent injury. I bear the scars, as do you.

The apostle Paul suggests to the church at Ephesus, "Do not let any unwholesome talk come out of your mouth, but only what is helpful for building others up according to their needs, that it may benefit those who listen" (Eph. 4:29). Proverbs 21:23 says, "He who guards his mouth and his tongue keeps himself from calamity." In other words, whatever you do, don't shoot anyone. If you do, you lessen yourself in the eyes and ears of those who watch and listen.

CHAPTER 8

A PERSONALIZED BLUEPRINT FOR MINISTRY

Holy Father, keep me faithful
to Kingdom priorities.
Use my gifts for Your glory,
my abilities for Your people,
my strength for Your service,
my weaknesses to show Your strength,
Amen.

> IT WAS HE WHO GAVE
> SOME TO BE APOSTLES,
> SOME TO BE PROPHETS,
> SOME TO BE EVANGELISTS, AND
> SOME TO BE PASTORS AND
> TEACHERS, TO PREPARE GOD'S
> PEOPLE FOR WORKS OF SERVICE,
> SO THAT THE BODY OF
> CHRIST MAY BE BUILT UP.
>
> EPHESIANS 4:11-12

YOU ARE UNIQUELY GIFTED FOR A SPECIAL MINISTRY

God loves variety. He designed infinite diversity into Creation. In nature, His originality shows in every maple leaf, every snowflake and every mountain peak. His humorous originality even shows in human noses, voices and toes.

God made you unique and different from every other human being. This fact shows in your deoxyribonucleic acid (DNA) profile, which looks like an expanded bar code that supermarkets use to check prices. It is, however, more than a price code. It is a detailed blueprint that answers questions about you, ranging from the color of hair to parentage to potential to the length of life.

Scientific researchers say your DNA makes you different from every other human being. Your DNA is as singular as your signature and can be used to establish your identity with more reliability than conventional blood-typing that is used to implicate suspects in criminal cases. In fact, geneticists can pinpoint more than 4,000 hereditary diseases from the study of DNA.[1]

God created you as a unique person so He could use you in a particular place to meet a specific need during this period of human history. Therefore, the Creator does not want you to imitate someone else. He does, however, want you to yield to His will and purpose so He can help you accomplish something important for the kingdom of God.

A TV commercial tells the story well. Four children are asked in the commercial what they want to be when they grow up. One says, "I want to be a fireman." Another says, "I want to be a doctor." The third says, "I want to be a basketball star." But the fourth responds in the biblical way: "I want to be myself."

Every pastor needs to grasp the insight behind that last remark. He must cherish his uniqueness and not try to copy anyone else. Neither should anyone expect him to be like another—especially not like a pastor before him.

Frustration by Unmet Aspirations

An urban pastor I (H. B.) know feels locked in to his suburban pastorate. It's a good place and a setting many of his colleagues would love to consider, but he doesn't feel like he fits there anymore. He is in midlife and feels he will never fulfill his dream of being a maverick pastor in an inner city.

In a letter he wrote to me about his frustrations, he said, "I have always wanted to work in the inner city. I dream of supporting myself with a secular job and serving as a bivocational pastor among poor people. The concept I wanted to try was to be a worker-pastor, different from any traditional ministries I have ever seen.

"I don't know if it would work, but the suburbs bore me more every day. Most of the time I feel like I am babysitting immature Christians; their money and tradition seem to make the problem bigger than it really is. The spark is gone. Now life is passing too quickly; I doubt I will ever get to try my idea."

How sad that what he desires most eludes him at a time when he is needed in the cities. How sad, too, for those pastors who would like to have what he has. He would gladly move to the city if he could figure out ways to raise the money and get started.

The lesson for all: Turning our back on curiosities and aspirations decimates satisfaction, causes long-term feelings of defeat, and undermines the effectiveness of our current ministry.

Trapped by Boring Assignments

Surveys show that many pastors feel locked in to their assignments. Perhaps they belong to a denominational system such as the Methodist governmental structure that sometimes places pastors in situations and locations they might not desire. Other pastors have been in an assignment for many years where the congregation or the neighborhood has changed but the ministries have remained unchanged.

Other pastors serve traditional churches that have remained unchanged while they themselves have grown or have changed perspectives. Still others want to move to a smaller church after their church has grown beyond their ability to cope. Some pre-retirement pastors wish to slow down, while their churches want to be more progressive and sponsor more activities.

Location frustration, whatever the cause, should be admitted and solved in one of two ways. If a pastor cannot change his feeling of being trapped in his current assignment, for his personal well-being and wholeness, he should seek to move to another assignment or to start a new ministry.

Another option available—one that is at the heart of this book—is for the pastor to stay where he is and make the place holy ground. Most of the time, location frustration is a problem in the pastor's psyche and is not well-known or even considered important by members of the congregation.

The solution for location frustration starts by developing a specific blueprint of ministry for your present setting that makes room for two things: the most pressing needs of the setting, and the maximum use of your personal talents and abilities.

Cultivate Your Uniqueness

When God created you, He made a blueprint of a distinctive ministry for you. He designed you to do something special for Him—something no one else does as well as you can. He likely wants it done where you now serve. Cloning is not the way God works in your ministry or in anyone else's. No other person is as capable or talented to accomplish what God has mapped out for you.

God believes so much in your gifts and devotion that He chose a risky strategy for changing His world through people like you. God allows you immense freedom to discover what ministry is suitable for you and how you will use the gifts He has given you. He even allows autonomy about where ministry is done.

This freedom creates confusion for the Kingdom and for us when it is misused. It tends to complicate a church's placement procedures for pastors. To bewilder matters more, we are often overly modest or shy about telling others what we know we can do best. We reason it could sound like self-promotion or could appear that we covet a particular assignment. Then, again, we might not know what we do well, so we have nothing to tell anyone else.

Ministerial tedium multiplies when a pastor buries his talents. Maximum fulfillment develops, however, from being at the right place at the right time with the right skills to accomplish a magnificent work for Christ. When a pastor fails to use his unique giftedness, the Kingdom and his specific congregation suffer. As a result, his disillusionment increases, his impact declines, and he denies a congregation the talents God intended to be used in his ministry.

Excellence Brings Satisfaction

God wants magnificent competence in every aspect of ministry. A personal commitment to competence determines the difference between excellence and mediocrity. God detests shoddy work and is always a little embarrassed when someone announces, "I want to be faithful even if I can't do ministry very well."

Why not do both? Why not give God a combination of competence and faithfulness? The Father multiplies satisfaction for those who do their work well. Competence is a habit, and so is shoddiness. Doing ministry well produces incredible impact for the cause of Christ, even as it brings indescribable exhilaration.

We Need a Divine Helping Hand

Playing the pastoral perfection game usually leads to a miserably shallow ministry. No pastor even comes close to being perfect in his performance of ministry. Although we might hate to admit it, most of us easily identify with a pastor who snorted, "I specialize in fallibility." The apostle Paul candidly rejoiced in the fact that ministry was essentially impossible for him without divine enablement. And the same is true for us.

A year or two ago, a district superintendent friend asked me to read a statement he wrote to lay leaders of a church in crisis. In essence, his excellent statement said, "I feel inadequate to help you, but I never want to be involved in any facet of ministry that I could not do without God's help." His message was crystal clear: I want to help, but I need supernatural assistance to do very much. His message sounds a lot like Jesus' words that we must be connected to the vine if our ministry is to produce anything worthwhile.

Although rarely discussed, this issue of presumed competence may be among the most compelling problems in the contemporary Church.

Competence is a habit, and so is shoddiness.

No matter how favorably educated or fervently zealous, no one is qualified enough, insightful enough or talented enough to do effective ministry without the energizing enablement of the Omnipotent One.

Sadly, too much ministry is attempted in human strength alone, and it goes nowhere. But supernatural resources are promised to those who seek and use them. God chooses to use people who depend on Him.

Team Effort Pays Dividends

Dependency on members of the congregation is also important. Admitting need and asking for help is not easy in our can-do world. In the Church, however, such an admission often begins a lovely experience of shared service in Jesus' name. Strange as it seems, the people of God are quick to offer acceptance and to assist when a pastor admits frailties and needs.

People naturally step forward to help a pastor who acknowledges inadequacies. Such self-revelation somehow motivates people to help. The results are wonderful: The helpers find satisfaction, the cause is advanced, and the pastor feels encouraged by the team effort.

Pastor Was Too Flawless

The all-too-common perfection game shackles a pastor with self-imposed paralyzing demands. In such circumstances, a pastor feels forced to act as if he knows everything or pretend to be more pious than he is.

One beginning pastor found out the hard way. He was young and handsome in a rugged kind of way. He had an excellent education and enjoyed a storybook marriage. With many impressive personal and professional assets, he started his first pastorate overloaded with confidence and expected perfection from everyone, including himself.

Although his pastorate was a near disaster from the start, this young pastor kept trying harder and harder. When he faced demands where he had no experience or training, he bluffed his way to make a good impression. Each time he encountered these kinds of situations, his self-confidence eroded a little more and his satisfaction dissipated.

He soon learned an excruciating lesson: No one can do ministry perfectly all the time. Much to his surprise, when the crunch came and he admitted it, his congregation overlooked his inadequacies with a shrug.

More than one volunteer said, "We're relieved to see you are not perfect. We like preachers who are human, like us." To relish sustained satisfaction, a minister must come to terms with his lack of experience, his weaknesses and his toxic need to be perfect.

Perfection Fuels Fantasies

Perfection sometimes shows up in other ways, too. For some pastors, by the time they come to mid-life, self-justification or denials have accumulated into mind-breaking loads. They cannot be perfect, but they pretend to be.

A weary minister is then no longer able to accurately evaluate his work and his ideas. So, without intending to do so, he creates a fantasy of who he is, what his church can be, and how important he is to the congregation. As a result, he takes up permanent residency in his mind on Main Street in Make Believe, USA. Recently, I met a 69-year-old pastor who has lived at such a phony address for more than 30 years.

Ministers of this kind have a frame of reference that resembles a medieval castle surrounded by a deep moat of water filled with angry alligators. Sadly, no drawbridge spans the moat to help pastors move into the real world or for others to rescue them. They live in a make-believe world where their contribution in ministry is greater than it really is. The pastor perfection game makes them that way.

Beware of Becoming a Fish Keeper

One pastor I know also lives by fantasies that are influenced by a need to be perfect. Although his congregation tolerates him like a friendly, aging great-uncle, he seems out of touch and unaware of the pivotal issues of contemporary Christianity. He takes comfort in being a keeper of a placid tiny aquarium. He seems satisfied to feed a few fish a monotonous diet every Sunday at 11:00 A.M. and to scour the fish tank now and then.

Sadly, he completely missed the excitement of ever doing ministry exceptionally well. Because of his perspective, the people he touches with his ministry consider Christianity too dull for a thinking person to consider.

Pathetically, many pastors who are infected with this chronic disease know something is cockeyed. But because they do not know what to do, they do nothing. For them, it just seems easier to brush off bad news than to deal with it. One overstressed leader remarked, "I don't know who the enemy is." The enemy was likely inside him and he didn't realize it.

Work Increases, Results Decline

My first conversation with a pastor I'll call Vince Delong dealt with his confusion about ministry. Delong asked me to be a sounding board as he thought out loud about his future. He felt unnerved and afraid as he explained, "I try harder but get fewer results now than at any time in my ministry. I keep working longer hours, but I get less and less response."

Thinking a few new members might fix his problems, he drove himself untiringly. He kept busy so he could dodge the tension his church problems caused at home. Draining bustle replaced meaning for him. He was tired and depressed.

As I listened, he moved deeper into his disappointments: "Six wonderful couples in their middle 30s moved out of our congregation to other area churches in the last four months. They represent the spiritual backbone and economic core of this congregation.

"The loss is simply staggering. The last couple blasted me with these words just before they left: 'You don't get it, do you? We all joined this church because of you, but you have changed, and not for the better. You used to keep up with the times, but you now operate the church in a tired old way you did 10 years ago. It just won't cut it anymore.' I worry that they may be right."

Vince's problems, like many current pastors, are not doctrinal or moral, but relate to outlook and methods. Although those members who deserted probably could not describe it, they sensed in him a great unwillingness—almost naiveté—to face the real world.

It appeared to them to be an unhealthy fixation on the past, which made them lose interest. They left because they saw no possibility for improvement. What a sad predicament for everyone—for those who left, for those who stayed, and especially for the pastor.

For the purpose of our discussion, it is necessary to deal only with the pastor and not with the laity. For Vince to enjoy spiritual and emotional wellness, he must be willing to recognize and to correct several weaknesses.

It is not in being perfect, but in striving for competence. Pastor-writer Robert Hudnut's comment speaks precisely to this problem: "Rather than being paralyzed by his faults, a pastor must acknowledge them and push ahead in spite of them. Fortunately, the job makes the person in the ministry even more than the person makes the job. Weaknesses can be forged into strengths. But facing and correcting weaknesses helps keep ministers effective."[2]

Facing Frailties Blunts Egotism

This tricky task of identifying and correcting weaknesses pays off with self-understanding and professional growth. Such an effort blasts an inflated ego and helps a pastor see ministry through the eyes of those who live life at the front lines of contemporary life.

Without such self-understanding, it is incredibly easy for an ego-driven pastor to form obnoxious attitudes and demonstrate self-centered behavior. Then he berates inflexibility, manipulation, compulsiveness or suspicious ethics in others without recognizing those same faults in himself.

Conversely, enduring fulfillments often grow out of an accurate assessment of a pastor's work and an awareness of personal identity. What a pastor learns in self-appraisal helps him to continue growing professionally, emotionally and spiritually. Sustained satisfactions usually follow.

The content of our ministry is always the truth of the gospel.

VIEW YOURSELF AS A TRUST OFFICER OF TRUTH

The rather startling, stretching idea of the pastor being a trust officer for truth is not an original idea with me—I found it first in James Massey's writings, and he traces it to Albert Outler. Massey uses the idea well when he makes a strong case for Christ founding the Early Church on truth. He reminds us that Jesus called Himself Truth because He brought us the truth about God, truth about our world, and truth about ourselves. Jesus, according to Massey, was so filled with truth and so fully shared the truth that He came to be known as Truth as well as Way and Light.

Massey's charge for the pastor is that as trust officers of truth, they "are passing on something that is not novel or new. It is something that was here earlier. It was established by our Lord, and it must continue with integrity. . . . The Christian gospel is God's invitation to an experience, an experience inclusive of moral effects, spiritual effects, and social effects."[3]

Two realities come together here. As we have seen earlier in this chapter, pastors are free and apparently encouraged to do their work according to their own unique gifts and interests. But the content of our ministry is always the truth of the gospel, and we are trusted with it.

MAINTAIN A HANDS-ON MINISTRY

Efficient delegation is an important element of contemporary ministry; hands-on ministry is decreasing. Without question, a congregation is healthier spiritually when a pastor shares ministry with church members. This useful trend means that empowering the laity increases their spiritual development, and more work gets done.

Such a partnership in ministry is necessary for efficiency and for increased fulfillment of laity. Consider the examples. Pastoral care is now being shared, and many lay leaders are doing this phase of ministry well and with satisfaction. Administrative functions are increasingly being assigned to laypersons, and they are doing them well. Bible teaching has been shared for centuries. Shouldering such responsibilities encourages an overdue renewal of the laity and gives them meaning once reserved only for the clergy. All of this is positive and useful—more of it is needed.

However, all ministry cannot be delegated to others. No pastor can fully bloom and grow when he only manages and assigns ministry to others. He, himself, must take the towel and the basin. He must rejoice with young families at the birth of their children and he must weep with the dying. He does not need to do all the ministry—nor can he—but he must do some of it.

A pastor forfeits a keen ingredient of ministry when he no longer ministers to others on a regular basis. He gives up a spiritually satisfying bond between pastor and parishioner that is not available in any other way. This essential connection is among the most satisfying motivations for being a pastor; to give it up completely is to give up something precious and needed for personal fulfillment.

Such commitment to a pastor's personal involvement does not deny service opportunities to others. It simply means the minister must keep in touch or he will be unfulfilled and out of sync. The paradox is to continue personal ministry while giving much of it away. Participation and delegation are needed in contemporary pastoral work. No minister who isolates himself from the sinful, hurting and dying can continue to bloom.

Don't Take Authority Too Seriously

Authority and influence do not make you special or different from other people. Such privilege simply places greater demands on the trusted leader. A pastor needs to remind himself often that ordination or installation in a church as pastor does not make him infallible.

Simply holding ecclesiastical, organizational or ordination authority does not mean a pastor knows how to make flawless decisions automatically. It does not mean he can think better than anyone else. Nor does it mean he is more spiritual than members of the group.

Admittedly, the person holding the highest position in church structures usually gets his way, regardless of who is right. Pastors sometimes resent this reality in relationships to their ecclesiastical superiors. But what happens in the upward organizational flow in churches also happens in a downward flow in local congregations.

As a result, pastors sometimes misuse authority. This means that a pastor who wants to be effective in a spiritual sense must sometimes willingly lose an administrative decision because his judgment is in error. Authority in itself never makes a leader unerring.

Use of authority is complicated even more when lay members of a church's decision group comply with their pastor's wishes simply because they want to be cooperative. Because complying is not commitment, organizational and relational disasters sometimes follow.

A pastor who insists on having his own way will then find himself followed by a group who submit to his domination but do not accept his leadership. He may hold a rope in his hand, but it is not attached to anything that matters. Such stubborn use of authority causes spiritual and organizational stagnation.

On the contrary, a spiritually aware leader will work for consensus, ownership and refinement of ideas. His ministry then blooms because he uses the best judgment he receives from advisers. He builds strong morale in the process.

Our Lord empowered others for greatness by loving them, trusting them and holding them spiritually accountable. His pattern helps us bloom, too.

Commit to Lifelong Development

Effective pastors learn from every possible source all the days of their lives. An example that comes to mind is a man in his late 30s who entered the ministry as a self-made country preacher. He brought exceptional people skills to ministry that had been developed when he was a small-business owner. But formal learning and ministerial development continued low on his priority list. He reasoned, "I already know how to get along with people."

Soon after launching his ministry, he realized he had to study to keep up with the demands. To his surprise, when he began to study, something amazing happened. He began to see the world as a wonderful learning place where people, events and situations taught him a great deal he could use in ministry. Now he says, "I love to learn, and I hope it shows." It does.

Many pastors plateau personally and professionally because they seldom consider a fresh thought. Others shut their minds the day they receive their diploma or degree. How sad to miss so much. Learning and personal development can be fun and always help a pastor bloom where he is planted.

Pay the Price to Lead

The church needs more real leaders. In his book *Today's Pastors,* researcher George Barna wrote, "During a decade of study, I have become increasingly convinced that the Church struggles not because it lacks enough zealots who will join the crusade for Christ, not because it lacks the tangible resources to do the job and not because it has withered into a muddled understanding of its fundamental beliefs. The problem is the Christian church is not led by true leaders."[4]

What a stunning indictment, and what a frightening appraisal. Apparently, administration, management and supervision are done reasonably well in many churches. But the call is for more *leaders*, not for more efficient administrators, managers or supervisors.

Leadership, for our purposes, might be defined as a pastor who generates positive spiritual achievement in a congregation. A genuine pastor-leader sees his task as much more than being a resident saint, showing up for church, preserving the establishment or spending the money.

In his book *Developing the Leader Within You*, Pastor John C. Maxwell describes a congregation that is led by a genuine pastor-leader: "Morale is high. Turnover is low. Needs are being met. Goals are being realized. . . . Leading and influencing others is fun. Problems are solved with minimum effort. Fresh statistics are shared on a regular basis with the people that undergird the growth of the organization."[5]

The Church of Jesus Christ at every level of her life and ministry needs leaders who are able to establish and communicate vision.

Let's realize that not all authentic leadership starts with being given an important post, although sometimes it does. Neither does genuine leadership automatically come with an appointment—a person can hold a pastoral position for a lifetime without being a leader.

Conversely, designated official leaders do not always exert the greatest influence in a church or organization. Tillich, Huxley and Oates—a strange trio—all speak with approval about a type of leader who lives at the periphery of an organization or congregation. A short sentence from Huxley explains, "It is not at the center, not from within the organization, that the saint can cure our regimented insanity; it is only from without, at the periphery."[6]

The peripheral leader's tools are friendly persuasion, unquestioned love, and loyalty for the cause of Christ. In times of confusion or crisis, the peripheral leader may be heeded for the strength of his ideas alone. Perhaps the Church needs an army of peripheral leaders for times like these.

From firsthand observations and personal correspondence, compelling evidence shows many pastors are not equipped, educated or experienced for the job typical churches need them to do. Neither are they able to lead effective outreach in the contemporary world.

Barna believes this leadership shortage revolves around the Church's ability to identify potential leaders, the way pastors are typically prepared, the way ministers are evaluated, and the way clergy are supported.[7] Barna's chapter in *Today's Pastors* on "Training Leaders to Lead" and numerous other books and magazine articles suggest massive reforms are needed in ministerial preparation.

Barna may be right. But something much more immediate is needed, because if his proposed changes were started at once in Bible colleges and seminaries, they would have little effect on people now active in ministry.

Consequently, pastors must strengthen their leadership skills in every imaginable way. Books, seminars and mentoring will help. But a closer, more convenient learning resource is often overlooked. Many never think to view the Church and the world as living classrooms.

To increase leadership competence, a pastor must keep alert to life. Such development demands listening carefully for leadership lessons from common people as well as from professionals. It means applying ideas from every source to the ministry. It quizzes trend-setting ministers. It observes and questions pacesetters in business and government. In fact, a developing leader will be open to insights and ideas from every source.

An achievement-driven leader takes what he learns from life and applies the data to ministry. An imaginative pastor-leader schools himself to consider how a concept, program or principle can improve his ministry.

Such a continual state of "how can I make it better" helps formulate a church's future. Such filtering of the environment helps a leader successfully ride the frightening waves of the future to new ways of thinking and doing.

Dedication to betterment of personal leadership keeps a pastor blooming anywhere, even in the winters of ministry. It prevents a pastor from becoming out of date. Such persistent individual development encourages laypersons to use their curiosity and imagination in Kingdom adventures. Beyond managing, influencing, directing, preaching, administering and teaching, a growing pastor-leader challenges people to hope, love, believe and experience compassion, wonder, reverence and grace.

By reaching deep into these never-dry, ever-fresh springs, we equip fellow pilgrims to be dreamers of dreams, to be passionate risk-takers who transform churches and communities, and to create Christ-alive churches.

All of these resources will produce stunningly beautiful blooms in any ecclesiastical leadership garden.

CONTEMPORARY CHALLENGE

Follow God's Blueprint

- God loves diversity.
- God expects competence.
- God uniquely created you.
- God empowers our best efforts.
- God resources growth.
- God enables us to be trust officers of truth.
- God sometimes uses leaders from the peripheral.

If you pastors don't know the absolutely essential, then you will do the merely important. And because so much of what you do is potentially important, you are apt to allow the important to crowd out the absolutely essential.
—Henri Nouwen[8]

What's on Your Calendar?

Musings from H. B. London, Jr.

A TV commercial in our viewing area ends with the question, "What's in your wallet?" The idea: We carry evidence in our wallet of what we most value—pictures, identification, receipts, credit cards, insurance coverage and money. The more I pondered the statement from the commercial, the more I realized the question for pastors should be, What's on your calendar?

As the psalmist wrote in the beautiful 139th Psalm, "All the days ordained for me were written in your book before one of them came to be" (v. 16). I sometimes wonder how my calendar compares with His. And I wonder about you—what's on your calendar?

Does each day note adequate time for you to spend with your Lord? Does your calendar provide sufficient time to show honor and concern for your family members? Does each month have a notation that reads "date with spouse," "quality time with my daughter," or "basketball game with my son Friday at 7:00 P.M."?

How about clearing an afternoon each week to walk in the "village" and rub shoulders with those in your community who need to see you from a perspective outside the pulpit? Oh, and what about your day off? Do you guard it, or do you allow other things to take away your Sabbath? Is your vacation scheduled? If you don't do it soon, the pages will inevitably fill up with other things.

I don't mean to belabor the point, but your calendar tells more about you than anything else. It speaks of your spiritual discipline, your priorities and, most of all, your intimacy with the God who called you and gave you a special gift called family.

CHAPTER 9

GROW A GREAT SOUL

God of wholeness and wellness,
walk with me in my pastoral pilgrimage.
Draw me to the mountain peaks of splendor.
Walk with me through the dark valleys of shadow.
Make me. Break me. Stretch me.
And use me.
Amen.

> # I URGE YOU TO LIVE A LIFE WORTHY OF THE CALLING YOU HAVE RECEIVED.
>
> EPHESIANS 4:1

GETTING IN SHAPE SPIRITUALLY

Going to the gym or working out on a treadmill wasn't even mentioned in the home where I (Neil) grew up. It was assumed that hard work would take care of any need for exercise. As might be expected in such an atmosphere, not much attention was given to exercises for the soul, either. The idea was to work hard for God, just as you do in other parts of your life, and your soul would be healthy.

So that's what I did—work, and work hard—when I started ministry. After a few years, I was spiritually and emotionally spent, winded, empty, shallow, lean and hungry. The demands of my pastoral work had grown well past my personal spiritual resources.

What was I to do?

I started searching the spirituality literature. It became a holy quest for God. I bought books, talked to mature believers, listened to audiotapes from seminars and Sunday morning worship services. And they all helped. As I read and researched and listened, I discovered that a hunger for God like mine was a common experience among persons of all theological traditions. That meant lots of material was available from many perspectives.

Soon, many books by favorite authors stood as sentinels on the shelves behind my desk as a kind of "cloud of witnesses." And what an impressive group of witnesses they were.

My list includes Richard Foster, who taught me about the disciplines. Francis Thompson pointed me to the simplification of life. Corrie ten Boom stretched my ideas about forgiveness. Vance Havner nudged me to see grace in parish life. Henri Nouwen shaped my thoughts about creative ministry and nonviolent teaching. Mother Teresa taught me the power of prayer. Oswald Chambers called me to personal holiness. A. W. Tozer rapped my spiritual knuckles. Paul Scherer pointed me to the spendthrift God. And what more could I say about Frederick Buechner, E. Stanley Jones, Hannah Whitall Smith, Dietrich Bonhoeffer, Eugene Peterson, Charles Spurgeon, Dwight Moody, Dallas Willard and Ken Gire?

The Frightening Dilemma

It is amazingly easy for pastors to become out of shape spiritually. They have used up their spiritual stamina in long hours of preaching, teaching and counseling. They have little available reserves to keep their souls

We burn out without ever getting fired up.

healthy. Without a dogged discipline, they often fall victim to the tyranny of the urgent and to overcrowded schedules.

From long bouts with empty souls, we find that if we try to function without spiritual energy, we feel stressed, spent and overextended. We fret over discrepancies between what is and what ought to be. The activity of ministry makes us dizzy, and we grow bone weary. We burn out without ever getting fired up. Sometimes we even feel forced to fake piety because it is expected—what John Henry Jowett calls "being professors but not pilgrims."[1] Then ministry turns into dreadful duty to perform or it becomes a frustrating job that can be cast off when the going gets tough.

When the flame of devotion burns low, a pastor's performance sinks to a shocking state. Every task requires too much effort. An accumulation of weariness corrodes a minister's soul, sabotages his ministry, and shatters his concept of who he can become in Christ. Ministry dies a slow, miserable death and is buried under a tombstone marked, "Died too young because he tried to do it in his own strength."

As the dilemma becomes more confusing, spiritual shallowness colors all of life. The pastor feels disheartened and is easily tempted. Then a warning from Alexander Solzhenitsyn comes to our minds: "The meaning of earthly existence lies not, as we have grown used to thinking, in prospering but in the development of the soul."[2]

We know and even preach that spiritual conditioning produces the best quality of life. But for some strange reason, pastors frequently compartmentalize personal faith and professional ministry so that the two cannot draw strength from each other. In such situations, the minister

To grow a beautiful life, the Father gives us forgiveness, grace, hope, love and faith.

soon starts functioning more like a religious robot than a caring pastor. Soon, he is overextended, reactionary and scared.

Growing a great soul promises so much more. It helps us remember that God intends every aspect of life and ministry to be intricately organized around Christ. This focus is for our own development as much as it is for vibrant ministry. To grow a beautiful life, the Father gives us forgiveness, grace, hope, love and faith. He wants life and ministry to be tied together with meaning, value and beauty.

RAW MATERIALS FOR SOUL DEVELOPMENT ARE EVERYWHERE

During a grueling church construction program—the kind that tries a pastor's soul—I (Neil) struggled to finish my Christmas sermon. For most of the morning, my sermon wrestling had been dealing largely with the conceptual aspects of the Incarnation accounts in Scripture. In an effort to clear mental cobwebs, I took a walk along the Atlantic Ocean a few blocks from the church I served.

Something supernatural occurred that morning. As I walked by the sea, all nature seemed to be singing the songs of Christmas. As I admired the moving tide and tried to take in the full range of colors of the sky and sea, an "aha" moment splashed at my feet and forever changed ministry for me.

At that moment, I experienced the birth of Christ in a profoundly personal way. Incarnation power was no longer a novel and seasonal Scripture to be preached at Advent. On that day, the Incarnation became an intimate treasure, something to share. Ministry began to enrich me and feed my soul in many new ways. From that time forward, though my ministry still served other people as it always had, it also fed my personal inwardness. Ministry developed me even as I offered it to others. That satisfying two-way process continues today. I am a better Christian because of the demands of ministry.

Try Maximizing the Opportunities for Spiritual Fitness

Think of the possibilities. Preaching exposes you to the great truths of Scripture and gives you opportunity to be shaped by what you discover even as you prepare to preach it to others. Pastoral care gives opportunity for you to see God coming alongside persons in crises and helps you believe God will care for you all your life through. Administrative tasks allow you to put faith into practice in relationships. Outreach and disciple development help you grow into the image of Christ even while you are introducing others to Him. All of this is something like a gourmet cook who, while busy preparing a scrumptious meal, is able to taste the food. The point of beginning is for you to view spiritual growth as an essential ingredient of your own faith and of your ministry.

Three principles apply: (1) Spiritual development does not come by osmosis—it must be intentional; (2) being near the fire is not the same as being on fire; and (3) it is possible to become overly familiar with the sublime provisions God has provided us.

Get Acquainted with the Saints

Dr. Maxie Dunnam—pastor, Upper Room editor and Asbury Seminary president—tells of accepting a ministry assignment that made it necessary for him to get better acquainted with the saints as well as to more intentionally tend his own soul. He began reading Julian of Norwich, William Law, Francois Fenelon, Francis of Assisi, Evelyn Underhill, Brother Lawrence and an array of others. He tells of his rich discovery of the characteristics many of the saints had in common:

- They passionately sought the Lord.
- They discovered a gracious God.
- They took Scripture seriously.
- Jesus was alive in their experience.
- They practiced discipline, at the heart of which was prayer.
- They were convinced that obedience was essential for their life and growth.
- They sought not ecstasy, but surrender of their will to the Lord.
- They were thirsty for holiness.
- They lived not for themselves, but for God and for others.
- They knew joy and peace that transcended all circumstances.[3]

What a standard those characteristics provide for a pastor to use as a guide for growing a great soul.

Use Spiritual Dynamite

Check the facts and reevaluate the opportunities. Pastors are exposed continually to spiritual development opportunities in their day-by-day ministry. Even the busiest pastor holds spiritual dynamite in his hands many hours every week.

Teaching and preaching take the minister to the Book of God—the oxygen line of spiritual health. Ministers pray private and public prayers often and everywhere, and they sometimes see unbelievable results. Counseling and pastoral care take them to the middle of spiritual action where they see lives changed, marriages healed and spirits transformed.

The challenge is to make fuller use of these close-at-hand opportunities to draw our souls closer to God.

Make Ministry More Than a Profession

For years, society viewed pastors as bumbling but harmless people. Everyone was expected to respect them, but not everyone took them seriously. Although this attitude still prevails in some places, it has radically changed in others.

Now, pastors are often well trained, skilled in their work, and professionally credentialed. Now, citywide ministerial associations sometimes look much like a professional meeting of doctors or lawyers. In such an environment, it is easy for pastors to allow ministry to become overly professionalized and spiritually undernourished.

Teaching and preaching take the minister to the Book of God—the oxygen line of spiritual health.

A balance is needed between call and competency, professionalism and character. No one need criticize or fret about a professional focus if improved skill, training, understanding and approval of peers are what is intended. Even the most highly trained, sophisticated pastor must remain close to the basics of faith and to the awareness that God has set him apart for a lofty, holy task.

For soul health, a minister must utilize the rich resources of prayer, Scripture and spiritual disciplines. He must keep his faith warm and assuring. He must love righteousness and show mercy.

We give up too much if we lose the soul passion out of ministry by overly professionalizing it. The desired objective is to conduct ourselves like competent professionals and to trust God like dependent servants.

Follow a Strict Spiritual Fitness Regiment

Try to view growing a great soul through a medical lens: A license to practice medicine, a thorough knowledge of pharmacology, and 30 years' surgical experience do not keep a physician personally well. He may practice medicine without being healthy himself. But a healthy medical doctor must apply the same rules of good health to himself as he gives his patients, or he will be as sick as they are.

One undebatable axiom for ministry must be faced: Personal spiritual growth is absolutely essential for a pastor if he wants to enjoy sustained satisfactions and effective ministry. A pastor must take his spiritual fitness seriously by applying the remedies and suggestions he prescribes for others to himself.

Retain Freshness

A pastor's spiritual fitness requires fresh encounters with God in traditional faith-formation exercises of prayer, Scripture reading, fasting, devotional reading, soul friendships and centering on Christ. Freshness may be more important than frequency. Eugene H. Peterson, a long-time pastor and an insightful eyewitness of present-day ministry, shares this perceptive observation: "Three pastoral acts—praying, reading Scripture and giving spiritual direction—are so basic, so critical, that they determine the shape of everything else in ministry. Besides being basic, these three acts are quiet and done mostly out of the spotlight of public ministry. Because they do not call attention to themselves, they are so often neglected. . . . Because almost never does anyone notice whether we do these things or not, and only occasionally does someone ask that we do them, these real acts of ministry suffer widespread neglect."[4]

When any of these pastoral acts is neglected, the minister and his congregation are seriously shortchanged.

Peterson amplifies his warning: "It doesn't take many years in the pastorate to realize that we can conduct a fairly respectable ministry without giving much more than ceremonial attention to God. Because we can omit these acts without anybody noticing, and because each of the acts involves a great deal of rigor, it is easy and common to slight them."[5] Vitality leaks out of ministry when a pastor makes his own spirituality ceremonial and perfunctory.

The task is to infuse spirituality with soul, spirit and expectation. The routines must be fueled by creativity, imagination, spontaneity, delight and even fascination. Consequently, spiritual wellness takes more than praying louder or longer. It also requires more than reading an additional 50 Bible verses each day. The point is to find personal spiritual nourishment in every expression of devotion.

This relationship is like family bonding that draws one close to the Father. Longing, originality and intention then become as important as sentiment, length or sameness. Cultivating an adventuresome closeness to God is the overriding goal. Without it, vigor and stamina burn low, or go out.

Cultivate a God-Permeated Life

A pastor who served a congregation of about 100 for more than two decades calls this Christ connection "a God-permeated life." What a word picture. The components consist of devotion to Scripture, intimacy in prayer, and friendship with saints who walk across the pages of devotional literature. It also esteems contemporary, ordinary persons who do heroic service for God in out-of-the-way churches or in unheralded settings.

Our effort to grow a great soul means we allow the discoveries of past pilgrims to shape us until the stories of biblical characters and devotional saints become a part of us. Their quest then becomes our own, so we grow as they grew, bloom as they bloomed, and we produce fruits of righteousness as they did. And we live what they lived—at home, in the church and everywhere.

Thus, spiritual formation means getting together often with God. To use teenage language, we hang out with Him. This God-closeness, like falling in love, creates attentiveness, togetherness and warmth. This deepening intimacy with God opens our eyes to see amazing mysteries of grace and provides fulfillment throughout a lifetime of ministry.

Such Christ-closeness is more than a private adventure for a pastor. It is like an electrical conduit through which divine enablement flows through us into our ministry. Pastors experience such empowerment as they welcome the One T. S. Eliot described in his prayer: "Oh, my soul, be prepared for the coming of the Stranger, Be prepared for Him who knows how to ask questions."[6]

CHRIST—THE SOURCE FOR LIFELONG SPIRITUAL GROWTH

How, then, is a great soul grown? Authentic ministry fitness comes from standing at full attention before the Chief—Peter Marshall's splendid phrase—and doing what our Commander orders.

The urgency for personal spiritual development is emphasized in Thomas Kempis's warning, "At the day of judgment, we shall not be asked what we have read, but what we have done; not how eloquently we have spoken, but how holy we have lived."[7]

This endeavor by a pastor to grow his soul motivates commitment in churches, inspires Christlikeness in laity, and generates incredible satisfaction for a pastor. Every effort to keep spiritually fit activates Christ's extravagant promise, "Blessed are those who hunger and thirst for righteousness, *for they will be filled*" (Matt. 5:6, emphasis added).

Personal Spiritual Growth Illuminates Vision

Ministry seems fuzzy these days. By this, I mean that current pastoral effort often appears to be fixed on empty traditions or habitual practices and gives almost no thought to fresh expressions of biblical mandates.

Perhaps God wants something different. Perhaps He intends a pastor's dedication to grow a great soul to help a congregation clarify its mission. It may also help illuminate God's will for a specific church at a particular time. The pastor's personal prayer efforts often ignite his ability to share his vision.

A 35-year-old pastor who served a small church for more than five years explains, "When my Scripture reading and intercessory prayer keep me close to God, I sometimes experience a pastoral guidance system, something like ESP, or perhaps it is more like radar. I am aware of what God wants done when and sometimes why. In trying to follow this guidance, I am in error often enough that I do not blame God for false impressions, but I have been guided enough times that I always act upon those directions."

Another minister describes a similar link: "I get specific assignments for ministry at old First Church when I pray and read Scripture. My prayer conversations invigorate my ministry. To my delight, I receive up-to-date prescriptions from the Physician of my soul."

What could possibly provide more satisfaction than having God's guidance as to how mission is to be carried out in a particular setting? How exhilarating to draw close to God so we experience His blank-check promise that He will draw close to us!

Personal Spiritual Growth Leads Us Along Well-Marked Trails

Spiritual formation generally makes use of established disciplines of the inner life. The disciplines take us along trails that saints have walked in all generations. However, the wide-awake pilgrim frequently discovers something incredibly new.

A hiking path in our old neighborhood offers a good example. The trail is paved and predictable and even has mileage markers along with a spectacular view of Pikes Peak. Spring wild flowers and winter snow sometimes decorate the path. But the view is different each time I walk the trail, because the sun changes the light so often.

Growing a great soul is like that. Although there are many familiar landmarks along the paths of righteousness, new richness keeps showing up as we travel these well-known trails. God keeps infusing eternal truth with new light and brighter color and richer texture.

Personal Spiritual Growth Prevents "Inner Kill"

Cynicism and distrust all add up to a climate of suspicion in our society. This attitude frequently seeps into the Church and causes what one psychologist calls "inner kill" in the pastor's soul. This graphic phrase offers an accurate assessment of what happens when a pastor suffers from dulled motivation or from superficial faith over long periods.

Prolonged scarcity of fulfillment intensifies inner kill for people in any profession, especially pastors. Playing it safe also destroys drive and initiative. Inner resurrection, one of God's amazing specialties, is the remedy. Inner kill thrives when a pastor curbs the prophetic directives of Scripture, when he sees his situation as hopeless or when he fails to find adventure in ministry. The fallout causes him to mark time, mires him in a time warp, and distorts his priorities.

To prevent this condition, the minister's spirituality must be intentionally personal and much more than a professionalized piety. Frail spiritual weaklings won't do for pastors.

Personal Spiritual Growth Heals Harmful Experiences

One pastor described his struggle in these words as he worked out his spiritual fitness:

> I was raised in a household where prayer was used to manipulate and restrict life. I had to go through a time of rebellion before I could come to know another kind of prayer, but I still can identify with feelings that make those who have been raised in the church turn away from religious words and practices. They have been turned off by the unreality of much of it.[8]

How devastating and distressing that anyone would even unknowingly pervert prayer for another, especially a child.

Unfortunate or counterfeit childhood experiences, however bad they seem or harmful their influence, do not invalidate our need for the holy.

We cannot give up knowing Jesus intimately as the central force for ministry just because childhood religious experiences were not ideal or because of a few bizarre Christians.

Personal Spiritual Growth Restores Balance

Pastoral ministry has many confusing expectations that originate from a wide variety of sources. All these changing expectations easily get us off balance. Conflicting priorities hound us continually. Expectations confuse us, too—theirs, ours and God's. Thus, every reflective pastor is frequently bothered by his use of time and by the fact that ministry is never finished. That being true, where does the possibility for balance come from? This issue of priority must be addressed if a pastor is to grow a great soul.

When a pastor prays and listens carefully to Scripture, he sees *being* and *doing* as two interrelated dimensions of ministry. Each informs the other. A student underscored this interplay on her Bible college senior exam: "We are human beings, not human doings. Therefore, we must be before we can do." Thus, when an activist pastor listens to God, he sees character flaws in himself that his Father wants corrected and healed.

Conversely, the introspective pastor, while reading the Holy Book and praying, feels sent into a more active involvement in the lives of people. This built-in creative tension between being and doing nurtures growth. Contemplative praying and redemptive doing are two sides of the same coin of ministry that must be constantly polished in a pastor's spiritual development.

Denominations, special interest groups and local congregations need to be introduced to this message again. Without spiritual energy, religious activism is nothing more than a round of beneficent activities that quickly run out of purpose, passion and support.

The opposite also is true. Christians who give their whole attention to personal character development can become so heavenly minded that they are of no earthly good. But pastors who carefully listen to Scripture, prayer and the devotional giants find resources for building a delightful balance between being and doing. Thus, they will hear the call of the people in the streets while cultivating their inner world. On the other hand, they will hear a call to be like their Master in the noise, in the hurry and in the crowd.

This balancing process stretches a pastor between rationality and spontaneity, grit and grace, piety and practicability, obligation and gladness, faith and fun.

EIGHT WAYS TO GROW A GREAT SOUL

To cultivate an effective, fulfilling ministry, let's get specific about how to grow a great soul. Try to view spiritual fitness as more than a high-octane spiritual additive to be poured into the details of ministry. Think of growing a great soul as nothing more or nothing less than an authentic Christian life—normal, whole, well adjusted and Jesus-focused—that is lived as God intends us to live.

The following section provides eight practical ways to grow a great soul. Note, however, that because spiritual growth can come from any activity or action that draws us nearer to God, this list is not exhaustive.

1. Cultivate a Soul Friend

Every pastor needs a trustworthy friend to whom he voluntarily makes himself spiritually accountable. A soul friend must be given permission to question him about motives, marriage and ministry. This soul friend must also be given permission to question him about his relationship with God.

A pastor needs a soul friend who loves him enough to be tender, yet tough. He needs someone to pray for him and with him. Ideally, the soul friend should be willing to listen redemptively to his hurts, affirm his strengths, and call him to authenticity. He must know when to pat the pastor on the back and when to kick him in the seat. This person should be a good friend as well as a demanding critic.

2. Resist the Seduction of Safety

Mere maintenance in church attendance, fund-raising or personal spiritual development sounds so good to us. Humanly, we want to hold on to what we have developed or inherited. It's good, we feel, to be safe.

Years ago, I knew one high-placed leader who, when faced with a potential recruit or a new program, would always ask, "Is he/it safe?" In his quest for safety, he rejected progressive ideas because they might be controversial, and he seldom appointed maverick ministers because they were too threatening. To the detriment of the Kingdom, he often missed the energy and achievement of new ideas and of innovative people.

We are often like that, too. Our reluctance to risk, pioneer new frontiers or reinvent ministry hinders the work of God and makes it mediocre and inane. The word "great," as in growing a "great" soul, frightens us. It is so much easier to be careful and cautious and predictable—words that do not seem to fit in the same paragraph with the gospel, missions and worldwide impact.

3. Solicit Prayers from the Faithful

Stamina strengthens ministry that is undergirded by prayer. Untapped prayer support surrounds us. We have more people than we realize who are interested in praying for us. We can have more prayer for the asking—and most of us need all the prayer we can get. Think of those people who might be willing to take your name and ministry to the Father.

People Who Nurtured Your Faith

Sunday School teachers, pastors and friends in your home church will feel highly honored if you ask them to pray for you every day. Power from these prayers cannot be hindered by miles, clocks or calendars.

People You Have Served with in Crises

Every person you helped through a crisis is a prospective candidate to support your ministry with prayer. Because of the difficulties you shared with them, they will have a built-in awareness of how much you need supernatural assistance as you seek to serve others as you served them. They are bonded to you forever by the tender compassion you once showed them.

People Who Need Attention

Every congregation has people who need and want more attention than a pastor is able to give them. A common example is shut-ins who regret they do not get more of their pastor's time. They may be frail or sick and believe they are unneeded because they cannot do what they once enjoyed doing in the church. Their limitations make them feel useless. Consequently, asking them to pray for you turns their focus to significant concerns outside themselves and makes them feel needed again. It involves them in something important they can do and something you need. Everyone gains.

People Who Serve with You
Christian workers can expect to receive power when they band together in prayer for a common cause. Examples are a local church staff meeting daily for prayer or a church board gathering early Sunday morning to intercede for the ministry of the day. Try enlisting committee members of your church to covenant to pray for each other every day. Emphasize this need as being more important than agenda decisions. As a result, a spiritual synergism develops so two will do much more than twice what you could have done alone.

Ministry Peers Who Can Share Your Prayers
Topping the list of all the inspirational sentences I have ever received in a letter were the words, "Let's trade prayers." What an energetic, enabling force for ministry.

4. Rekindle Affection for the Bible
Use Scripture to energize your ministry. Saturate your life with Scripture by active Bible reading. Let your encounter with the Bible shape the details of your ministry. Enter into mental conversation with Bible characters. Synchronize your thinking with its message so you hear, respond and apply new truths to this moment of your life. Use Scripture to energize your ministry.

Read for Relevance
Be open to insight about your life and ministry. Develop a continuous friendship with the Author. Go for quality as well as for quantity. Listen closely to what the Spirit is saying. What does God want you to hear through Scripture about your service for Him?

Interrogate Scripture

Walk around its message and its meaning. Check similar ideas in various passages by using a concordance and commentaries. Probe the passage. Explore, research, study, compare and contrast. As you read, ask questions about how this passage affects your life.

Personalize the Passage

Put your name in a promise or a command. What affirmation does the Scripture say about your ministry? Does it seem to have your name and ZIP code written on it? If you were present at the particular biblical event, what would you feel and what would you do?

5. Grow Past Your Prayer Hang-Ups

I (Neil) love the old story about lightning striking a nightclub in a tiny western town after the Christian people had an all-night prayer meeting, asking God to destroy the "den of iniquity." When the nightclub owner heard about the prayer meeting, he sued the church. Immediately, the church people denied any responsibility. The judge threw the case out of court after he observed, "Apparently, the night club owner believes in prayer more than the church people." This is an interesting parable for pastors.

Like other believers, pastors sometimes suffer from prayer hang-ups. As a result, they focus on problems about prayer without experiencing its possibilities. Most of us have at least one or more of these prayer dilemmas, but a single obstacle should not keep us from earnest conversations with our Lord.

Unanswered Prayers

Although we do not have much light on why some prayers are not answered, God has proven Himself to be the dependable One. Therefore, why not pray in an act of intentional Christian commitment: "I trust You, even though I do not understand why a particular prayer was not answered. I love You. And I want to serve You all the days of my life—in the storms as well as in the sunshine."

Delayed Answers

Delayed answers often seem unnecessary, even cruel. However, because God knows tomorrow as well as He knows yesterday and today, His wait-awhile answer is always best. Remember that delay does not mean denial.

Guilt About Not Praying Stalks Lots of Good People

In their inwardness, many people carry a picture of God as a harsh, heavenly timekeeper who inspects their time cards every day. They believe God would be more pleased if they prayed longer and louder. Of course, we all could pray more, but the quality of our relationship with God affects our prayers, too. To stop praying because we did not pray enough last week or last month does not move us nearer to God.

Unrelinquished Concerns

Every genuine believer sometimes feels handcuffed by people or issues he cannot control or change. These concerns may perhaps be the consequences of past sins.

Then, too, people from our past have complicated our lives in ways we cannot shake. Some feel defeated by lies told about them, even by good people. Some have been cheated by duplicity or outright stealing. Others have been locked out of "what might have been" by parents, spouses or children. A victorious relinquishment of these concerns will liberate us to live satisfying lives and have an improved ministry. This may be the precise time to pray for the grace of relinquishment—to take your hands off for all time.

6. Enjoy God

Many believers dread spending time with God. They are afraid because they picture Him as an authoritative judge, accusing parent, perfectionist professor, unbending boss or absentee landlord. Accordingly, their meetings with God are dreadfully unpleasant.

If we want to grow a great soul, however, it is essential to wholeheartedly embrace the fact that God champions us. More than the most loving human parent, God wants us to succeed so we can find joy in service and do our adventuresome part to advance His kingdom.

Recently, I (Neil) heard a pastor tell about an early morning appointment he kept with God. Being a night person, he has difficulty getting up. After dragging himself out of bed to pray on a particular morning, he started back to bed with sleepy eyes and a sluggish brain. Then he experienced an impression as real as an audible voice: "So you would rather sleep another hour than keep your appointment with Me. Who would miss for anything in the whole world a meeting with the King of the Universe, the Lord of resurrection life and the Lover of your soul?" God's friendly chastisement transformed the pastor's devotional duty into winsome fellowship with the Father.

Ministry, by definition, makes us partners with omnipotence. Even though we are junior partners, we are important, needed and essential. The mental pictures we have of God provide affirming inspiration we too easily overlook:

- *The Judge* sets us free when we deserve imprisonment or death.
- *The Parent* affirms us as a member of God's family.
- *The Professor* teaches us truth about the world and ourselves.
- *The Ruler* stands as sovereign Lord of our lives.
- *The Landowner* provides us with shelter and security.

Although the possibilities of enjoying the Father are thoroughly rooted in Scripture, the Westminster Catechism summarizes it in beautiful shorthand language: "What is the chief end of humankind? To glorify God and enjoy God forever."

Look for ways to enjoy God continually. Discover fun and fascination and exhilaration in prayers, Scripture reading, people to whom you minister, hymns, and the magnificent examples of grace all around you. Great souls enjoy the sparkle and satisfaction of friendship with God and His people. Cultivate a sense of joyful ministry for the sheer adventure of it.

Take the glumness out of ministry for a week, and it might never return. Build an enjoyable relationship with God into the fabric of every pastoral effort. Pastoring links you with God's mighty power. Let's act like it.

7. Pray Risky and Adventuresome Prayers

Some prayers seem like tough exams that show us what we do not know, what the professor expects, and what significant issues we have overlooked.

Spiritual directors and devotional saints across the centuries have cautioned believers against prayers that request miracles with no effort on their part. Prayers are generally not answered that way.

Far from being magic formulas, prayers are usually answered by receiving an assignment that can be achieved only with divine aid. God answers prayers by empowering us after we have done our best.

Human experience offers many examples. You will have your patience tested when you pray for patience. You will be given a peacemaking task when you petition for peace. Pray for generosity and God will ask you to give more than you have ever given. In a similar vein, genuinely great sermons usually grow out of human anguish or even travail before they receive divine anointing.

Here are five risky, adventuresome prayers that will add a supernatural dimension to your ministry, send you into specialized tasks, make you more Christlike and require more than your best efforts. These prayers could change your ministry forever:

1. *Search me.*
2. *Break me.*
3. *Stretch me.*
4. *Lead me.*
5. *Use me.*

Seldom does a person pray even one of these petitions without incredible growth happening in his inner relationship with God or in his outer expressions of Kingdom service. These petitions produce authentic achievement in the front lines of ministry.

8. Commit to Spiritual Self-Care

Adequate spiritual self-care is a little-understood secret of a flourishing ministry. To adequately care for his own spiritual fitness, a pastor must buck busy schedules, priority pressures, unreasonable expectations and secular values. But it must be done.

Like everyone else, pastors should desire the best possible life: Christ-directed living centered on our Lord's teachings, energized by His nearness, and steeped in His will. The center of a minister's responsibility is to find such a life for himself and then share it with those he serves. Thus, self-care multiplies his ministry rather than being a favor he does only for himself.

Seeking such a satisfying life may be the main reason people come to church week after week. Sadly, many seekers believe it is a spiritual mirage or an unobtainable ideal because such a Christ-quality life is so seldom modeled before them. Perhaps more people would want this valuable life if we reminded them that Christ brings eternal newness to people of every generation as they welcome Him into the details of their lives. Perhaps more people would thirst for such a quality life if the Church did not keep faith safely embalmed in ancient words or yesteryear's creeds.

We have the privilege to show them authentic Christian living at its best. Shout it from the housetops and live it in the streets. Nothing faintly compares with the Jesus way of life. The people we serve will be significantly affected by its relevance and sweetness as they observe it working so well in our songs, in our catastrophes, in our ambiguities, and in our victories.

Remember: To teach and live a Christ-quality life is the most gratifying style of life anyone has discovered or enjoyed.

Too many pastors feel their personal spiritual development is hindered by problems, difficulties or limitations. Sometimes they blame their shallowness on a power-hungry matriarch or patriarch in the congregation. But a pastor must look past every impediment to realize a Christ-quality life can be cultivated anywhere. Even tough pastoral assignments offer enough stretching points and affirmative influences for a pastor and spouse to build a Jesus-permeated life.

To nourish this kind of life, a pastor must realize continuously that he is a grace consumer, not a producer. To make this happen for himself, a pastor must value and celebrate the momentous serendipities of pastoral service. Reading, praying and knowing God are part of his job description—something very different from the occupational demands of average Harry in the parish.

Self-care is not only beneficial for the pastor, however, but the congregation also benefits. Such bonding with Christ deepens a pastor's devotion to ministry and helps him portray Christlikeness in the expressions of his ministry. It positively affects his preaching, counseling and worship leadership. A holy contagion will then ignite his congregation.

As a result, church members move nearer to Christ because they see spiritual adventure at work in their minister. As they see the life of Christ embodied in their leader, their spiritual appetites increase. They begin thirsting for a life of love and trust and grace. This spiritual interplay between pastor and laity is spiritual blooming at its best.

However, without vibrant personal spiritual self-care, a pastor sentences himself to leading a well-intended religious business enterprise, a do-goodish relief agency, or an affable social club. That's not much fun, and it produces a boring life.

A GREAT SOUL REVITALIZES MINISTRY

Grow a great soul so that supernatural strengths of character will enrich and energize every expression of your ministry. Your personal spiritual strengths can become a mighty combined force for curing the discord, disharmony and confusion that prevail in the Church and in society.

Therefore, fill your inner life with the spirit of Jesus so His character shows in your ministry. Then the work of Christ will survive and thrive or even flourish under your leadership. And remember:

- Great souls *preach* powerfully, warmly and redemptively.
- Great souls *care* for hurting, broken people and point them to the Savior.
- Great souls *lead* worshipers into God's awesome presence.
- Great souls *build* strong families, cherish their marriages and see the Church as the family of God.
- Great souls substitute supernatural achievement for cheap, empty talk.

Consider the incredible possibilities. God intends that your ministry will profoundly affect those you serve. But He plans much more. God wants your ministry to shape you into Christlikeness and to add adventure to your life in ways beyond your fondest imagination. Ministry takes you to adventuresome places. Ministry allows you to rub shoulders with people you would otherwise never know. Your junior partnership with God allows you privileges and permits you to receive grace in a measure no one experiences in other occupations.

Genuine greatness expands your credibility and kindles your passion for Christ. Growing a great soul blasts away the corrosion that, like acid, eats away at the Church's achievement and vision. A thousand pastors with growing souls can rekindle fires of principle, hope, devotion, conviction, magnanimity, servanthood, imagination, creativity and holy living.

CONTEMPORARY CHALLENGE

How to Keep in Shape Spiritually

- Go beyond a professionalized ministry to a personal pilgrimage with God.
- View ministry as a colossal opportunity to grow a great soul.
- Apply to yourself principles of spiritual wellness that you preach to others.
- Refuse to allow your own spirituality to become ceremonial.
- Renew the adventure of being a spokesperson for the resurrected Lord.
- Model the God-permeated life.
- Balance your ministry between being and doing.
- Resist the seduction of safety.
- Solicit prayers from the faithful.
- Enjoy God.

In the middle of the bad, it has never been so good! —Student Prayer[9]

God Loves You—You Matter a Lot

Musings from H. B. London, Jr.

In every worship service I conducted, I always found some way to remind worshipers, "God loves you as though you were the only one in the world to love, and that makes you a very special person."

Although St. Augustine had a similar phrase, I think the apostle John crystallized the thought when he said, "For God so loved the world that He gave His only begotten Son" (John 3:16). John was saying that Jesus came in person for each of us—as though we were the only one!

This is a truth that the people in our churches should hear over and over again: They are loved in a unique way by an Almighty God. What a great message! If people could embrace that truth as little children, the Christian walk would be so much easier for them.

What about you? Do you understand that God loves you as though you were the only pastor-teacher-leader in all the world to love? The battles you engage in are His battles. The circumstances you face are familiar to Him. The burdens you bear may be placed on His shoulders with His permission.

So many influences in our world seek to discourage us by telling us we are simply one in a billion. Don't ever believe that, my friend. God's love for you is the greatest story ever written.

Live in this great inspiration: "How great is the love the Father has lavished upon us that we should be called the children of God—that is what we are!" (1 John 3:1).

CHAPTER 10

A FRESH
ENCOUNTER
WITH GOD

Father, send revival and renewal
to my soul and church.
Invigorate, rejuvenate and revitalize every
phase of my ministry.
Help me live by the reality that I can
do nothing without You.
Amen.

> IF MY PEOPLE, WHO
> ARE CALLED BY MY NAME,
> WILL HUMBLE THEMSELVES AND
> PRAY AND SEEK MY FACE AND
> TURN FROM THEIR WICKED
> WAYS, THEN WILL I HEAR
> FROM HEAVEN AND WILL
> FORGIVE THEIR SIN AND WILL
> HEAL THEIR LAND.
>
> 2 CHRONICLES 7:14

"IT'S ME, IT'S ME, O LORD"

"A few members of any church must get thoroughly right with God," was evangelist Dr. R. A. Torrey's first rule for revival. However, if a pastor is serious about renewal in his ministry and church, the rule must be personalized with his name and address and ZIP code.

Then the rule reads: "Let [insert your name] get thoroughly right with God as a first step of revival." To reinforce the revival rule, we sing, "It's me, it's me, O Lord, standing in the need of prayer."

Pastor Shares His Need for Revival

A life-changing renewal came to me after I (H. B.) had been a pastor for 15 years in Salem, Oregon. I was a pastor of a spiritually vibrant church, but I still saw myself as a phony. I went through the right motions without the right motives. I saw myself accomplishing about what anyone could do if given the same opportunities. My success, however, was not comfort enough. I needed healing, revival.

One night in a dark, silent church when no one was present, I fell across the altar in a mood of spiritual desperation. I began to pray the most humiliating prayer you could imagine.

I prayed, "O God, I want out of this. I want out of the ministry. I'm not worthy of this church. I'm artificial and a play actor. You need to get me out of this. I would appreciate it if you could get me out gracefully. But if it is not graceful, that's okay, too. I just can't go on with this pain inside."

At that point, I humbled myself. I admitted to God that I was not authentic. I acknowledged that I was inadequate. I confessed that I was an unworthy vessel, full of cracks and holes. I admitted that I was running on spiritual empty.

At that moment, the presence of Christ came over me with empowerment and meaning. The Lord seemed to say in that moment, "Now I can use you." The results of that encounter with the Lord changed my whole life. It revolutionized my ministry.

Personalizing Torrey's rule may seem a bit uncomfortable at first. But spiritual development never works for "them" before it starts with "us" or "me." Like so many things in ministry, revival is a matter of leadership, priority and visibility.

A genuine spiritual awakening causes a pastor to feel a holy dissatisfaction with things as they are.

From what you know about God and about how churches function, you know that few congregations will become spiritual power-
houses until their pastors first experience a fresh personal encounter
with God. Consequently, the first step for authentic revival is personal renewal of the pastor at any cost.

The second step follows the first automatically: A genuine spiritual awakening causes a pastor to feel a holy dissatisfaction with
things as they are. Thousands of ministers who become fed up must
speak up in kindly but unmistakable ways about what needs to be
changed.

Our legitimate discontent centers around playing church, cod-
dling emotional infants, worrying about personal security, preaching
arid doctrinal scholasticism, baby-sitting trivia, being controlled by
spiritual pygmies, and living by savage schedules that leave no time
for prayer, study or outreach.

It's time to face the fact that the nation's moral malaise and the
Church's navel-gazing apathy are sobering, serious spiritual issues.
It's time to seek reality in knowing God. It's time to fast, receive God's
perspective and insist on authenticity in ourselves and in church leaders above and below us. It's time to get serious about holy living so
that it becomes a personal and congregational obsession.

It's time to move beyond puny image building about small successes to accomplish truly supernatural exploits for God—the kind
that transform individuals and revolutionize society. It's time to rally
all the church's facilities, finances and personnel to win the war
against evil and godlessness.

For such a revival, we must pray Habakkuk's prayer for ourselves,
our assignments, our denominations, our colleges and our publishing
houses: "O Lord, revive thy work" (Hab. 3:2, *KJV*). And we must march
and sing:

O Breath of Life, come sweeping through us;
Revive Thy Church with life and power.
O Breath of Life, come, cleanse, renew us;
And fit Thy Church to meet this hour.[1]

MAKE REVIVAL A USER-FRIENDLY WORD

Revivals have a bad reputation in many places. Because a spurt of religious enthusiasm soon plays out, it is argued that planned and calendared revivals accomplish little. The conclusion seems overly jaded, however, when you consider that some renewal is better than none. A Methodist bishop said in a conversation in which revival meetings were being criticized, "I agree that revivals are often ineffective, but that's how I got into the Kingdom."

The revival we need will take us back to the basics of faith and reactivate a no-reservations commitment to the cause of Christ. Such a revival will require us to humble our souls before God, to question our egos and to get serious about personal righteousness. Such a revival will stimulate fresh love and soul-stretching adoration for Christ and will energize selfless service to God and neighbor.

Such a contagious revival will make the life of God satisfying, joyful and fun again. And it will anoint our preaching with a holy contagion so we are able to make the gospel inviting and invigorating to a broken world.

Norman Vincent Peale painted a clear picture of the kind of revival we seek when he described his father's ministry as a revivalist: "What he [Peale's father] wanted was in-depth life-change in which not only emotion but the mind combined in a commitment bringing spiritual growth and lifelong Christian discipleship."[2]

That's real revival—an in-depth life-changing commitment involving the emotions and mind that makes believers in our churches and in ourselves spiritually different and growing for a lifetime.

Look Beyond the Wrappings

More slick substitutes, maneuvering manipulations or extreme emotionalism are not what we desire from revivals out of the past. Rather, it is the God of revival and renewal that we seek.

Like stories from our childhood, it's fun to retell revival experiences from our past. I remember an evangelist who displayed an open casket with a mirror in place of a corpse at the front of the church. I recall singing 34 verses of "Just as I Am." In my college years, I remember being tricked into admitting in public that I had not surrendered to Christ.

In my mind, I can still see eccentric evangelists from the past with big cars, garish ties, giant Bibles and flashy suits. Those itinerants sometimes sold study Bibles, records, books or ceramic eagles to help them make a living. But these are just the wrappings. There is so much more to real revival.

Let's try looking past the externals to the essential. What is the essential nature of revival? What is the driving force for authentic revival?

For real revival to take place, God wants a minister and a church to thoroughly examine their relationship to Christ and continually evaluate ministry in light of Kingdom priorities. Depth and obedience are to replace shallowness and playacting. God intends for revival to impact the heart of a pastor and the heart of a congregation.

For an individual, such a renewing welcomes God into the citadel of the soul. It joyously allows a loving Father to forgive outward sin and remedy inner corruption. Genuine revival makes us willing to turn from sin, rebellion and disobedience. Genuine renewal requires humbling ourselves, seeking God's face, turning from wicked ways and changing in any way He suggests. Real revival helps us make the wonderful trade of giving up embarrassing self-sovereignty to receive God's guidance, grace and will.

Follow Scriptural Directions

From Genesis to Revelation, the Bible is a book about reality, renewal and starting again. It encourages us to eagerly hope for revival and commands us to earnestly seek revival. We are to yearn for renewal as if it all comes from God. At the same time, we are to seek renewal as if its coming depends completely on us.

Scripture teaches that revival is more than a desirable wish or an idealized spiritual state of being. Rather, genuine revival is a revitalized faith God wants us to enjoy, a supernatural new vision for every church and a favor we give ourselves.

Consider these scriptural directives for seeking authentic revival and kindling genuine renewal.

Peter Proclaims the Necessity. At Pentecost, Peter proclaimed revival ingredients: "Repent, then, and turn to God, so that your sins may be wiped out, that times of refreshing may come from the Lord, and that he may send the Christ, who has been appointed for you—even Jesus" (Acts 3:19-20).

Jesus Explains the Source of Revival. Even after two centuries have passed, Jesus' immortal words at the Feast of Tabernacles still call the Church to authentic renewal: "If anyone is thirsty, let him come to me and drink. Whoever believes in me, as the Scripture has said, streams of living water will flow from within him" (John 7:37-38).

Revival Impacts a Nation. Scripture teaches a connection between a genuine revival of God's people and the spiritual salvaging of a nation. In the events surrounding the dedication of the Temple, Solomon prayed earnestly for God to honor the Israelites' worship with His presence in the new location:

> When your people Israel have been defeated by an enemy because they have sinned against you and when they turn back and confess your name, praying and making supplication before you in this temple, then hear from heaven and forgive the sin of your people Israel and bring them back to the land you gave to them and their fathers (2 Chron. 6:24-25).

Note the relationship of the land to Israel's sinfulness.

Places of Worship Need the Reviving Presence of God. Solomon understood that it is possible to build a magnificent house of worship without much of God's presence. Solomon also knew he could never revive himself. His seeking after God shows he agreed with Charles Spurgeon, who wrote centuries later, "You would just as soon expect a wounded soldier on the battlefield to heal himself without medicine, or get himself to a hospital when his arms and legs have been shot off as you would expect to revive yourself without the help of God."[3]

After the Temple was completed, God answered Solomon's prayer: "If my people, who are called by my name, will humble themselves and pray and seek my face and turn from their wicked ways, then will I hear from heaven and will forgive their sin and will heal their land" (2 Chron. 7:14). A common theme keeps appearing: Although revival comes from God, we have an important role in bringing it to pass.

John Gives God's Formula for Revival. A pattern for revival is clearly spelled out in the apostle John's warning to the church at Ephesus. He begins by complimenting the noble achievements of the congregation. He commends them for good deeds, hard work, persevering tenacity, refusal to follow false apostles, and willingness to endure hardships. That list of admirable qualities is desirable for any church!

"Yet . . ." John tells them, "you have forsaken your first love" (Rev. 2:4). All their impressive achievements had little significance without a return to their first love. After issuing a solemn warning, John tells the Ephesian church members they will be renewed if they (1) remember the heights from which they have fallen; (2) repent; and (3) repeat the things they did at the beginning (see Rev. 2:1-6).

The warning, intended especially for the Ephesians, also applies to us: "He who has an ear, let him hear what the Spirit says to the churches" (Rev. 2:7). A first love lost is the problem. Rediscovering first love is the solution.

The Ancient Prophet Has a Demanding Word, Too. A renewal passage in Hosea speaks to contemporary churches: "Sow for yourselves righteousness, reap the fruit of unfailing love, and break up your unplowed ground; for it is time to seek the Lord, until he comes and showers righteousness on you" (Hos. 10:12).

Many Churches Need a Heart Warming

Many churches are orthodox in doctrine and are busy in worthwhile activity but, like the Ephesians, have lost their first love. Some of these churches have pastors who know Scripture well and preach sermons decked out in impressive scholarship, generously seasoned with secular self-help suggestions. But something is missing, so neither pastor nor parish glows with childlike faith, unpretentious obedience and holy joy.

Because of lost love, outsiders regrettably find little warmth or nourishment in these fellowships. Years ago, Baptist evangelist Vance Havner described our current situation in words that sound like this morning's newspaper: "While we cry out against liberalism and loose living, are we not blind to the perils of lukewarmness? . . . Call it what you will, we need a heart-warming."[4]

Today, some churches toy or trifle with revival. Like a small child with a short attention span on Christmas morning, many contemporary churches keep checking the ecclesiastical smorgasbord of the latest fads, looking for easier ways to do ministry. Magic quick-fix programs that cost little soul passion and require less commitment are sought.

Sometimes, an entire congregation tries to make itself believe that a religious performance is an actual revival or that a highly energetic worship service is genuine renewal. Performance, great crowds and noise are not in themselves useful criteria. It is amazingly easy to fool ourselves into believing we are being renewed when we are dried up inside.

Most of this is like fool's gold—a shoddy substitute for the real thing. Inside, we are dying for a fresh infilling of God. Inside, we are dry and barren, and we are a long way from what God wants us to be.

Ministry Is a Dangerous Occupation

I recently talked with an insurance underwriter who ranks pastors among the safest actuarial risks from a physical point of view a life insurance company can have. Yet ministry can be among the most dangerous of all occupations spiritually.

The cause of this risk, of course, is the enemy of our souls who ambushes ministers with sly snares and subtle temptations. An ineffective, compromised or fallen pastor makes the devil's labors easier and more convincing. The enemy gets more credit than he deserves.

All of a church's impressive achievements have little significance without a return to their first love.

Often, our problems are self-induced by neglected prayer life, self-sufficiency or professional pride. The prophetic words written by Charles Spurgeon in the last century should cause us to stand at full spiritual attention:

> We too often flog the church when the whip should be laid on our own shoulders. We should always remember that we are a part of the church, and that our own lack of revival is in some measure the cause of the lack of revival in the church at large. I will lay the charge before us; we ministers need a revival of piety in our lives. I have abundant grounds to prove it.[5]

REVIVALS START WITH HOLY DISSATISFACTION

Earlier in this chapter, we considered how God builds the need of revival and the hope for renewal into the fabric of Scripture. The Bible frequently warns us about the tendency of spiritual fire going out.

It reminds us, too, that organized religion nearly always continues its rituals, rules and regulations long after it has lost its soul. But in those six words, John the apostle clinches the truth and stops all our defenses: "You have forsaken your first love."

Regardless of our theological label—evangelicals, liberals, conservatives, independents, charismatics, Catholics, reformed, Calvinists, Wesleyans—we all know John is right. The Church's first love has been forsaken. Incriminating evidence is everywhere. Every segment of Christianity has in some measure forsaken its first love and has lost its spiritual influence in society in the process.

How bad will it get before every pastor personally begins to stir up holy dissatisfaction with the way things are in his own soul and in the church?

Dissatisfaction 1: Loss of First Love

A long time ago, a ministry examination board asked a student pastor, "What does repentance mean?"

The young man replied, "To have a godly sorrow for sin."

The chairman of the examination board said, "You are only partly right.

Repentance means to have a godly sorrow for sin, but it also means a willingness to forsake one's sins forever."

Sorrow and a willingness to forsake sin are important directives for the modern Church. The Church in general, and local congregations in particular, have many reasons to repent. You can list your own convincing reasons. But even a short list must include confused priorities, lukewarmness, shallowness, sin, diluted message and inappropriate use of monies contributed for ministry.

For too long, contemporary congregations have given themselves high marks because they worked hard, persevered and refused to follow false prophets. But John clearly told the Ephesians that was good but not good enough for God. The church at Ephesus did those things well, but John still called them to repentance and insisted that they needed to return to their first love.

Dissatisfaction 2: Leaders with Sin in Their Lives

A church is never what God wants it to be when those who lead are living in sin. God's holy standards apply both to laity and clergy. To the Corinthians, Paul wrote about sexual immorality in the church: "And you are proud! Shouldn't you rather have been filled with grief and have put out of your fellowship the man who did this?" (1 Cor. 5:2).

In God's expectations for His Church, willful sin disqualifies a person for leadership. The Father's serious concerns likely include sins we do not often worry about in church leaders, such as lying, cheating, doublespeak, gossip, stealing and greed.

Every segment of Christianity has in some measure forsaken its first love and has lost its spiritual influence in society in the process.

Biblical standards of the holy life must be applied to all who lead the Church in any way. Otherwise, the Church becomes a sham, pretense and travesty in the eyes of her people and the community. Teachers, singers, decision makers, worship leaders, praise-team members must all live lives that are pleasing to God and inspiring to the congregation.

Pastors must rid their churches of sin. It must be done carefully, redemptively and tenderly—but it must be done. Too often, people are allowed to lead when they are spiritually unqualified because their talents are so badly needed. But yieldedness to Christ is the first key to Kingdom service, not talent alone.

Six facts must be faced in dealing with sin in leaders:

- God wants leaders to be holy.
- People in the pews know more about a leader's lifestyles than we think.
- Spiritually unqualified leaders often get right with God when a pastor urges change.
- If spiritual charades are allowed to continue, the offenders may eventually lose their souls.
- Spiritually unqualified leaders generally create an unwholesome drag on a church's ministry.
- Outsiders may never come to church because they know leaders are not living as they should.

Dissatisfaction 3: The Church Becomes Worldly Minded

Worldliness chooses secular values rather than Kingdom priorities. Worldliness allows sophistication, security and self-sovereignty to press us into secular ways of thinking and acting. Worldliness is playacting, leaving the impression of being holy, separate and devoted when we are not.

For 2,000 years the Church has crippled itself whenever it allowed the spirit and values of the world to shape its ministry. For some sad reason, each new generation has to learn this lesson. The secular world and the spiritual Church do not mix any better than oil and water.

Worldliness sometimes shows in churches as a group pride of achievement, a pride of spiritual commitment, or a pride of worship practices.

Pride of achievement has been the downfall of churches that allow themselves to be distracted by their prominence, their talents, or even their missionary efforts. In the process, some great old churches and some contemporary emerging congregations have become only an echo of what they could be in the kingdom of Christ.

Some congregations pride themselves on their piety. Being super-spiritual, these churches easily drift into becoming a holy club that admits only those who act and look a certain way—usually some weird way. They are separate for the sake of being separate but fail to realize that spiritual pride is actually sly self-deceiving worldliness.

Worship practices also can become a subtle form of worldliness for churches. Some churches are proud of worn-out worship forms that no longer inspire anyone or that are little understood. Other churches are proud, believing they are special to God because of the energy, enthusiasm or noise level of their services. Why the pride in either extreme? Worship forms are nothing more than channels to help people into the presence of God. Worship forms are never an end in themselves.

Worldliness can also infect a church's methods. In a day of shifting paradigms with many innovative ways of thinking and doing, many church leaders assume any method that is new or produces visible results is acceptable to God. A not-so-holy pragmatism sometimes makes us believe any means justifies the end when the means and the end often need to be reevaluated in light of the New Testament. Although worldliness may not be in the method, it can be in the attitude of those who use the method.

Dissatisfaction 4: A Church Loses Its Sense of Wonder

Your church has amazing reasons to praise God. According to Peter, "you are a chosen people, a royal priesthood, a holy nation, a people belonging to God, that you may declare the praises of him who called you out of darkness into his wonderful light" (1 Pet. 2:9).

That too-good-to-be-true news renews our sense of wonder. Think of it: The Father makes nobodies into a chosen people. If God says we really are a royal priesthood, a holy nation, a people belonging to God, then we must be. That means every congregation has lots of reasons to praise God.

Peter says believers are no longer ordinary folks. God has made us different and alive and new, so we have incredible reasons to praise Him. Every church needs more praise to God for whom He is helping them become.

Thousands of churches could be revolutionized in a week if they began to practice the motto "Praise changes things." Or maybe the motto should be adjusted a bit: "Praise changes people who praise God." Rejoice in the wonders of God's grace that surround you in your congregation.

WHEN IS REVIVAL NEEDED?

Charles G. Finney offered a list to determine when a church needs a revival. This list from his revival lectures is timeless. He believed revivals were needed when these conditions prevailed:

- **Lack of love:** "When there is a lack of brotherly love and Christian confidence among professors of religion, then revival is needed."
- **Disunity and division:** "When there are dissensions and jealousies and evil speakings among professors of religion, then revival is needed."
- **Worldliness:** "When there is a worldly spirit in the church, then revival is needed."
- **Sin in the church:** "When the church finds its members falling into gross and scandalous sins, then revival is needed."
- **Controversy and disagreement:** "When there is a spirit of controversy in the church, then revival is needed."
- **Wickedness controls society:** "When the wicked triumph over the churches and revile them, then revival is needed."
- **Sinners are careless:** "When sinners are careless and stupid, then revival is needed."[6]

Genuine Revivals Start with Prayer

Seldom have great spiritual awakenings come to pastors, churches or countries without intercessory prayer. Before an awakening in India near the turn of this century, John Hyde, a praying missionary, asked Christians these questions to stimulate faithfulness in prayer for revival:

- Are you praying for quickening in your own life, in the life of your fellow workers and in the church?
- Are you longing for greater power of the Holy Spirit in your life and work, and are you convinced you cannot go on without this power?
- Will you pray that you may not be ashamed of Jesus?
- Do you believe that prayer is the great means for securing this spiritual awakening?
- Will you set apart one-half hour each day as soon after noon as possible to pray for this awakening, and are you willing to pray till the awakening comes?[7]

REVIVAL REVOLUTIONIZES A CHURCH

Real revival restores an individual and a church to spiritual health and well-being. For individuals, genuine revival enables them to live out their faith in the daily details of life.

Such a renewal brings a church from a subnormal, barely-making-it Christianity to a supernatural empowerment, a refreshing, a renewal, a sense of anointing, and a growing awareness that the Church is a unique organization owned and energized by God.

It stirs a congregation and challenges and empowers them to live out the radical demands of Christianity in every phase of life inside and out-side the church.

Spiritual Normalcy Is Restored

The main purpose of renewal and revival is not to produce super-saints or souped-up churches, although that sometimes occurs. Revival more often directs a church to its original purposes, making it more whole-some, healthy, robust or even redemptive. After restitution, forgiveness and reordering of its priorities are experienced by a church. Renewal and revival help believers sharpen their commitments to the church's unique roles and functions of prayer, worship, witness and service. Spiritual normalcy then returns so that a church is more than a feeble imitation of a garden club, a service club or a well-intentioned welfare organization.

Recently, a Southern California pastor shared a story of his personal journey of faith. He told about joyous renewal in the congregation he serves and expressed the belief that pastoral renewal and congregational revitalization grow in the same spiritual soil. He believes renewal in one person encourages renewal in the others.

Revival made incredible changes in his church. Early prayer meetings following the Korean pattern of morning prayer replaced a cluttered whirl of purposeless activities. His entire church was permeated with evidence of answered prayer. A new love for Scripture moved like wildfire through the fellowship so people, wherever they gathered, applied the meaning of the Bible to their contemporary lives. A changed, energetic worship atmosphere is so common that parishioners often sing with meaning, "Surely the presence of the Lord is in this place." The pastor's sermons have a new passion and vitality.

No one can explain the amazing change, because the church has the same preacher, the same songs, the same meeting times, the same worshipers and the same sanctuary. Holy living has become the routine practice of many people in the church. The pastor suggested, "My people often say the Early Church must have been a lot like the present environment in our church."

Extraordinary Prayer Is Activated

Evangelists and devotional writers are not agreed on whether prayer brings renewal or whether renewal engenders new power in prayer. It is like the chicken or the egg question. Either way, genuine revival always brings with it a component of extraordinary prayer.

This is a supernatural and satisfying kind of prayer in which believers approach God with a sense of humility and urgency. They stay until they know that they have communicated with God. Then they depart, fully aware they have had an audience with the King of the universe. It is the closest of all possible contacts with God.

Prayer is among the most popular discussion topics in church circles. We talk about prayer. We read books about prayer. We preach about prayer. We teach about prayer.

Meanwhile, it seems that the Church does not pray much. Today, the Church needs a bold urgency and fresh fervency in prayer until we know the answer is on the way because the Lord has heard us pray. It is still true and God will continue to respond, because "the prayer of a righteous man is powerful and effective" (Jas. 5:16). Magnificent answers to critical needs for renewal come when believers really pray.

Sin Feared as a Spiritual Cancer

Revival forces a person to face sin and its incredibly damaging consequences. Sin, like cancer, requires radical surgery if a person or church is to experience spiritual health. But worse than the dreaded effects of cancer on a human being is the not-so-obvious damage that individual sins have on a congregation. The outcome impacts a church, sometimes hindering its ministry for generations. Sin is serious business that must be acknowledged, forgiven and forsaken.

Although it may not make us comfortable to think about it, many churches are crippled, anemic, handicapped, feeble and too weak for spiritual warfare because of known and unknown, inner and outer, and respectable and vile sin in their fellowship. Sometimes even in the ministry.

The remedies are the same as they have always been: intercessory prayer by everyone who cares about the spiritual wellbeing of the church, anointed preaching on the subject that is clearly based on Scripture, and an atmosphere of deliverance in the church where recent converts are encouraged to freely tell of their transformations from the sins of their past.

Miracles Are Experienced

Many debates among ministers and scholars center around the meaning of the term "signs and wonders." Some consider signs and wonders as flamboyant and absolutely unexplainable events, while others believe that the days of miracles ended with the apostles. Sincere Christ followers can be found on both sides of the issue.

Wherever you stand on the debate, it is time to admit that the contemporary Church needs more of the supernatural and miraculous. More ministers need to put themselves in places of courageous commitment that are so demanding and so near the cutting edge that it requires God's supernatural enablement to survive or thrive.

A veteran pastor remarked recently, "Don't expect a miracle until you have gone way beyond your own resources. God doesn't waste the supernatural on what you can do on your own."

Peter, the coward before Pentecost, did this in the Early Church. In Acts 4:29-30, Peter's (and the church's) prayer for "signs and wonders" asked God for boldness to speak convincingly before Herod and Pontius Pilate and for supernatural results in the Early Church.

Peter received boldness—and results. He wanted the Early Church to be so unique and so remarkable that no one could doubt it was an instrument of God. He prayed for results to impress those who watched the Church from the outside and to inspire those on the inside.

God answered Peter's prayer. The Bible says the place was shaken. They were filled with the Holy Spirit. They spoke the Word of God boldly. They were united. They shared everything they had, including their material possessions. They testified with great power of the Resurrection. They fed the needy. They sold their land for the cause of Christ, and all of them received much grace.

When you consider what the Church would have been without this miraculous answer to prayer, Acts 4:32-35 is a model of God giving a church exactly what it needed, more than it expected, and more than members of the congregation thought they needed. It started when Peter prayed.

Peter prayed for results to impress those who watched the Church from the outside and to inspire those on the inside.

Results will be like that in our revivals. God will give us what we need. The work of God in the human heart and in the Church may not always be spectacular, but it will be supernatural.

The Supernatural Continues Today

What about those close-at-hand and less sensational miracles that seldom are noticed? Here are a few that changed someone's world:

- Recently, a Bible college student's family in our town received $200 in the mail from an unexpected source on the day their cupboards were empty.

- A few months ago, a rebellious teenager who had been living on the streets called her Christian parents and asked to come home after being led to Christ by a street preacher.

- A short while ago, a group of laypersons confronted a church controller and told him they were tired of him dominating the church, forcing pastors' resignations, and giving the church a bad name in the community. The controller left in a mad huff. Now in sweet fellowship, the lay leaders have concluded they will never again be ruled by one person.

- A few months ago, a minister who falsely accused a brother minister of stealing money from the church called to try to make things right. Although damages to the accused's reputation can never be fully restored, healing has started.

- Five years ago, a key layman in a middle-size church was gloriously called to the Christian ministry at age 35. His wife, unwilling to give up her home and security, openly opposed the idea. Wisely, the man simply said, "I won't make efforts to prepare until you agree wholeheartedly." He loved her and never badgered her, but just waited for God's timing. God did a wonderful work in her heart and they are now students at a seminary.

Contemporary pastors need to pray Peter's prayer for their ministry setting. Who knows what God wants to do for you where you are? It might not be spectacular, but it could be supernatural.

What might happen if contemporary congregations received and used what God gave to the Church in Acts 4:32-35? Consider the possibilities for renewal in our time. They preached with supernatural power, they were filled with the Holy Spirit, they were committed to a common cause, they testified to the resurrection of Jesus, they had great grace, they gave up their security and greed by selling their land, and they cared for the needy.

Sounds like the power of God working in a local congregation, doesn't it?

Love Becomes Magnetic

When a revival of love occurs in a church, people treat each other as they would treat Christ. The golden rule becomes spontaneous. Differences are confessed, splintered relations are repaired, and restitutions are made.

Forgiveness is requested and granted. One person says, "I'm sorry" while another says, "It's okay; I should have grown past our disagreement months ago."

The glorious gift of hospitality gets dusted off. They babysit for each other. They become surrogate grandparents to children and love their young parents. They begin praying for each other and with each other. Love flows like a quiet river into every nook and cranny of the church so everyone sings better, smiles more and criticizes less.

Like a holy epidemic, renewed love at a church automatically spreads outside to offices, factories, gas stations, convenience stores, schools, Fortune 500 companies—wherever Christ lovers find themselves. Holy love flowing through the people of God to the unsaved is a powerful force for evangelism. Even though spiritually needy people may not be scolded out of their sins or reasoned into the Kingdom, they can often be loved to Jesus.

In this renewal of love, a believer's witnessing becomes delightful and natural. It shows on the tennis court, on the golf course, in shopping malls, in family rooms, in PTA meetings and anywhere else he or she meets someone who needs the Savior. Outsiders who feel that love want to attend the church. And they come again and again to experience the love of Christ flowing through a Christ-exalting church.

IT'S TIME TO LIGHT REVIVAL FIRES

While pleading for revival, Charles Spurgeon challenged laypeople to stop complaining about their pastors and to stop finding fault with their churches.

He challenged laity to cry out in intercessory prayer, "O Lord, revive thy work in me!" He told laity, "You don't need a new preacher, another kind of worship, another type of preaching, new ways of doing things or even new people. You need life in what you have."[8]

Pastors need to hear a comparable message. This might be the time to get past the common and destructive "if only we had" syndrome. I've said it often and heard it many times and in many places: Oh, if only we had another building. Oh, if only we had more trained laypersons. Oh, if only we had more money. Oh, if only we had a higher class of people. Oh, if only we had more commitment among the laity. Oh, if only we had a different style of worship. Oh, if only we had better or different music. Oh, if only my spouse were more involved. Oh, if only we had more Bible teachers. Oh, if only we had more social standing in the community. Oh, if only we had . . .

Spurgeon prescribes a cure for our "if only we had" debilitating virus. With a passionate heart burden, he says:

In this renewal of love, a believer's witnessing becomes delightful and natural.

If you want to move a train, you don't need a new engine, or even ten engines—you need to light a fire and get the steam up in the engine you now have. . . . It is not a new person or a new plan, but the life of God in them that the church needs. Let us ask God for it! Perhaps He is ready to shake the world at its very foundations. Perhaps even now He is about to pour forth a mighty influence upon His people which shall make the church in this age as vital as it ever was in any age that has passed.[9]

Let's light the fire and get up steam in the engines we already have. Let's pray, "O Lord, revive Thy work in me!"

A SPIRITUALLY RENEWED PASTOR

The following testimony must have been written by a renewed pastor— the kind the Church and the world need now. I (Neil) regret the source is unknown to me.

A Christian leader saw it on the wall of a pastor's home in rural Africa. I have a copy from a radio preacher dated 1981, and a Bible college student found it in the notes of a pastor who has been with the Lord for several years. At any rate, it needs a wide reading and a wider replication in contemporary pastors. My appreciation and thanks to the unknown author.

I am a part of the "fellowship of the unashamed." I have Holy Spirit power. The dye has been cast. I've stepped over the line. The decision has been made. I am a disciple of His. I won't look back, let up, slow down, back away or be still. My past is redeemed, my present makes sense and my future is secure. I am finished and done with low living, sight walking, small planning, smooth knees, colorless dreams, tame visions, mundane talking, chincy giving and dwarfed goals!

I no longer need preeminence, prosperity, position, promotions, plaudits or popularity. I don't have to be right, first, tops, recognized, praised, regarded or rewarded. I now live by presence, lean by faith, love by patience, lift by prayer and labor by power.

My face is set, my gait is fast, my goal is heaven, my road is narrow, my way is rough, my companions few, my Guide reliable, my mission clear. I cannot be bought, compromised, detoured, lured away, turned back, diluted or delayed. I will not flinch in the face of sacrifice, hesitate in the presence of adversity, negotiate at the table of the enemy, ponder at the pool of popularity or meander in the maze of mediocrity.

I won't give up, shut up, let up or burn up till I've preached up, prayed up, paid up, stored up and stayed up for the cause of Christ.

I am a disciple of Jesus. I must go till He comes, give till I drop and preach till everyone knows.

And when He comes to get His own, He'll have no problems recognizing me . . . my colors will be clear.

That makes it clear, doesn't it?

CONTEMPORARY CHALLENGE

Genuine Revival Must Start with the Pastor

- Revival begins with a holy dissatisfaction.
- Revival can be a user-friendly word.
- The Church is crippled with worldliness.
- Revival starts with prayer.
- Revival requires humility and repentance.
- Revival brings a willingness to change.
- Revival restores love in a church.

I ask no dream, no prophet's ecstasies, no sudden rending of the veil of clay, no angel visitant, no opening skies, but take the dimness of my soul away.
—George Croly[10]

Compassion Fatigue

Musings from H. B. London, Jr.

Sometimes I think I get compassion fatigue. Do you? It usually occurs when you come to the place where there is so much to care about that you just can't care any more.

As clergy, we deal with heartbreak all the time—so much so that we must guard against growing calloused or cynical. We can't lose our empathy or take for granted other people's suffering. Our hearts must remain sensitive—even though sometimes we just want to stick our fingers in our ears and say, "No more!"

How do we do this? For one thing, we should pray for a heart like Jesus. For another, we should never come to a place in our ministry in which we can walk away from suffering without letting people know of God's love. We must attempt to be an answer to our prayers and do what we can to help. We cannot do what we do for others out of selfish motives, but as unto the Lord. We also should place a high priority on getting enough rest and spiritual food, or we will wear down very quickly. We are reminded to "cast all your anxiety [care] on him because he cares for you" (1 Pet. 5:7).

There are times when I feel helpless, but then I remember it is not about me but those for whom our Lord called me to serve—to be His compassion in a world that hungers for solutions. And when I remember this, I again feel His power to do whatever I need to do.

Stay strong, my colleagues!

CHAPTER 11

CREDIBILITY— MAKING GOOD ON OUR TRUST

Holy Father,
empower me for ministry
that is
authentic in every act;
holy in every intention;
pure in every relationship;
genuine in every word;
and devoted in every expression of worship.
Amen.

> HIS DIVINE POWER HAS
> GIVEN US EVERYTHING WE
> NEED FOR LIFE AND
> GODLINESS THROUGH OUR
> KNOWLEDGE OF HIM WHO
> CALLED US BY HIS OWN
> GLORY AND GOODNESS.
>
> 2 PETER 1:3

God places trust in you as a pastor that is mind-boggling, humbling and even frightening. This trust includes His gospel and the local branch of His everlasting Church where you serve. He trusts you with folks in your geographic area who have not yet come to faith. And He trusts you with the spiritual care of your own family. Trusting pastors like this has been His strategy for more than 2,000 years—since the birth of the Christian Church. The results have been pretty astounding, and in the process some pastors have been stretched into becoming great souls.

CREDIBILITY IN AN ATMOSPHERE OF TEMPTATIONS

Credibility is not everything in ministry, but little can be accomplished without it. It is developed and maintained by doing the right thing for the right reason over and over. It means keeping our word and being true to our values.[1] It is the place in which promise—what we say we will do—and performance—what we actually do—meet. It means telling the truth and being what we claim to be. Credibility comes from being the best Christian we can be.

Credibility has to do with who we are on the inside. Although Ralph Waldo Emerson may not have been thinking about pastors when he wrote the following, his insight nails this issue for us: "What lies behind us and what lies before us are tiny matters compared to what lies within us."[2]

Credibility takes years to build and can be diluted or even destroyed in a moment. And it is under constant scrutiny every day by almost everyone we meet. Mark Twain helps us understand how credibility works when he advises, "Always do right. This will gratify some people and astonish the rest."[3]

Obviously, the Lord, the Church, the family and the community are all stakeholders in a pastor's credibility. Thus, these three key points must be considered in developing and maintaining credibility: (1) please the Lord, and most people will be satisfied; (2) credibility grows in direct proportion to our accountability; and (3) everyone has an opinion about the pastor's credibility or lack of it.

Credibility has four close cousins in the dictionary and in life, especially in ministry: integrity, authenticity, temptation and accountability. Think how this foursome helps us to be all God wants us to be and all the people need us to be.

- **Integrity** has to do with motives—why we do what we do. It comes from an attitude and commitment of steadfast adherence to a high ethical standard or code. For a pastor, it is being who we say we are when no one is looking. It has a spin-off benefit of giving us moral authority so we can ask followers for any

sacrifice because they know we have been there before them or
are willing to go with them now.

- **Authenticity** has to do with genuineness. Like an authentic
painting, it's the real thing—not a copy, imitation or counterfeit. Applied to a pastor, it means we practice what we preach.
It allows no duplicity, no playacting and no double speak.

- **Temptation** means having our credibility put to the test in
the details of living and serving. For the pastor, temptation
most often arises in areas such as power, money and sex.
Martin Luther believed three things were necessary to create
an effective minister: prayer, meditation and temptation.[4]
Help for overcoming temptation can be found in the biblical account of Jesus' temptation in the wilderness (see Matt.
4:1-11).

- **Accountability** is the necessity and willingness to open the
details of your life and ministry to someone whom you can
trust and to someone whom you have given the right to ask you
questions about the three big *M*'s—your motives, your ministry
and your marriage. Accountability is also sometimes written
into reporting and formal evaluations systems.

What a foursome—integrity, authenticity, temptation and accountability—to help us keep our credibility robust and well. What a source to
ask us the hard questions when *looking* spiritual becomes more important than *being* spiritual.

After thinking about the strength and hope these components of
credibility provide every pastor, let's start a parade or a Jesus rally and
carry placards. The messages on the placards could read something like
these: Down with duplicity and up with integrity. Down with seeming
and up with being. Down with image and up with authenticity. Down
with persona and up with personhood. Down with building a reputation and up with developing a Christlike character.

On second thought, why not develop your own placard message. God has trusted you with a branch office of His everlasting kingdom. And you can make good—in fact, you likely are already making good—on your trust from the Lord.

HOW TO MAKE GOOD ON THE TRUST

Keep in mind the powerful foursome that keeps our credibility robust and well: integrity, authenticity, temptation and accountability. Each of these feeds into one or more of the following exercises designed to help pastors make good on the trust God has given them.

Victory Exercise 1: Keep Your Resistance Up

The Bible boldly declares, "Resist the devil, and he will flee from you" (Jas. 4:7). In the context of that verse, James tells us that God gives grace to the humble (v. 6). Then he instructs us to submit to God (v. 7) and assures us that if we draw near to God, He will draw near to us (v. 8). Two verses later, we are told to humble ourselves before God and He will lift us up (v. 10).

Spiritual health requires that we avoid exposure to viruses of evil and germs of sin and infections of discouragement. That at least means keeping our distance from the infection sources, as we do with what we read and what we view on television. But it also means living the holy life that we preach and demonstrating the Christian virtues of forgiveness, grace, kindness and *agápe* love.

When we keep our spiritual resistance high, the devil cannot overcome us (see 1 John 5:18). Although the enemy is cunning and strong,

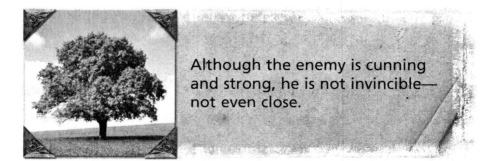

Although the enemy is cunning and strong, he is not invincible—not even close.

he is not invincible—not even close. When temptation comes, go to the Word of God. You will find amazing strength there.

Victory Exercise 2: Develop a Code of Integrity and Live by It

Dr. Archibald D. Hart explains why a code is needed: "A healthy concern for morality is not enough to maintain a ministry of integrity. Each pastor has a responsibility to develop a personal code of ethics tailored to his unique set of circumstances. Simply wrestling with such a personal code begins to sensitize one to important issues. Over time, there begins to develop an 'ethical sense'—a natural ability to tell if any action is likely to become a problem."[5]

Developing a personal code of integrity starts when you commit yourself to self-imposed guidelines that provide moral control of your life. Such an effort sets your will on God's will so you know your answer will be *no* to temptation when it comes. Then, when the tests come—as they inevitably will—there will be no need to reconsider, negotiate or fantasize about giving in.

Such a code builds holy conduct into the fiber of your life before the temptation appears.

These guidelines are not so much to protect your public persona, reassure your spouse, impress your children or convince your church—although they will accomplish all of this and more. Rather, components of the code are a commitment you make to yourself and to God that you are what you say you are.

All this becomes an inward strength that shapes thought and behavior and makes people say when a pastor is falsely accused, "His high standards of behavior prevent him from such conduct."

You can develop a personal code of integrity by personalizing the rules John Wesley used in the early days of Methodism to establish converts in a group atmosphere of active faith and personal accountability. Wesley asked five searching questions in his class meetings:

1. What known sins have you committed since our last meeting?
2. What temptations have you met with?
3. How were you delivered?

4. What have you thought, said or done of which you doubt whether it be sin or not?

5. Have you nothing you desire to keep secret?

One retiree was heard to joke when this process was explained in a pastors' meeting, "Sure would keep people awake in those meetings." The purpose, however, is not to embarrass anyone but to give solid encouragement for making holy living a reality.

Victory Exercise 3: Strive for Balance

Surveys show a direct correlation between exhausting burnout and moral failure. Dr. James C. Dobson warned in a radio broadcast that the pastorate is built for burnout, it's built for exhaustion, and it's built for trouble. He is right.

Fatigue, burnout and frustration make us more vulnerable to bad judgments and moral lapses. The guard tends to go down much more quickly when we feel tired, overworked, or full of self-pity. Frightening temptations also come when we wonder if our work is worthwhile or when we quit praying.

Because role expectations for pastors are not likely to change, we must find ways to create balance of those expectations for ourselves. Here are some starting points:

- **Family:** Schedule time with your family just as you would schedule any other priority. Establish a date night each week with your spouse and schedule individual time each week with

Fatigue, burnout and frustration make us more vulnerable to bad judgments and moral lapses.

each child. Years pass at breakneck speed with the children. You can miss a lot before you know it.

- **Personal soul care:** Plan specific times for personal soul care. There are many ways to do this, but it must be done. A half day per week away from the office for the sole purpose of developing your interior life works best for many pastors. Others take two days per month to get away for prayer and Scripture saturation. Be sure to review some of the many books about spiritual disciplines so you have a variety of helps.

- **Work commitments:** Arrange your schedule so you do not give more hours to your ministry than an active layperson gives to the church and his position or profession. For example, if an active layperson invests 20 hours a week to the church in addition to working a 40-hour job, try to limit yourself to that same time commitment of 60 hours.

- **Office hours:** Keep office hours so your work routines and your time at home are predictable. Organize your time. Get to work on time and remember Who your Boss is. Effective ministry is hard work.

Although achieving complete balance is seldom possible, the simple act of trying tends to make your ministry more balanced than it would be without such an effort.

Victory Exercise 4: Shift Priorities

Learn how to shift priorities. For example, if you have a heavy day of hospital ministry with the sick and dying that falls on the day you normally spend with your family, shift the time with the family to another day. And not just any day, but a *specific* day so your family understands that you are working for balance but also realizes your desire to be with them. The trick is to shift and reschedule rather than to shift and ignore. Some pastors keep one day a week open so they are able to shift demands.

Victory Exercise 5: Establish Accountability Relationships

Accountability, whether formal or informal, is essential because so much of ministry is done alone or in one-on-one relationships—places in which reality checks are not often found.

The idea is to establish a trust relationship with a person of the same gender to whom you give permission to ask you questions about your motives, your marriage and your ministry. This person is called by several names—mentor, coach, accountability partner, soul friend, prayer partner—depending on the intensity of the friendship and level of the accountability.

Prayer Partner

This relationship is a covenant between two persons of the same gender who are seeking a special empowerment of God's power on their ministry. The covenant should be an agreement for at least six months and be based on mutual trust. Both persons commit to pray for each other on a daily basis.

These partners meet at least once every two weeks for a time of sharing. They also keep in touch by e-mail or brief phone calls.

The process can be uncomplicated, even simple. The key is to trust enough in the other person to say, "I believe in you enough that I will allow you to really know who I am in Christ."

In such a covenant relationship, both persons receive strength through intercessory prayer, spiritual accountability and an active commitment to help another servant of the Lord.

Soul Friend

I (H. B.) often rejoice about the five soul friends in my life whom I have known and cherished for years. These five would go to the mat for me, and I would do the same for them. One of them is Dr. James C. Dobson. The others are spread across the country, and we stay in touch on a regular basis. It seems the older the friendships become, the more honest and vulnerable we are with one another.

I feel unbelievably blessed in having these relationships with these lifelong friends who would put their life on the line for me. These relationships have developed over long years of interaction, jousting, time spent together and sharing honestly and openly with each other.

We've shared pain and heartache as well as joy. We've been through rough spots in parenting and problems in marriages. One lost his wife in death. Another had children who were out of control. One had a moral breakdown.

But still there is a bond that cannot be broken. And these friends make me more real and authentic with their questions and warnings. They say, "Be real, H. B. Stop playing games, H. B. Get authentic, H. B." And they ask, "Tell us what is really going on, H. B."

We have this confidential, supporting, warning, bonding relationship that says we can count on each other unconditionally. These friends sustain me, support me and make me accountable to them and to the Lord Jesus.

Soul friends provide invaluable inspiration, correction and spiritual-growth cultivation. They make me sing the old hymn with new meaning, "I would be true for there are those who trust me. I would be pure, for there are those who care."[6]

Next to pleasing the Lord Jesus, my soul friends might be the strongest possible source of accountability. They trust me and care about me.

Victory Exercise 6: Develop Outside Interests

Ted Engstrom, a Christian statesman of a previous generation, summarized the issue clearly: "For a leader to excel, he must find avocations and interests in his life away from the job. He must not only provide materially for his family, but give them much of himself as well."[7]

Find a rhythm to work and play. Commit to down time.

LESSONS FROM ONE WHO FAILED TO KEEP THE TRUST

Put the ears of your heart down to this autobiographical story of a pastor who failed to keep the trust. Catch his grief and listen for his sadness. Then check his suggestions on what he would do differently if he had it to do all over again.

Pastors, hear my story.

Today, I am looking for a job, daily scouring the newspaper, sending out resumes and waiting for phone calls. A few months ago, I felt securely placed in a new church, so much so that we even purchased a house, thinking that we'd spend many years ministering there. It was not a down time. I loved my people. The church was growing. I had a good relationship with my leadership group and with members of the congregation.

This all began to come apart when a counseling situation became a "gripping relationship." I knew I had to do something drastic. I knew this situation would only get worse if I didn't stop it quickly and decisively. It could ultimately lead to the destruction of two families, a church and my ministry.

Up until this time, on two occasions the counselee and I had agreed together that we could go no further. God could not honor what was happening. But we happened to get into several kinds of situations alone again. Many of these situations were not planned. The fire continued to blaze.

I began to acknowledge to myself the possibility of a sexual relationship. I was afraid—afraid of my own feelings, afraid to tell someone, afraid not to tell someone and get accountability, and afraid of what would happen if I did tell.

When I considered all the angles and prayed beyond my emotions, I felt led to call the area supervisor of my denomination to tell him that I was in trouble and to risk whatever the end result would be. I really didn't think my world would fall apart, and I really did desire to be right with God and right with people.

I looked at the phone for about an hour, dialing all the numbers but the last and stopping. Suddenly, I dialed all the numbers, and he answered on the first ring. Of all times, this time the secretary didn't answer! "Dr. ——, this is ——. This is not a normal call. I'm in trouble."

Nervously, I went on with my story.

His advice was to tell my wife. Maybe we could keep the whole thing within the circle of the two couples and go on with what appeared to be a profitable ministry. That night I told my wife. That night the "other" woman told her husband. I'll never forget that night. All hell seemed to break loose. It was clear that this was not going to be contained between the two couples.

The previous Sunday was the last Sunday I spoke in that pulpit, except for my resignation.

I shared with my board honestly and with a repentant heart. I did all I knew to do. They accepted my apology and believed I was right with God, but they felt that my ability to minister there was diminished. Some said they still loved me, but to them something was now missing. They could never see me as their pastor again. My heart was broken. I loved these people.

The church and my superiors have treated me fairly. I still hold my ordination certificate with good standing in my denomination, but I am wounded and shy about rushing into another pastoral assignment.

The denomination offered counseling. It has been good, because some things that had never been dealt with in our marriage (and maybe never would have been dealt with) have been brought to light. Issues came from my wife and myself.

As I look at all that has happened in recent months, I feel a loss and lack of direction, as it seems I must change occupations.

Since I faced down temptation without sin, I wonder about the ability of the church and people to be redemptive. I question the rightness of being cut off from all our Christian friends in our town at this troubled time. At times, I question God and wonder why we must face such financial hardships and loss of self-esteem when at a time of extreme temptation I did what I felt was right.

Perhaps some good can come out of this situation if I can share with fellow pastors how I believe the Lord is showing me this troubling situation could have been avoided. Maybe my story can help some pastor avoid ruin and realize how high the stakes really are. Maybe some pastor will realize that we, as ministers of the gospel, are on a pedestal in the minds of the people and therefore are judged by a different standard. Maybe someone who hasn't discovered this will realize the very appearance of evil must be avoided.

I offer the following thoughts for my fellow pastors:

The stakes are high. Consider the high price of any inappropriate action. In our day, many are losing their ministries purely on the basis of suggestion or accusation.

People in the Church don't know how to handle trying to be redemptive, especially if they are faced with two families from two sides of the same situation. People on the outside of the Church are suspicious and untrusting of the Church and its leaders, looking for any flaw or failure in it or its leaders.

Consider not counseling members of the opposite sex alone. If it must be done, structure as much accountability in your life as possible. Have not just one accountability partner, but three or more if necessary. I had two. With one partner, it was becoming hard to get together, and our schedules wouldn't mesh. With the other, we had been talking about it, but we never sat down to ask the tough questions.

You might consider these options: Refer counseling of the opposite sex to a person of the same sex. Counsel with your spouse present. If you have an associate, counsel together in some cases or plan occasions in which you alternate with the associate. Report weekly to someone and have them ask tough questions like, "How is your thought life?" and "Is there anyone outside of your marriage that you have been sexually attracted to this week?" and, if yes, "What are you going to do about it?"

Consider a buddy system for counseling. Have the counselee come to the sessions with a friend you can both trust if the spouse cannot be involved. Stick to the subject in counseling.

Don't fool yourself into thinking you are too strong to be tempted. Nothing is foolproof. You have to make your safeguards work. Don't think you

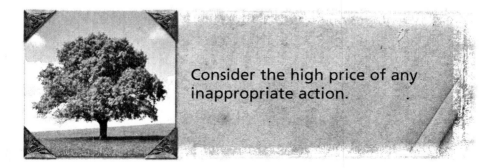

Consider the high price of any inappropriate action.

can manage tempting situations. In my case, I knew the counselee had been molested. I was aware this offered a greater likelihood of one who had that background acting out sexually. I knew she might transfer my role as a caring counselor to that of a lover. Just because I knew it, I thought that I could manage it. Remember, the times you believe you will stand are the times you are likely to fall.

Don't swap stories when counseling. Swapping stories is a means of creating a bond. It takes away from the professionalism of the situation and tends to make you "pals." Focus on the counselee's situation in the light of the Word of God. Keep yourself a professional counselor in the eyes of the counselee. Steer away from answering questions like, "How is it at your house or in your marriage?"

Don't take nonverbal signs lightly. They usually precede unwholesome involvement. Some of these are lingering looks or an appreciative hug at the end of the session. Often "accidentally on purpose" body contact takes place. Some counselors start to receive little gifts of appreciation like cookies and coffee or a spoken desire to be together. Be careful if you find yourself calling on the phone just to talk without a real reason.

Get accountability. Speak loudly, if you must. Speak loudly, clearly, quickly and to someone who matters. Even though my world seems to have fallen apart and right now I am not in the pulpit anymore, I don't regret my phone call to my church superior. He has been gracious and loving.

But there is a greater reason why I am glad I called him. See, I have a little boy. He's two. The other day, I was headed out of the house with a briefcase in each hand, as I have done often lately. I didn't know it, but he was behind me following me to the door. He had a lunch box in one hand and a small plastic file in the other. He was heading into the world to do what his dad does.

He deserves to have a godly father and mother bonded together, rightly relating to each other with Christ in their hearts to lead him in a fallen world. I am so glad I resisted temptation and called for help so I didn't mess up his life and his mother's. Preserving your marriage and your family is worth whatever price it costs.

Establish safeguards before you need them. The decisions about how you will counsel need to be made before you get into the counseling relationship. In many cases, if you have to ask, "Is this going too far?" it has, and it will be hard to turn back.

I am trusting two promises these days: "A broken and contrite heart, O God, you will not despise" (Ps. 51:17) and "The Lord upholds all those who fall and lifts up all who are bowed down. The eyes of all look to you, and you give them their food at the proper time" (Ps. 145:14-15).

A MOMENT OF THANKS FOR THE STRETCH

To think about living up to the standards of credibility and being trusted to lead the local branch of the everlasting family of God tests our skills and stretches our soul. We, of course, take the Bible seriously when it says, "Now it is required that those who have been given a trust must prove faithful" (1 Cor. 3:16). But the stretch makes us better people, more attractive Christians and more effective pastors, and we are grateful.

CONTEMPORARY CHALLENGE

Living Above Reproach

- God trusts the gospel to human beings.
- Credibility is doing the right thing for the right reason.
- Credibility can be destroyed in a moment.
- Every pastor needs to develop a personal code of integrity.
- Soul friends encourage accountability.
- Fatigue and burnout make a pastor more vulnerable to moral lapses.
- Accountability must be self-imposed.
- Vocational hazards do not absolve moral breakdowns.
- Temptation can be resisted.
- Establish safeguards before you need them.

Credibility is a by-product of a Christlike character. —Retired pastor

About Flying on Airplanes and Surveys

Musings from H. B. London, Jr.

As I was getting settled just before takeoff on United Flight #1217 bound for San Jose, California, the announcement was made that they would be conducting a passenger survey. To those who participated, there was a chance to have as many as 60,000 air miles credited to your frequent-flyer account. I never win anything, but I decided I would go ahead and offer my opinion.

I'm telling you, they asked about everything! How did you like the seats? Was the aircraft clean? Did the flight attendants treat you nicely? What was it like when you checked in? Was the ticket fairly priced? And the questions that really caught my attention: Would you fly on United again? Would you recommend United to someone else?

Now, I am sure you can see where I am going with this. What if, about once a month, you put a survey into the hands of your church attendees and asked them to consider a few simple questions: Were you made welcome when you arrived? Did the music point you to the preached Word? Was the message relevant? Were your children well cared for? Was the Lord's house neat and in order? Was the service performance-oriented or Christ-centered? And the big questions: Will you return? Would you invite someone else to attend with you?

I know churches are not airplanes, but sometimes it is good to know how your people are feeling. Don't you agree? "Plans fail for lack of counsel, but with many advisers they succeed" (Prov. 15:22).

CHAPTER 12

MAINTAINING PERSONAL PURITY

God of the holy heart and the pure life,
cleanse me from self-will that seeks my own way,
purify me from wicked lust and misdirected passion.
Empower me to live so Your grace
and peace and transformation make my life
attractive, loving and useful to others.
Amen.

> AMONG YOU THERE MUST
> NOT BE EVEN A HINT OF
> SEXUAL IMMORALITY, OR ANY
> KIND OF IMPURITY, OR
> OF GREED, BECAUSE THESE
> ARE IMPROPER FOR GOD'S
> HOLY PEOPLE.
>
> EPHESIANS 5:3

GOD EXPECTS PERSONAL PURITY

A life of purity—I mean personal holiness—may not be easy in our kind of world, but for the spiritual leader, it's more important than anything else. It's important because it gives authenticity to every phase of ministry. It's important for our self-respect. It's important so our family knows they can count on us in every situation. It's important for the confidence of our congregation and community. It's most important because that's what God expects. And what He expects, He also provides enablement to meet His expectation.

The biblical standard is clear. The apostle Paul wrote, "Among you there must not be even a hint of sexual immorality, or of any kind of impurity, or of greed, because these are improper for God's holy people.

Nor should there be obscenity, foolish talk or coarse joking, which are out of place, but rather thanksgiving. For of this you can be sure: No immoral, impure or greedy person—such a man is an idolater—has any inheritance in the kingdom of Christ and of God" (Eph. 5:3-5).

That's a pretty high standard, but one that gives others a reason to believe in us and for us to believe in ourselves.

IT'S TIME TO GET PAINFULLY HONEST

Sadly, even some of the best and brightest of our ministry colleagues sometimes fall prey to the attacks of the enemy of our soul. The fallout is unbelievable. New converts give up. Families are wrecked. Ministries are destroyed. Churches are divided. The credibility of all ministers is undermined. Future opportunities for the gospel are lost. And the pastor lives under a cloud of suspicion for the rest of his life. The cost is too high—much too high. And it's time to call it what it is: sin.

Flirtation Sets Off Alarm

The temptation to have an affair provided a wake-up call for this pastor. He described his situation and his feelings to me (H. B.) at Focus on the Family:

"Last Sunday, I was reminded that my feet are still clay. Usually I find the flirtation of women other than my wife to be offensive. The last four weeks have been most demanding: I put in 76, 64 and 59 hours, respectively. Needless to say, I've neglected and been neglected at home. Little time for physical or emotional intimacy. The positive feedback from my wife is low. No hostility. No arguments. No fights. But just simply the quiet of autopilot.

"Sunday, an attractive young lady asked to head up VBS. She also commented on what a wonderful pastor I was. She flirts with every man in sight, and usually I find it repulsive. But this Sunday, I found it exciting. Even more than that, I found she kept coming to mind, and that bothered me very much. I took time Tuesday to make myself accountable to three people—to two fellow pastors and my wife.

"To the pastors, I confessed openly and asked them to hold me accountable. They will call me at unexpected times every week and ask the hard questions."

Preventative Action Established

The pastor went on to explain in his letter the steps he took to prevent this from happening again:

"Step 1: I took my wife into the picture, and I am glad. We went to lunch and talked for a long time. She had been experiencing similar things in our relationship, and we decided improvements have to be made. Think of how much joy we will find in a date every week, no matter what.

"Step 2: I put a 60-hour limit on my workweek.

"Step 3: My wife and I will have open conversations about attractions to members of the opposite sex.

"Step 4: The final step was to place our young attractive VBS director under the leadership of an older elder.

"It's not over and done with, but your broadcast was the thing that stimulated me to do something about this problem. Thanks. You may have saved my ministry and marriage."

Let's Make It Personal

In case you are not fully convinced of the terrible fallout caused by moral failure, listen to the pain and be warned as you read this heart-breaking story from *The Minister's Little Devotional Book* by H. B. London and Stan Toler:

"He was my mentor for preaching. As a young ministerial student, I followed his ministry with great enthusiasm. He could sprinkle the stardust with his oratories. Without question, he will be remembered as one of the greatest camp meeting speakers of the 20th century.

"Recently, my hero sat across the breakfast table from me. Having been removed from his pulpit, he was a broken man—a life in shambles and a ministry ruined by years of illicit sexual behavior that had finally caught up with him. At his age, there was little hope for restoration to ministry.

"As the tears flowed freely, my fallen preacher hero asked for my forgiveness. I reminded him that I loved and forgave him. I emphasized that God in heaven had also forgiven him. He acknowledged that he was forgiven through the shed blood of Jesus Christ.

"As I watched him walk away, shoulders slumped, I thought of the mighty cleansing power of God's forgiveness and grace. I then thought of the people who might never hear one of his inspirational messages because of his sin."[1]

God Expects More Than Moral Purity

Go back to Ephesians 5:3-5 again. The personal purity God expects has to do with avoiding sexual immorality, but there is more. He opposes any kind of impurity or greed because these are improper for God's holy people. He opposes obscenities, foolish talk and coarse jokes. Then He calls those who are involved in these sins idolaters who have no inheritance in the kingdom of Christ and of God.

Sins of the inner life are hard to admit but easy to rationalize or deny completely. That's why a pastor who wants to be pure must know his heart and commit to what some rugged old-time tent-meeting preachers proclaimed: "To others a heart of love and to myself a heart of steel."

A friend of mine reports attending a conference where Pastor Rick Warren was one of the presenters. During the question and answer period following Warren's message, someone asked, "Sir, is there anything you need us to pray about for you?" Warren answered immediately,

God opposes any kind of impurity or greed.

"Yes, pray for me that I might have humility rather than pride, integrity rather than power, and generosity rather than greed."

As the Ephesians passage says, the life of holiness is a life of holy wholeness—the best way of life anyone in the human family has ever discovered or lived. It's a life that delivers us from so many of the dead-end streets that many others have been determined to experience. It's the life of peace, caring, grace, nobility, opportunity and satisfaction.

PLANT HIGH HEDGES

The idea for planting hedges to help pastors live above reproach comes from Jerry B. Jenkins's book *Loving Your Marriage Enough to Protect It.* His suggestion helps immensely: "One of the major causes of marital breakups in the Christian community is the lack of protective hedges that spouses should plant around their marriages, their heads, their hearts, their eyes, and their hands."[2] With a little effort, anyone can build safety hedges and protective guardrails around his ministry.

Hedge #1—Keep Home Fires Burning

A happy marriage is the pastor's best insurance for sexual purity. Invest more time, money and creativity in your own marriage. Let your spouse enjoy your selfless surrender, tender vulnerability, honest communication and lusty pursuit. Keep your sexuality under the lordship of Christ just as you do with every other part of your being. Give your church a model of a strong, satisfying marriage. Without being gushy or sentimental, tell your congregation how much you love your spouse and family.

Scripture gives directions for keeping your marriage satisfying:

Be good husbands to your wives. Honor them, delight in them. As women they lack some of your advantages. But in the new life of God's grace, you're equals. Treat your wives, then, as equals so your prayers don't run aground. Summing up: Be agreeable, be sympathetic, be loving, be compassionate, be humble. That goes for all of you, no exceptions. No retaliation. No sharp-tongued

sarcasm. Instead, bless—that's your job, to bless. You'll be a blessing and also get a blessing" (1 Pet. 3:7-9, *THE MESSAGE*).

While leading a four-session seminar on clergy marriage in a district
consisting of about 80 churches, I (Neil) discovered many surprises.
I asked participants to write questions they wanted discussed in the seminar. That strategy provided an easy way for them to raise issues without
embarrassment. It allowed me to assess what they needed. And it gave
me time to think through my answers so they were orderly and accurate.

When the questions came in, I was surprised by how many couples
were living a kind of quiet desperation. I was surprised by how quiet
the room was when some subjects were being discussed. I was amazed
that a couple in their 80s and a couple in their 20s were the first ones
to ask for a private conversation. I was startled when several couples
began to weep quietly when I said God deserves our most profound
praise for giving us the beautiful gift of intimacy in marriage—the only
place in all creation in which wife and husband can have a meeting of
the physical, emotional and spiritual. I was surprised by the reactions
I received in the mail from people after the conference. This seminar
and other experiences since that conference convince me that much
more is needed to help clergy couples understand the basics of growing a strong marriage.

Letters from pastors and their spouses to Focus on the Family and
honest, candid conversations with ministry couples also show much
more attention is needed regarding the issues of affection, intimacy and
sexual harmony.

Too often, clergy couples carry
unresolved intimacy frustrations
from their bedrooms into ministry.

Too often, clergy couples, without even realizing it, carry unresolved intimacy frustrations from their bedrooms into ministry.

One pastor's wife said, "I carry on a cold war of pettiness and small terrorist acts because my husband flirts with a woman in church and never meets my physical and emotional needs at home."

Another pastor in his late 50s wrote, "My wife and I both had brief emotional flings with people in the church. It could have been avoided so easily if we had gotten help. She needs more affirmation and affection from me and I need more sexual gratification from her."

He continued, "The sad part is that with a little effort, we could be more for each other than anybody outside our relationship. We're working on that, and our marriage is a whole lot better."

To prevent such hurt, distance and misunderstandings requires an increased concern for the needs of our spouse. Sexual frequency and techniques, important as they are, are not as important as mutual satisfaction and an eager willingness to please each other.

"Recovering the Heart of True Intimacy" is the beautifully accurate description of a wonderfully positive Christian view of sex in marriage produced by Focus on the Family (the web address is www.pureintimacy.org). Examples of the topics available under the "couples" link include: "The Sexual-Spiritual Union of a Man and Woman," "Sexuality in Marriage," "Restoring Marriages," "Intimacy and Basic Trust," and "To Be Known and Loved: (Re)Building Intimacy in Marriage."

Hedge #2—Sabotage the Sex Revolution with Purity and Prevention

A sex-saturated society like ours presents an incredible challenge to the Church and her ministers. The challenge, of course, includes going against the views of society to oppose abortion, pornography, TV filth, homosexuality and same-sex marriages.

At the same time, the challenge also has a much more positive side—to help people maximize the fulfillment of their sexuality under the Lordship of Jesus.

In the past, when sex was hush-hush in society, the Church was not expected to speak about these issues—and she said almost nothing. As a result of this silence, the Church's congregants, especially her youth, were often sexually ignorant, and some lived with a sense of quiet desperation their whole lives. Guilt about sexual feelings haunted them from puberty to senility. Unwed pregnant women put their children up for adoption or became the most visible partner in a shotgun wedding. Divorce was frowned upon. All of these problems made one wonder what went on behind closed doors that produced such large families—often eight or more children.

Things are different now. In response, the Church is teaching her people how to apply their faith to personal relationships, especially in marriage and parenting. A flood of books, seminars, teaching videos and other training programs are now available, and Christian counselors are now available to help people work through their issues.

Now the question is how and when we will teach people the possibilities of the beauty, balance and wholeness that God intended for our lovemaking in marriage. In a survey conducted by *Christianity Today* that included 1,972 churchgoers and 680 pastors, it was discovered that almost half of the congregants (44 percent) wanted to hear more biblical teaching on sexual issues. However, only 22 percent of pastors surveyed believed they should spend more time preaching on the subject.

Speak up—the people are eager to hear.

Hedge #3—Keep Your Maleness Under the Lordship of Christ
"Real Men Don't Have Affairs." Although the phrase comes from an essay written by Steve Farrar, the truth is as old as the Word of God.

He-men in ministry are not victims of their glands or slaves to their seductions.

He-men in ministry are not victims of their glands or slaves to their seductions. They control their appetites. They allow God's power to keep them from senseless sin and moral stupidity. What right-thinking man would ever choose infidelity rather than longtime affection and intimate satisfaction in marriage?

The Church must stop softening her outrage against adultery by calling it an affair. Sexual sin is heinous and devastating. Although the stigma may be acceptable in society, the sting is as painful in church and family as it always has been. It's time to shout, "Stop!"

To be heard and heeded, however, a pastor must live beyond reproach before he can denounce adultery as the deadly treason it is to the family and to the church.

Farrar's strong paragraph needs to be personally faced by every pastor:

When a man leaves his wife and children for another woman and acts as impulsively as an aroused junior high kid on his first date, it's not an "affair." It's adultery. Real men don't have affairs because real men are responsible. Real men keep their commitments, even when their personal needs are not being met the way they would hope.[3]

Help for dealing with lust can be found in Dr. Archibald D. Hart's book *The Sexual Man*. He offers these hints for controlling lust:

1. Own up to your lust and admit it is a problem that needs to be controlled.
2. Don't feed your lust. Dispose of all sources of stimulation that provoke your lust.
3. Develop alternative diversionary strategies.
4. Change your belief about sexual lust. Remind yourself that you don't have a right to take anyone you desire in your imagination to bed with you.
5. Try to find the underlying reason for your lust, beyond just blaming it on your strong sex drive.

6. If you cannot bring lust under control by yourself, get professional help.

Hedge #4—Wake Up to the Porn Tsunami

Pornography is causing a destructive tsunami in the soul of America, and not enough is being done to warn people of present and future dangers. This rising use of Internet pornography is causing marriages to fail, jobs to be terminated, family breakdowns to increase, and ministries to be destroyed. Cybersex has found its way into all parts of American society, including the Church.

Although the temptation of pornography may be very old, technology now makes it only a click or two away on every computer. And lots of clicking is going on in work places, family rooms and even pastors' offices.

The Increase in Pornography Is Astounding

Hollywood releases 11,000 adult movies each year—more than 20 times the mainstream movie production.[5] As a $12 billion a year industry, revenues for the porn industry are bigger than the combined revenues of the NFL, NBA and Major League Baseball combined.[6] According to the Justice Department, in 1998 there were 28,000 X-rated websites; within three years, the number had increased to 280,000.[7] In May 2004, *Business Week* printed the results of a ComScore Networks survey in which 44 percent of U.S. workers with an Internet connection admitted to accessing an X-rated website at work in the month of March 2004, as compared with 40 percent of home users and 59 percent of users at universities.[8]

Virtually everyone is affected by this evil—spouses, children, neighbors and fellow-workers—and that includes persons who sit in the pews of our churches.

Surprises in the Pornography Picture

Much of the profit from porn is being generated by businesses not traditionally associated with the sex industry. Mom and pop video stores, long-distance carriers, cable companies and hotel chains now reportedly earn millions of dollars each year by supplying adult films to their guests.[9]

There are other surprising trends in the overall pornography picture:

- **Women.** Women are involved, too. Seventeen percent of all women struggle with pornography, and 9.4 million women access adult websites every month.[10]

- **Acceptance.** Thirty-eight percent of adults in the Church believe there is nothing wrong with pornography use.[11]

- **Clergy.** In a 2000 *Christianity Today* survey, 33 percent of clergy admitted to having visited a sexually explicit website. Of those who had visited a porn site, 53 percent had visited such sites "a few times" in the past year and 18 percent had visited sexually explicit sites between a couple of times a month and more than once per week.[12] In March 2002, Rick Warren conducted a survey of 1,351 pastors at the pastors.com website and found that 54 percent had viewed Internet pornography within the last year. Thirty percent of those respondents had visited within the last 30 days.[13]

Hedge #5—Wage War Against Pornography

Start with the fact that pornography is omnipresent. It assaults people in hotel rooms, in airports, in convenience stores and in their homes. And the sales and profits support the assumption that millions are addicted, including some pastors.

For those who struggle with any form of addiction to pornography or know of someone who does, please be encouraged—there is hope. But the war is fierce and it must be fought on four battlefields simultaneously: (1) personal purity, (2) sexual evil in society, (3) prevention in the Church, and (4) rehabilitation of victims.

To help in this effort, Focus on the Family provides useful material called "Battle Plan Against Pornography," which can be located on the web at www.family.org.

As a pastor, there are several things you can do in your church to combat the spread of pornography:

1. Face pornography and denounce it as you would any other sin.
2. Be sure the issues regarding pornography and its damage are understood clearly.
3. Lead from strength of personal purity.
4. Organize positive, Christ-exalting retreats and workshops on the wonderful possibilities for fulfillment in marriage.
5. Contact government officials and register your protests against pornography.

Hedge #6—Commit to the Shepherd's Covenant

You can pledge with thousands of other pastors to live out the details of a godly life and a fruitful ministry by signing the Shepherd's Covenant. The covenant reads:

> *We are joined together by a common call of God to feed His sheep, but we are also tied by a common commitment to purity, holiness, righteousness and faithfulness. Our agreement to submit to the Shepherd's Covenant transcends theological differences, denominational connections and local congregational constraints. We are bound to one another by our calls, mutual accountability and by the knowledge that one day the Great Shepherd will be our final Judge. We further believe that when clergy are more focused on mission than on profession, we will see a renewed interest in the churches we serve and a genuine acceptance by those we seek to influence. It is through God's grace that commitment to this covenant is made possible.*[14]

The actual pledge deals with five basic principles, built on the acrostic "G.R.A.C.E.":

G   Genuine accountability
R   Right relationships
A   A servant-shepherd's heart
C   Constant safeguards
E   Embrace God intimately

Details and pledge cards for The Shepherd's Covenant can be secured from Focus on the Family. Our book *The Shepherd's Covenant for Pastors* is a support manual for the five parts of the pledge. It is published by Regal Books and can be purchased from www.amazon.com or on Regal's website at www.regalbooks.com. In many ways, the book is a summation of chapters 11 and 12 of this book.

Hedge #7—Live Above Reproach

Holy character is the bedrock foundation of ministry. Character made pure and empowered by God has magnetic attraction to all to whom we minister. Such a manner of living does not squeeze adventure out of ministry but gives us a singing heart that stands without shame before God and without regret before the people. This gives a minister sensibility, stability and stamina in a world where so much is uncertain, alienated and morally unstable.

An authentic current relationship to God is the source of pastoral power that impacts every phase of ministry. It is the fountainhead for a Christlike character, a joyous Christian experience, a soundness of doctrine and an effectiveness of preparation.

Now, three questions about living above reproach need your answer: (1) If not you, who? (2) If not where you're planted, where? (3) If not now, when?[15]

HIGH HEDGES AND OPEN HEARTS

Sturdy hedges help protect the gospel, our congregations, our ministries and our families. They prevent us from actions that are cheap, questionable or immoral. While we are building hedges in positive and upbeat ways, we need to communicate what we are doing and why. We can, for example, remind our parishioners from the pulpit that our marriage is among our most cherished relationships in life. We can also demonstrate how a healthy home energizes ministry.

Hedges to help us live beyond reproach are proper and necessary because they help us please the Savior, authenticate our ministry in the minds of our congregation, reassure our spouses and families, and generate fulfillment in ourselves.

A caution is worth noting: Care must be taken in our hedge building to avoid shutting people out of our lives. Ministry, at its heart, is always about relating to people. Hedges need not become fences to keep us away from the people in the parish. Our hearts contain enough room to love people in our congregations while we are loving our spouses and our children.

Build the hedges high around your ministry, but do it in ways that allow you to welcome those you meet as potential best friends. Love people even as Christ loved them and demonstrate that affection. Serve people, even unusual ones, as if you were serving Christ.

Most parishioners trust and feel secure with a pastor who openly speaks and demonstrates his affection for them while he is showing devotion and love for his wife and family. To be fulfilled, a pastor needs the love of family and congregation, and he needs to love both family and congregation.

CONTEMPORARY CHALLENGE

Maintaining Personal Purity

- God empowers personal purity.
- Every clergy marriage needs a high hedge.
- Remember the biblical standard: "Not a hint of sexual immorality."
- Real men don't have affairs.
- Cybersex has invaded all levels of American society.
- Prevention is in short supply.
- Sexual sin is heinous and devastating.
- Satisfying marriages are a resource for ministry.
- Accountability must be self-imposed.
- Authentic ministry requires pure motives and holy character.

My strength is as the strength of ten, because my heart is pure. —Alfred Tennyson[16]

Is Anybody Being Saved?

Musings from H. B. London, Jr.

It's a really big world, isn't it? When you think that there are more than six billion people who populate our planet, the whole thing seems staggering. And I am often reminded that probably two-thirds of the world's population do not know Jesus, and some say the prospect of that figure changing is a real step of faith.

Some of those same feelings came when I met recently with leaders in the American Chinese Church. They are delightful men and women of God who carry a spiritual burden for their people in the United States and Canada as well as the more than one billion Chinese who live on the mainland.

I can't say for sure, but I heard recently that one-half of our churches in North America did not receive one new member by a profession of faith. Could that be true? What is it like in your fellowship?

My question in light of all this: "Is anyone getting saved?"

Do we still ask that question? Do we preach for conversion? Do we give people an opportunity to accept Jesus Christ as Savior? Or have we become so contemporary that a straightforward invitation is too much of a threat to people? Oh, I know times have changed, but have words like "conviction" . . . "repentance" . . . "surrender" . . . and "confession" lost their significance?

Is anybody getting saved? Jesus said, "Do not marvel that I said to you, 'You must be born again'" (John 3:3, *NKJV*). Is anybody being saved in your world? I pray so!

DON'T TRY TO DO IT ALONE

We hope you have read this far. If not, you may want to begin here. What we have shared with you represents a love letter from our hearts concerning your ministry. We know it's tough out there, and the chances of it getting much better without a genuine revival are not very good. What that means is that you, the pastors, have your work cut out for you. Yet we must constantly be reminded that the Church is His Church. He will build His Church. We must acknowledge the problems but look past the threat to the empowerment of God. We dare not deny the diagnosis but we must also apply the cure—the gospel.

Remember the promise of Jesus: "And I tell you that you are Peter, and on this rock I will build my church, and the gates of Hades will not overcome it" (Matt. 16:18).

Sometimes, we think pastors and Christian leaders forget this and feel as though we must resort to theatrics and personality to make it happen. We beg you not to fall into that trap. In many ways, the Church in North America is like a struggling athletic team—we must return to fundamentals: prayer, faith, humility, repentance. Those same things that moved the Early Church out of the doldrums and into a world that watched in amazement are available to us today. Even then it will not be easy. Take courage, exercise hope, and redouble your efforts.

We in the Church are engaged in a real battle and at times it seems the troops are unaware of the stakes. We have grown passionless. Not so unlike the church at Ephesus, we may be in danger of losing our first love (see Rev. 2:4). At least that's what a lot of observers of church life feel. Please don't let this happen. We must regroup and press on. Remember, you're a winner on the winning team. You must never forget that.

We have attempted to say several things to you in this book that possibly bear repeating, or at least a review.

God's call. You are very special. In His own wisdom, God laid His hand upon you unlike any other person in the world. He prepared you for such a time as this. "You did not choose me, but I chose you and appointed you to go and bear fruit—fruit that will last" (John 15:16).

God's heart. Like David, who was a man after God's own heart, God wants your heart to be broken by the things that break His heart. We represent a clergy that is bottom-line motivated rather than by love for Him and His creation. We urge you to bind up some wounds, walk the back streets, put your arms around "lepers" and have a cup of coffee with some nameless, faceless people. Be Jesus to those you meet along the way, and you will never be the same again!

God's place. Moses had a place. David had a place. Paul had a place. Peter had a place. And God has prepared a place for you. We have often used a statement in this book: "Bloom where you are planted." Please do not look over God's shoulder for the next place or the next move. Look into His eyes, and you will know what He wants for you, where He wants you. We sense in our interaction with pastors a restlessness not unlike a person climbing the corporate ladder. We see pastors playing the climbing game rather than paying the price of longevity. Perhaps, like Peter, it is time to let down your nets (see Luke 5:4). See what miracle God has in mind for you. "No eye has seen, no ear has heard, no mind has conceived what God has prepared for those who love him" (1 Cor. 2:9).

God's gift. You are uniquely qualified for the opportunity God has allowed you. So you may not have as many gifts as the guy down the street. So what! You can become gift-greedy if you are not careful. That's why so many of you spend so much time on your lesser gifts. This explains much of your frustration, and it could be why you are easily distracted by minor things. Spend time doing what you do best. Give it your best. Come home in the evenings with a good tiredness. It sounds trite, but we heard it somewhere: It's better to run the risk of wearing out than rusting out. Make the most of every God-given opportunity. The time is short.

God's dream. Remember the phrase we used in chapter 3? "The dream never dies, just the dreamer . . . the song never stops, just the singer." Well, it's true. Lose your dream, lose your song, and you will find yourself terribly frustrated. Get in touch with God's dream for you, and remember, nearly all of His dreams seem impossible at first, but if they are His dreams for you, He will make a way. The world will stomp on your flowers. It may even destroy some of them, but it can never take away the power that caused those flowers to grow in the first place. The world will play with your dreams and even cause you to wonder if it will pay to dream again. We guarantee you it will. Dream on!

God's grace. Yet we know without God's grace, all that we have attempted to say to you will appear hollow and empty—even self-serving. In one of our recent books, *The Shepherd's Covenant for Pastors,* we wrote:

"When faced with decisions that carry major consequences, which road will we take? The road most dangerous and fleeting? Or the road that leads to the applause of our Lord? So many of our colleagues have missed the gift of grace because their mind-set and aptitude fell victim to the enchantment of the world.

"Yet His grace is sufficient (see 2 Cor. 12:9). God looks at our arrogance, yet He loves us like a father loves his child. The Lord sees our faults, but He envisions us as holy. He sees when we've hurt Him by our selfishness and our prideful ways, yet He patiently waits for the right moment to slip His arms around us and say, 'I love you, My son, My daughter. Please don't destroy your effectiveness.'"[1]

The Lord could walk and be done with us, but He doesn't. He could turn His attention to a more gifted and talented child, but He doesn't. He could say something like, "Why did I ever call you in the first place?" But He doesn't. He could even say something like, "Do you know how much you've hurt me?" But He doesn't.

Now that's grace.

Through His grace, He makes His presence known. And like a gentle breeze or a soft kiss or a loving arm around our shoulder, He is there.

Now, that is grace!

We believe in you. The *Heart of a Great Pastor* is our letter of affirmation to you. What we hope you feel from us is support. We are in your corner. What happens to you matters to us. Call us. Write us. Pay us a visit. We may not have all the answers, but we do have a genuine desire to listen.

So don't play the competition game. Don't get into a ladder-climbing contest. Don't look over God's shoulder for the next move. Don't feel insignificant—ever! Bloom where you are planted. Defy the troubling reports. Stay the course. Straight ahead. Don't ever quit—dream on! Keep hope alive. Endure hardship, if necessary, for the most important cause in the world.

We believe in you, and we pray that you will take all the strength you need from God for the journey. We have been doing the "pastor thing" for many years and, in many ways, the words of an anonymous writer express our hope:

We've dreamed many dreams
that never came true.
We've seen them vanish at dawn.
But we've realized enough
of our dreams, thank God,
    To make us want to dream on.

—H. B. and Neil

ENDNOTES

Introduction
1. John Frye, *Jesus the Pastor* (Grand Rapids, MI: Zondervan Publishing, 2000), p. 18.
2. See William Barclay, *The Letters to the Galatians and Ephesians* (Philadelphia, PA: Westminister Press, 1954), p. 175.

Chapter 1
1. Luis Palau, quoted in Bill Bright, ed., *The Greatest Lesson* (San Bernardino, CA: Here's Life Publishers, 1991), p. 173.
2. Bishop Joseph McKinney, quoted in Keith Miller, "Revolution or Abdication?" *Leadership*, vol. XXVII, no. 4 (Winter 2006), p. 127.
3. David Hansen, *The Power of Loving Your Church* (Minneapolis, MN: Bethany House Publishers, 1998), pp. 106, 108.
4. William Willimon, "Pumping Truth to a Disinclined World," *Leadership*, vol. XI, no. 2 (Spring 1990), p. 136.
5. Elizabeth Barrett Browning, *Aurora Leigh* (Oxford, UK: Oxford University Press, 1998), bk. 7.
6. Eddie Gibbs, *Church Next* (Downers Grove, IL: InterVarsity Press, 2000), p. 47.

Chapter 2
1. H. Dale Burke, "Even Healthy Churches Need to Change," *Leadership*, vol. XXVI, no. 3 (Fall 2005), p. 45.
2. Albert E. Day, *An Autobiography of Prayer* (Nashville, TN: The Upper Room, 1952), p. 53.
3. John R. O'Neil, *The Paradox of Success* (New York: Putnam and Sons, 1993), p. 163.
4. George Gallup, as quoted in *Racing Toward 2001* by Russell Chandler (San Francisco: HarperSanFrancisco, 1992), p. 313.
5. C.S. Lewis, quoted in Wayne Martindale and Jerry Root, *The Quotable Lewis* (Wheaton, IL: Tyndale House Publishers, 1989), p. 270.

Chapter 3
1. Advertisement from *Monday Morning*, July 1993, General Assembly Council of the Presbyterian Church (USA), Louisville, KY, p. 45.
2. Georges Bernanos, *Diary of a Country Priest* (New York: Carroll and Graf Publishers, 1937), p. 28.
3. Francis Bacon, *A Strategy for Daily Living* (New York: The Free Press, 1973), p. 22.
4. John W. Gardner, *On Leadership* (New York: Free Press, 1990), p. 198.
5. Warren Bennis, *Why Leaders Can't Lead* (San Francisco: Jossey-Bass, 1989), p. 27.
6. Ibid.
7. Katharina A. von Schlegel, "Be Still, My Soul," first published in *Neue Sammlung Geistlicher Lieder*, 1752. http://www.cyberhymnal.org/htm/b/e/bestill.htm (accessed April 2006).

8. Tony Snow, *Colorado Springs Gazette Telegraph,* Aug. 28, 1993, p. 15B.
9. Macrina Wiederkehr, *Seasons of Your Heart* (San Francisco: HarperSanFranciso, 1991), p. 73.
10. Alan Wolfe, *The Transformation of American Religion* (Chicago, IL: The University of Chicago Press, 2003), p. 3.
11. Bennis, *Why Leaders Can't Lead,* p. 13.
12. Mother Teresa, *A Gift for God* (San Francisco: HarperCollins, 1975), p. 37.

Chapter 4

1. Material for this section is from *Wikipedia*: "Hurricane Katrina," http://en.wikipedia.org/wiki/Hurricane_Katrina; "Columbine High School Massacre," http://en.wikipedia.org/wiki/Columbine_shooting; and "Oklahoma City Bombing," http://en.wikipedia.org/wiki/Oklahoma_City_bombing, (accessed April 2006).
2. Wade Clark Roof, quoted in Steve Rabey, *In Search of Authentic Faith* (Colorado Springs, CO: WaterBrook Press, 2001), p. 44.
3. Material for this section is from "Emerging Church," *Wikipedia,* http://en.wikipedia.org/wiki/Emerging_Church (accessed April 2006); Andy Crouch, "The Emerging Mystique," *Christianity Today*, November 2004, http://www.christianitytoday.com/ct/2004/011/12.36.html (accessed April 2006); "The Emerging Church," *Religion and Ethics*, PBS, part one, July 8, 2005, episode no. 845, http://www.pbs.org/wnet/religionandethics/week845/cover.html (accessed April 2006).
4. David Kinnaman, "Americans' On-the-Go Lifestyles and Entertainment Appetites Fuel Increasing Reliance Upon Technology," *The Barna Update,* February 7, 2006. http://www.barna.org/FlexPage.aspx?Page=BarnaUpdate&BarnaUpdateID=217 (accessed April 2006).
5. Ibid.
6. Dallas Willard, *Renovation of the Heart* (Colorado Springs, CO: NavPress, 2002), p. 251.
7. Anne Frank, *Anne Frank: The Diary of a Young Girl* (New York: Bantam Books, 1993), n.p.

Chapter 5

1. George Bernard Shaw, *Back to Methuselah* (Oxford, UK: Oxford University Press, 1947), n.p.
2. Joe Darion and Mitch Leigh, "The Impossible Dream (The Quest)," © 1965 Helena Music Corp./Andrew Scott, Inc. quoted from *1001 Jumbo Song Book* (New York: Charles Hansen Educational Sheet Music and Books, 1975), p. 208.
3. Phil Johnson, "Give Them All" (Nashville, TN: Benson Music Group, 1985).
4. Dr. Timothy George, *Christianity Today*, December 13, 1993, p. 15.
5. Sue Bender, *Plain and Simple* (San Francisco: HarperSanFrancisco, 1989), p. 63.
6. Oscar C. Eliason, "Got Any Rivers?" © 1973 Singspiration, Inc.
7. Daniel and Carol Ketchum, "The Molder of Dreams," © 1991. Used by permission.
8. C.S. Lewis, quoted in Wayne Martindale and Jerry Root, eds., *The Quotable Lewis* (Wheaton, IL: Tyndale House Publishers, Inc., 1989), p. 167.

Chapter 6

1. *Facts on File* (New York: Rand McNally and Company, 1993), p. 759B1.
2. Henri Nouwen, *The Way of the Heart* (New York: Seabury Press, 1981), p. 27.

3. Robert Schnase, *Your Call to Ministry* (Nashville, TN: Abingdon Press, 1991), p. 54.
4. Gary Fenton, *Your Ministry's Next Chapter* (Minneapolis, MN: Bethany House Publishers, 2003), p. 26.
5. Catherine Marshall, *The Prayers of Peter Marshall* (New York: Guideposts Association, Inc., 1954), p. 208.
6. William Sloane Coffin, quoted in Robert G. Cox, *Do You Mean Me, Lord?* (Philadelphia, PA: Westminster Press, 1985), p. 26.
7. J. Winston Pearce, *God Calls Me* (Nashville, TN: Convention Press, 1958), p. 25.
8. James McCutcheon, quoted in Cox, *Do You Mean Me, Lord?*, p. 24.
9. John Baillie, *A Diary of Private Prayer* (New York: Charles Scribner's Sons, 1977), p. 15.
10. Milo Arnold, *The Adventure of the Christian Ministry* (Kansas City, MO: Beacon Hill Press, 1967), p. 21.

Chapter 7

1. Gene Fowler, quoted in James B. Simpson, comp., *Simpson's Contemporary Quotations* (Boston, MA: Houghton Mifflin Co., 1988), p. 227.
2. C. S. Lewis, *The Weight of Glory* (San Francisco: HarperSanFrancisco, 2001). Quoted from *Christianity Today*, vol. 37, no. 6 (May 17, 1993), p. 40. Italics added.
3. Dr. Robert Coles, keynote address to the Provident Counseling Annual Conference in St. Louis, Missouri, April 30, 1993, quoted in Martha Shirk, "Trauma Can Build Strength, Conefrees Told," *St. Louis Post-Dispatch*, May 1, 1993, p. 4B.
4. Paul Pearsall, *Power of the Family* (New York: Bantam Books, 1991), p. 4.
5. Ibid.
6. Richard Lovelace, *Dynamics of Spiritual Life* (Downers Grove, IL: InterVarsity Press, 1979), p. 16.
7. Fulton Sheen, *On Being Human* (Garden City, NY: Image Books, 1983), p. 211.

Chapter 8

1. *Colorado Springs Gazette Telegraph*, February 21, 1994, p. 1A; *U.S. News and World Report*, January 27, 1992; *National Geographic*, May 1992, p. 112.
2. Robert K. Hudnut, *Surprised by God* (New York: The Associated Press, 1967), p. 125.
3. James Earl Massey, *The Pastor's Guide to Growing a Christlike Church* (Kansas City, MO: Beacon Hill Press of Kansas City, 2004), p. 22.
4. George Barna, *Today's Pastors* (Ventura, CA: Regal Books, 1993), p. 137.
5. John C. Maxwell, *Developing the Leader Within You* (Nashville, TN: Thomas Nelson Publishers, 1993), p. 9.
6. Aldous Huxley, *Ape and Essence* (New York: HarperCollins, 1948), p. 6.
7. Barna, *Today's Pastors*, p. 137.
8. Henri Nouwen, quoted by William Willimon, "Building a Spiritual Church," *The Pastor's Guide to Growing a Christlike Church* (Kansas City, MO: Beacon Hill Press of Kansas City, 2004), p. 13.

Chapter 9

1. John Henry Jowett, *The Preacher and His Work* (New York: Doran and Company, 1912), p. 45.

2. Alexander Solzhenitsyn, "What I Learned in the Gulag," excerpt from *Christianity Today,* September 13, 1993, p. 96.
3. Dr. Maxie Dunnam, quoted in Dale Galloway, *Taking Risks in Ministry* (Kansas City, MO: Beacon Hill Press of Kansas City, 2003), p. 127.
4. Eugene H. Petersen, *Working the Angles* (Grand Rapids, MI: Wm. B. Eerdmans Publishing, 1987), p. 2.
5. Ibid., p. 3.
6. T. S. Eliot, *Choruses from "The Rock," Collected Poems, 1909-1929* (New York: Harcourt, Brace and World, Inc., 1930).
7. Thomas Kempis, quoted in Derf Bergman, "Sermon Preparation by Doing," *Circuit Rider,* September 1993, p. 17.
8. Elizabeth O'Conner, *Journey Inward, Journey Outward* (New York: HarperCollins, 1968), p. 12.
9. Henri Nouwen, *Intimacy* (San Francisco: HarperSanFrancisco, 1969), p. 59.

Chapter 10

1. Bessie Porter Head, "O Breath of Life," first published circa 1914. *The Cyber Hymnal.* http://www.cyberhymnal.org/htm/o/b/obreathl.htm (accessed April 2006).
2. Norman Vincent Peale, quoted in Bill Bright, ed., *The Greatest Lesson I've Ever Learned* (San Bernardino, CA: Here's Life Publishers, 1991), p. 177.
3. Charles Spurgeon, quoted in Richard J. Foster and James Bryan Smith, eds., *Devotional Classics* (San Francisco: HarperSanFrancisco, 1993), p. 334.
4. Vance Havner, *Day by Day* (Grand Rapids, MI: Baker Book House, 1953), p. 16.
5. Charles Spurgeon, quoted in Foster and Smith, *Devotional Classics,* p. 332.
6. Charles G. Finney, *Revival Lectures* (Grand Rapids, MI: Fleming H. Revell, 1979), pp. 17-19.
7. John Hyde, quote from a letter to Focus on the Family, January 12, 1994.
8. Charles Spurgeon, quoted in Foster and Smith, *Devotional Classics,* p. 335.
9. Ibid.
10. George Croly, "Spirit of God Descend Upon My Heart," first published in *Psalms and Hymns for Public Worship,* 1864. As quoted by Tony Campolo, *Wake Up America!* (San Francisco: HarperSanFrancisco, 1991), p. 179.

Chapter 11

1. Lorin Woolfe, *Leadership Secrets from the Bible* (New York: Barnes and Noble, 2002), p. 2.
2. Ralph Waldo Emerson, quoted in Watts Wacker and Jim Taylor with Howard Means, *The Visionary's Handbook* (New York: Harper Business, 2000), n.p.
3. Harry Beckwith, *What Clients Love* (New York: Warner Books, 2003), p. 251.
4. Bob Briner and Ray Pritchard, *The Leadership Lessons of Jesus* (Nashville, TN: Broadman and Holman Publishers, 1997), p. 12.
5. Archibald D. Hart, *Leadership,* vol. IX, no. 2 (Spring 1988), p. 29.
6. Howard A. Walter, "I Would Be True," *Sing to the Lord* (Kansas City, MO: Lillenas, 1993), p. 493.
7. Ted Engstrom, *The Makings of a Christian Leader* (Grand Rapids, MI: Zondervan Publishing, 1976), p. 117.

Chapter 12

1. H. B. London and Stan Toler, *The Minister's Little Devotional Book* (Colorado Springs, CO: Honor Books, 1997), n.p.
2. Jerry B. Jenkins, *Loving Your Marriage Enough to Protect It* (Chicago, IL: Moody Press, 1993), n.p.
3. Steve Farrar, quoted by Bill McCartney, ed., *What Makes a Man?* (Colorado Springs, CO: NavPress, 1993), p. 80.
4. Archibald D. Hart, *The Sexual Man* (Nashville, TN: Word Publishing, 1994), n.p.
5. *LA Times Magazine*, 2002, quoted at *Blazing Grace.org*, "Statistics and Information on Pornography in the USA." http://www.blazinggrace.org/pornstatistics.htm (accessed May 2006).
6. *Family Safe Media*, quoted at *Blazing Grace.org*.
7. *MSNBC Survey 2000*, quoted at *Blazing Grace.org*.
8. *Business Week*, May 2004, quoted at *Blazing Grace.org*.
9. CBS News Special Report, November 2003, quoted at *Blazing Grace.org*.
10. *Internet Filter Review*, quoted at *Blazing Grace.org*.
11. "Morality Continues to Decline," *Barna Research Group*, November 3, 2003. http://www.barna.org (accessed May 2006).
12. Christine J. Gardner, "Tangled in the Worst of the Web," *Christianity Today*, March 5, 2001. http://www.christianitytoday.com/ct/2001/004/1.42.html (accessed May 2006).
13. *Pastors.com* website survey conducted by Rick Warren, quoted at *Blazing Grace.org*.
14. H. B. London, Jr., and Neil B. Wiseman, *The Shepherd's Covenant for Pastors* (Ventura, CA: Regal Books, 2005), p. 27.
15. Stan Mooneyham, *New Every Morning*, compiled by Al Bryant (Dallas, TX: Word Inc., 1985), p. 149.
16. Alfred Tennyson, quoted in Hannah Ward and Jennifer Wild, compilers, *The Doubleday Christian Quotation Collection* (New York: Doubleday, 1998), p. 195.

Epilogue

1. H. B. London, Jr., and Neil B. Wiseman, *The Shepherd's Covenant for Pastors* (Ventura, CA: Regal Books, 2005), pp. 16-17.

MEET THE AUTHORS

H. B. London, Jr., is vice president of church and clergy for Focus on the Family in Colorado Springs, Colorado. A fourth-generation minister, he was a pastor for 31 years before joining Focus on the Family. H. B. communicates with thousands of pastors and church leaders each week through "The Pastor's Weekly Briefing" (a fax network) and produces a bimonthly "Pastor to Pastor" audioseries. While pastoring, he hosted a daily radio program, "Lifeline to Truth," and a weekly television program, "A New Way to Live." H. B. is author, with Neil B. Wiseman, of *Pastors at Greater Risk*, *For Kids' Sake* and *The Shepherd's Covenant for Pastors*.

Neil B. Wiseman is a veteran pastor, clergy educator, writer, editor and small-church consultant. Perhaps his foremost passion in life and ministry has been the development of pastors. He has been a pastor's advocate through his writings, editing and publication of more than 30 books. He has also worked in the area of pastoral development in clergy education at Nazarene Bible College in Colorado Springs, Colorado. Beyond the classroom, Dr. Wiseman founded the quarterly magazine *GROW*, was the founder of Preaching Today—a monthly audio-sermon resource now produced by *Christianity Today*, founded and directed Small Church Institute and served as pastor to local congregations for 20 years.

The Shepherd's Covenant ®

Are you protected by G.R.A.C.E.?

Pastors are under unbelievable assault today. As a result, we in ministry are facing a crisis of integrity and righteousness as never before.

The Shepherd's Covenant is a strategy for victory. It is a covenant with God and one another to pursue a life of holiness and righteousness. The essence is a five-point acrostic:

G enuine Accountability
R ight Relationships
A Servant's/Shepherd's Heart
C onstant Safeguards
E mbracing God Intimately

Sound good? When you join thousands of your colleagues in this covenant relationship, you'll be promising God, your church and those you love most that you are committed to pursuing purity, holiness, righteousness and faithfulness in the midst of the daily assaults in ministry.

To request an information packet, log on to our Web site
www.parsonage.org
or call us at
(800) A-FAMILY.
(232-6459)

Also from H. B. London and Neil B. Wiseman

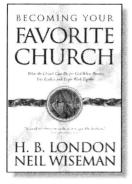

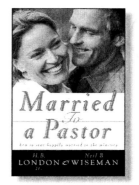

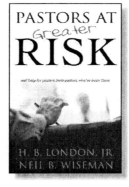
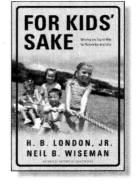

God's Word for
a Pastor's World

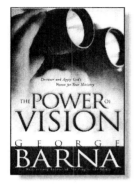

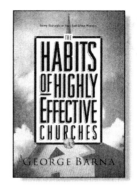
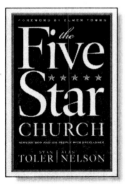
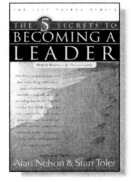
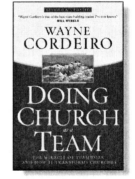